RETHINKING EVERYTHING

When Faith and Reality Don't Make Sense

Tim Rymel

CK Publishing

Rethinking Everything: When Faith and Reality Don't Make Sense

By Tim Rymel
1. SEL032000 2. REL004000. 3. REL078000 ISBN: 978-0-9857580-4-2
Cover design by Predrag Capo
Developmental editing by WriteNow
Copy editing by PeopleSpeak
Interior design by Jera Publishing
Printed in the United States of America

CK Publishing
A subsidiary of Corporate Kindergarten
Elk Grove, CA
Info@CorporateKindergarten.com
CorporateKindergarten.com

To rethinkers who change the course of their destiny.

Contents

Preface

As I was writing this book, it became increasingly clear I was going to make some enemies. I expect long reviews detailing where my "theology" went wrong, though I don't use theology anywhere in the book, except to point to what most evangelicals take for granted as "truth." And I have to admit, writing some of what you're about to read made me uncomfortable. Some of the information included in this book, which has been greatly condensed for readability, comes from research by archaeologists and historians and is sometimes contrary to everything I'd been taught in Bible school and church. I second-guessed whether I should even address some of those topics at all because I certainly don't want to come across as a disgruntled, backslidden crackpot who'd gone off the theological deep end. Nevertheless, I'd find myself researching one thing and run across an intriguing, seemingly unrelated comment. I'd dismiss it only to find it appearing elsewhere again and again. I chased many more concepts than those that made it into the book. Some were indeed written by disgruntled, backslidden ex-Christians with an axe to grind. I am not one of them.

I look back on my time in the evangelical church with mostly fond memories. I have lifelong friends as a result. These people are loving, kind, and gracious and represent what I would like to believe is at the heart of the gospel message. I spent most of my life growing up or participating in the fundamentalist faith. My view of Christianity formed my world-view. For better and for worse, it's made me who I am today. I can't change the past, nor do I hold a grudge against the people who shaped and influenced me in profound ways.

Before I became a minister, I sat through my fair share of Bible classes on everything from Greek to covenant theology to eschatology. I was a credentialed Assemblies of God minister who attended a Church of Christ Bible school and eventually wound up ordained at an independent, non-denominational, Pentecostal-leaning church in Memphis, Tennessee. My training started with a statement of faith. I was there because I believed in the "full gospel" message (e.g., speaking in tongues) of the evangelical church. As a result, the theological studies of my fellow classmates and I only confirmed what we already "knew" to be true. No one questioned the virgin birth, the second coming of Christ, or Christ's death and resurrection. If any discussion was to be had, it was on theology that had little impact on a person's salvation, such as if the second coming of Christ was pretribulation, midtribulation, or posttribulation.

I've seen the same approach among fundamentalist theologians. As a general rule, they start with what they believe to be true and then apply historical and archeological evidence that supports their theology. Evidence to the contrary is quickly dismissed or reconstrued. As a case in point, Bob Seidensticker noted the skewering of evangelical New Testament scholar Michael Licona when Licona denied that dead people literally rose from the dead after Jesus died, as stated in Matthew 27:52. Licona was pressured out of his job at the Southern Evangelical Seminary for denying the "full inerrancy of Scripture."[1]

When our minds are made up with our version of truth, without sufficient evidence to back up our claims, it is impossible to be objective. The problem with almost any religious belief, however, is that little to no evidence exists to support its claims. This leaves the door wide open for practically any religion or religious variant to claim it alone is true. Whether that religion believes that a galactic ruler named Zenu dropped humans off on the earth seventy-five million years ago, as Scientologists believe, or that the afterbirth must be buried to keep Satan from cloning a recently born child, as Nuwaubians believe, belief alone provides the "evidence" for followers to substantiate their own claims. This book looks beyond evangelical scholars and theologians to gain perspective from those who have less interest in spouting theological dogma and more interest in discovering facts as multiple sources of history show how they unfolded. Dogma and theology have no place here.

I based this book on physical and psychological sciences as far as we understand them today. The amount of information available to us is astounding, and many of the scientists, authors, and writers I quote throughout the book are some of the best in their fields. My personal field of study is education, which focuses on how people learn, process information, and think. Much of my research has focused on neurocognition, or the connection between the physical brain and the environmental and biological input that shapes our thoughts, behaviors, and beliefs. That said, I am an avid supporter of evolution because *theory*, in the scientific sense, means a "comprehensive explanation of some aspect of nature that is supported by a vast body of evidence,"[2] and there is overwhelming evidence to support evolution. Yet because of its intricacies and my ineptness to explain it, I don't attempt to do so here. Instead, I encourage readers who have been told that the earth is only six thousand years old to learn some of the basic blocks of science and then pick up a copy of *Why Evolution Is True*, by Jerry Coyne. Many other resources are available that start more simply than Coyne's book, but I found his book to be especially helpful.

Those of us raised in fundamentalist evangelical homes were fed a very specific menu of theological explanations for why things happen and how things are. If you're reading this book, those explanations likely didn't work for you. You've probably become disillusioned with the way your faith, and perhaps your politics, has turned out. Maybe your life, like mine, didn't end up where it was supposed to, based on the pray-read-go-to-church formula we followed. In the first part of the book, I address many of the questions that plague us while we stumble through life trying to make our theology fit our existence, making excuses for God, and dismissing obvious signs pointing us in a different direction. Honestly addressing the shortcomings of our faith is far more involved than simply dealing with facts. We are highly emotional beings whose emotions have been massaged or manipulated by church leaders or our own experiences. I'm not suggesting any maleficent intentions but merely stating that we are products of our environment. Intended or unintended consequences are the result.

Nevertheless, when we're ready to think differently, we go searching for facts. We try to figure out what is true and how we got here. In the fourth chapter of the book, I take you on a journey into faith and religion to explain the origins of the Judeo-Christian world-view and how those beliefs became *our* world-view. Historical and archaeological truths paint a very different picture than what many of us were taught in Bible school.

Once we've built our lives around a certain set of beliefs and discover that things didn't turn out the way we believed they would, we begin to question our own reality. In light of new information, we wonder, "Who is God, what is truth, and who am I?" In the second part of the book, I address the mental conflict that is so common in believers struggling to make sense of faith and reality and figure out who they are without it or with a set of beliefs that are different.

Former fundamentalists often find themselves sitting in a whirlwind of emotions as they rethink what they believed to be true. Anger, depression, and shame are not uncommon. These feelings seem to come from nowhere and at times seem unresolvable. But as we work through them, addressing them as they come, we begin to rediscover who we are. We find significance and passion in a life that is unfettered by the chains of legalism. I spend the last part of the book addressing each of these areas.

"But what if I'm wrong?" we often ask ourselves. The fear of being wrong can paralyze us. In the back of the book, I've included five appendices, which provide a detailed look at how religion developed and, more specifically, how Christianity evolved into what it is today. The last appendix covers the theology and beliefs around hell, a topic that holds emotional sway over recovering fundamentalists. The appendices were separated from the main chapters so more detail could be provided without interrupting the flow of the book.

Several years ago, I opened the bottom drawer of my armoire, where I keep the photo albums I'd collected before smartphones made them obsolete. I was looking for pictures of my kids. At the bottom of the drawer, however, I came across old photos and newsletters of my time at Love in Action, an "ex-gay" ministry where I spent seven years of my life, first as a client and then as a leader.

By this time, I'd been divorced for two or three years, and I was isolating myself from anyone who might have known me. I'd started drifting away from church and cutting off nearly all my relationships. I felt an overwhelming sense of embarrassment and shame. Each picture reminded me of what I was supposed to be. I didn't know who or what I was any longer.

I gathered up the pictures and other mementos, walked with them down the hall and out the back door, and threw them into the garbage can with purpose. I wanted nothing to do with that life. Memories of it reminded me that I had failed. My decades of effort had led to a dead end. With resolve, I swallowed my overwhelming sense of loss and walked backed into the house. I was already suicidal, and I didn't believe I'd ever recover from my sense of failure. With the slamming of the garbage can lid I lopped off the past like an infected limb and went back to my disconsolate existence by sitting on the floor next to the armoire. Years would pass before I saw the light of hope again.

Refusing to acknowledge my past locked me in a prison of immense pain, depression, and shame. The experiences I had, the people I met, and the years I'd spent in ministry were a part of who I had become. Trying to become something else without those experiences was like trying to bake a cake without most of the ingredients. Who we are is already beautiful, already worthy, and already valuable. Our experiences don't define us; they simply add color and flavor. The outcome of rethinking our beliefs doesn't change our intrinsic self-worth. To the contrary, it helps us recognize the importance of our place in a world that is sometimes filled with confusion.

PART I

Questions

CHAPTER 1

When Life Stops Making Sense

If you've got a religious belief that withers in the face of observations of the natural world, you ought to rethink your beliefs–rethinking the world isn't an option.

– PZ Myers

After my book *Going Gay* was released in 2014, I attended a conference for LGBTQ+ Christians in Houston, Texas. It was my first experience with so-called gay Christians. I had a difficult time wrapping my brain around this concept after spending most of my life in the fundamentalist faith. I wasn't even sure where I stood on the issue of faith at all when I went to the conference, but I had a book to sell and an audience I thought would be interested in buying it.

When I learned the conference offered a class on what it meant to be a transgender Christian, I was all in. I knew very little about the transgender issue, and I anticipated a confluence of Bible verses and science, intellectualism and faith. I wasn't expecting a symposium on the issue, but I was hoping to get a basic understanding and hear how the presenter came to her conclusions.

Going Gay is about my personal journey from living as a social, political, and religious conservative evangelical Christian to attaining self-acceptance as a gay man. My journey was long–*very* long. I was a tormented soul pulled toward my biological sexual orientation and equally pulled toward a belief system just as intrinsically ingrained. I'd tried changing my sexual orientation for over twenty-five years, joining what was once the world's most renowned "ex-gay" organization. I became a leader in the movement for six years and held fast to its ideologies, even after losing my marriage and ministry over the struggle. Eventually, against my will, I deconstructed everything I believed to be true and started over. I didn't just think outside the box, I questioned the entire box itself. My transformation was slow, thoughtful, and intense, leading me to experiences I wasn't looking for and conclusions I never imagined.

I walked into the transgender Christian class a few minutes late, as I'd spent lunch reconnecting with my former ex-gay ministry friends, now also out and having gone through their own transformation process. Together, we snuck into the room, where we were quickly ushered to the only available seats left, toward the front of the class. The presenter conspicuously passed us handouts, which I eagerly scanned. To my disappointment, they had no quotes or references to any research. Nothing explained transgenderism. The Bible verses were few and the class focused mostly on how to treat transgender people from a Christian perspective. Questions from participants were just as benign. The presenter, a transgender woman, came across as a likable grandmotherly type with pearls of wisdom for her grandchildren about how to treat people. For all practical purposes, the class was like a Sunday school lesson for adults. I left perplexed.

I'd spent years thinking about, reading, researching, and sorting out the social, historical, religious, psychological, neurological, and biological influences around homosexuality and religion. I studied the source of my own faith and the cultural influences that made it what it was. Abandoning my faith, which I'd been convinced was true and right, was emotionally tormenting. Eventually, my research led me to the opposite conclusion of everything I believed: homosexuality is indeed a normal variation on human sexuality. Its "sinfulness" doesn't make sense in light of science. What I'd been taught about it from my faith made God look and sound ridiculous. Based on all my research, I could explain exactly how I reached my conclusion. Yet, I had just sat through a ninety-minute session presented by someone who surgically altered her body to match her gender identity, seemed to just mindlessly swap out "transgender is wrong" for "transgender is right," and ostensibly barely bat an eye while she did it. Her faith, evangelical at that, was intact and remained paradoxically unquestioned.

Perhaps I should have thought "More power to her!" But I was incensed. I built my entire life on a faulty platform of unreasoned ideals that crumbled under my feet when I needed it the most. "Treat me nicely because God said so" didn't work for me and, quite frankly, was a little insulting.

My journey began early. While I grew up in the Pentecostal faith, I didn't officially become a Christian until I was fifteen years old. The struggle to reconcile my sexual orientation with my family's Midwest values began earlier than that, however. By the time I realized what my sexual orientation was and that it wasn't likely to change, only six years had passed since the American Psychiatric Association determined homosexuality wasn't a mental disorder after all. But I didn't know any of that. The APA's seemingly sudden change of mind had no impact on my conservative, religious family. In fact, I doubt my family even knew what the APA was. Furthermore, homosexuality wasn't something we talked about. We were Christians; why would we?

My only context for homosexuality was negative. I'd been called a fag, but so had my friends. It was like calling someone a weirdo or a jerk. As I entered my teens, though, I began putting the pieces together. I realized I didn't have the same interest in girls my friends did. The mental conflict began weighing on me early. I struggled to hide my truth and fit in. After committing my life to Christ, I believed God could, and would, fix whatever was broken. This was in the era following the 1960s Jesus Movement, when fundamentalists were softening their approach from fire and brimstone and focusing more on God's love. Still, the name-it-and-claim-it theology taught us whatever we asked of God in faith and belief, he would grant us. Since homosexuality was clearly wrong in the Bible, as our New International translation said, asking God to heal it seemed like a perfectly reasonable request. Why wouldn't he? I knew I was sinful by nature and the blood of Jesus was just the cure for my sinful condition.

The first few years ticked by with no changes in my sexuality. I dwindled down to 115 pounds on my five foot ten-inch frame by my late teens.

Anxiety left me in a state of near constant panic. I couldn't keep food down. I felt continuously nauseous. I'd been to gastrointestinal doctors who poked, prodded, and stuck tubes and cameras in nearly all the orifices in my body trying to figure out what was wrong with me. When a physical condition was ruled out, I was sent to psychiatrists and counselors. I didn't yet know just how powerful the brain could be on physical and mental health. I was hopelessly frustrated that no one had any answers. Exhausted, following yet another doctor's appointment, I walked with my mother into our house and dropped onto her floral couch in the living room. "Why is this happening to me?" I cluelessly asked.

The why question is a natural one. We all ask it when times get tough or we have a bad day. Sometimes, however, the questions are bigger than why. When life isn't working as it's supposed to, the questions shift from looking at the content of our lives to examining the box in which our lives reside. If we look closely enough, things are not always as they appear.

You've probably heard the phrase *think outside the box*, but that's an impossibility. We can only work with the tools we have inside our mental toolbox. Certainly we can come up with multiple combinations based on our experiences and knowledge, but our brains can only use the information it has received, pulling from the inputs of our five senses. For example, when my oldest daughter worked on a school project, my spouse, Abel, took out one of our ceramic plates for her to place the hot glue gun on to avoid ruining the wood on the kitchen island. When my daughter finished her project, I reminded her she needed to get the glue off the plate. She stared at me blankly, quickly pointing to Abel as the culprit since it was "his idea." Removing dried glue from a plate would take some thought, as this was something she had never encountered. Her thoughts spun in a circle as she tried to figure out how to undo what had been done, rather than thinking to do something that had not been done before. She scrubbed the plate with a sponge and hot water, the only way she knew to clean dishes, but the glue would not budge. I left her in the kitchen that night to figure it out while I went to bed.

In the morning, she had gone to school and I was left with a single plate, sitting on the counter, splattered with hot glue droppings. Her efforts the night before proved fruitless and she gave up. As much as I wanted to let her figure it out, I couldn't stand the thought of letting that plate sit there all day. So I covered the plate with a paper towel and stuck it in the microwave for one minute. After the hot glue heated up, I wiped it off with the paper towel, washed the plate, and put it away. It's not that I'm that much smarter than my daughter, but my life experience has taught me ways to look at some problems differently. I wasn't thinking outside the box, I was using the experiences and tools I'd acquired to deal with a problem I was having.

Questioning the Box

What's inside the box–our knowledge, experiences, and beliefs–can help us solve problems and get us out of tough situations, or they can trap us when our beliefs don't match our realities. Our realities are quite often different from our ideals or what we *say* we believe. For example, a friend told me he dated a woman who ate only healthy salads when they went out, and he couldn't figure out how she kept gaining weight. He later discovered that her desire to appear thin, and the public actions she took to prove she *was* thin, veiled an emotionally fueled food addiction that she couldn't control. Her belief that she needed to be thin to be valuable drove her uncontrollable and unhealthy secret behavior. Her behavior of eating salad when on a date with her boyfriend made her think she was making healthy choices and soothed her conscience. But her secret habits belied her ideals of what it meant to be healthy. She is no different from the rest of us. We are finite human beings with limited experiences and limited interactions, often unconsciously directed and controlled by our environment and internalized idealism. These influences start early.

Advertising began around the 1840s, primarily designed to inform consumers what was available for purchase.[1] However, by the 1880s, companies were creating slogans consumers would remember, specifically targeting women with the purpose of telling them what they couldn't live without.[2]

By the early twentieth century, the ideal American family had been carved into the national consciousness. According to Kevin Allor, "Progressive reformers and businessmen alike appealed to and propagated the idea of virtuous households, carrying a theme from the culture of sentimentalism in the 1850s that stressed the value of nuclear families with morally upright–if submissive–mothers."[3] Furthermore, the populist version of Christianity in the mid-1950s had commingled with the values of consumerism.[4] What emerged was a picturesque, middle-class family with the newest of amenities, seamlessly adopting corporate ideals and societal expectations, defining what it means to be an American Christian.

The 1950s concept of Dad as the breadwinner and Mom as the homemaker was relatively new.[5] It first emerged in the 1920s but was short-lived in light of World War I and the Great Depression. It made its way back into the culture as wages soared and house prices dropped following World War II and quickly became a favorite genre with Hollywood producers.[6] Television shows such as *I Love Lucy, Father Knows Best, Leave it to Beaver*, and *The Adventures of Ozzie and Harriet* were huge hits, setting the tone for what happy, prosperous Americans looked like if only white Americans.

In the United States today, advertising and entertainment shape much of the culture in America, which tells us how we should look, what we should wear, and what success looks like. The news media, 90 percent of which is owned by just six corporations,[7] controls what we see and hear. Only ten corporations control nearly everything we buy.[8] We are spoon-fed uniquely American information by our families, churches, schools, and environment.

Therefore, many of us have adapted to our American culture without much thought. We attend American schools and American colleges, work for American companies, and attend American churches. We subscribe to American theology, believing, like so many people of faith, that our version is the correct one and that it has always been that way. Our politics tend to follow our American values, regardless of which side of the aisle we find ourselves on. We blindly accept and assume that, whatever we believe, we are right and they, the people on the other side of the aisle, are wrong.

But what if *we're* wrong? What if the box we snuggle into, like a kitten nestling next to its mother's belly, doesn't look at all like we imagine? Perhaps it's a different shape, a different size, or a different material than cardboard, plastic, or concrete. Regardless of what it's made of, it's cozy and safe to us. It's comfortable because it's familiar. But it may also confine us. It may trap us into believing the ideals that we are told, even if covertly, are the best for our lives. The box tells us "it has always been this way," though that is seldom true.

When we accept at face value what we're told, we forfeit control over our own lives and destiny. That's what I did for decades. I inanely tried to conform my biological and natural existence into a societal, religious, and political box that told me that's what I needed to do to fit in, to be normal. I wanted nothing more than to be normal. But the box in which we live can define us only as long as we allow it to. When we ask ourselves who we really are or who we really want to be, we are not only questioning the box but questioning its authority. What's stopping us from doing that? While we may not be able think outside the box, we can ask the questions that open doors to possibilities we never imagined, dreams we never considered, and lives we truly want to live. Those questions have the power to free us from the box altogether.

Faith Is Changing Again

Since my journey began, I've met others, including parents, pastors, struggling Christians, and former Christians, looking for answers their faith did not give them. They give their questions context in light of their faith, but the answers leave them wanting. Some still find themselves trying to maintain their system of beliefs although their realities don't match up. Others, like the transgender presenter, decide that their lives and circumstances aren't sinful after all, realign themselves with people who agree with them, and move on.

The landscape of faith is changing in America. People are beginning to question faith and the existence of God. For example, 92 percent of Americans believed in God, and 71 percent believed in God with absolute certainty in 2007, but by 2014, 89 percent believed in God and just 63 percent believed in God with absolute certainty.[9] Believers in the United States, a predominantly Christian nation, dropped from 78.4 percent in 2007 to 70.6 percent in 2014.[10] While most faiths show declining membership, the population of those who are "religiously unaffiliated" or in non-Christian faiths has risen.[11]

That place of mental conflict where we try to align our view of God with the reality that is life is the most difficult. It creates an uneasy feeling that shakes us to the core. We ask ourselves, What if I'm wrong? Yet even some people who are convinced they are *not* wrong admit to visions of hell reverberating in their minds years after finding resolution to their question.

Not everyone is willing or able to question the box of ideals in which they reside. It's not a task for the weak of mind because the cost can be high. People lose families, social networks, church friends, and, in some cases, even jobs. Social pressure to maintain the status quo, even when we're adults, is strong. We don't like change and we don't like to question what appears to be working, even if it's working for only some people. We start to see things we can't ignore. We start to hear nagging questions that demand answers, and we feel forced into an existence that feels foreign to us. Yet we resist because the walk can be lonely and the people we love don't always go with us.

In the movie *Suffragette*, the main character, Maud, a twenty-four-year-old laundry worker who is a mother and wife, unwittingly finds herself in the middle of London's suffrage movement in 1912. She's determined to keep her head down, but while delivering a package one day she gets caught in a protest and recognizes Violet, a coworker, as one of the protesters. Violet is a vocal and outspoken proponent of the suffrage movement and encourages her coworkers in the laundry to speak out. As Maud's friendships develop with Violet and others in the movement, her eyes are opened to the unjust treatment these women face for merely seeking equal status. Maud's husband, Sonny, disapproves of Maud's involvement with the women and eventually throws her out of the house. In a poignant turning point in the movie, Sonny, disgraced by his wife's activities, puts their child up for adoption and reminds Maud she has no legal rights to their son. The pain of her personal loss becomes the motivation for trying to change her future.

Like Maud, most of us work our daily jobs, keeping our heads down and focusing on the tasks at hand. We may *feel* something is wrong, but as long as we don't make eye contact with it, we can mostly ignore those uneasy feelings. But the constant unease that builds leads us closer and closer to the problems or issues we're trying to avoid. Eventually, we're forced to face them and make a very conscious choice to sweep them under the rug or address them.

After a class I taught on how to effectively approach the hot topics of politics, religion, and sexuality, a young man came to the front of the room and said, "I have a difficult situation I could use your advice on." After listening to several of his statements, I assumed he was going to tell me his wife was a lesbian. I jumped in the conversation and suggested this was the crux of the matter. "It's worse than that," he said. "She's an atheist." He went on to tell me stories of their discussions about God, which he usually concluded by telling her to "just pray about it and get back to me." Her mind was already made up. She wasn't budging. The man's question to me, after dancing around the issue, really was, "How do I get her to become a Christian again?" He was uncomfortable with her being any other way.

After our fifteen-minute discussion, I laughed out loud. I didn't mean to, but the poor guy was banging his head against the wall and it was almost cartoonish. I envisioned his wife smacking her forehead after every conversation because he refused to acknowledge or honor her decision. "This is where everything you have ever learned about love and acceptance as a Christian comes into play," I said to him. "Just love her where she is. Respect her and be kind." I'm sure her decision to become an atheist was not one she made lightly. Seeing the wedge it drove between her and her husband was probably just as excruciating for her as it was for him. That said, our journeys are not always so black and white.

"Some days I'm an atheist"

At a conference I met a woman who had been doing a significant amount of work to end conversion therapy–the attempt to change someone's sexual orientation from gay to straight–for minors. We'd had several online conversations and spoken on the phone, but this was the first time we met face to face. I was curious to hear where she stood on issues of faith since she so often found herself battling the Christian right in court. "Some days I'm an atheist and some days I'm an agnostic," she said. "I don't know what I believe about God." Both of us had come to a similar conclusion–that there really isn't a conclusion.

Perhaps one of the most unnerving aspects about questioning our box of ideals is the lack of conclusions. If I'm "certain" about anything, it is that the version of fundamentalist Christianity I was taught simply isn't true. Christian fundamentalism is another iteration in the ever-changing definition of the Christian faith. Does God exist? It can't be proven one way or the other. Humans have attributed many things to God for lack of other explanations.

Scientists call this the God Gap. As we learn more, we see those things for what they are: not miracles but nature or sheer chance. The choice to live in this quagmire of uncertainty, removing right and wrong from our vocabulary and considering all the opportunities that present themselves, truly requires faith. For example, after being raised to believe that swearing was wrong, I taught my kids that words in and of themselves have no moral value. But using them to hurt or devalue someone is an immoral choice. Changing my view on swearing was a colossal undertaking as it went against everything I'd been taught. "It sounds uneducated," my dad would say. However, some of my best friends are PhDs with the dirtiest mouths. They are also some of the kindest and most compassionate people I know. Some research even suggests that people who swear are more honest.[12]

People who question their faith don't all become atheists, and it's important to remove labels and conclusions along the journey. Just as Christianity doesn't have one set of rules, faith and belief are also on a continuum. Atheists in America are often demonized and accused of having no moral compass. Extremist views of atheists have linked them with Adolf Hitler and the Holocaust, though a 1939 census of Germany and annexed Austria showed that 54 percent of the population identified as Protestant Christian and 40 percent Catholic.[13] In other words, Hitler's war was overwhelmingly supported by those who identified as Christians. Only 1.5 percent identified themselves as nonbelievers at the beginning of World War II.[14] Yet even the term *nonbeliever* can be misleading, as researchers Brittany Page and Douglas Navarick discovered. In a survey of hundreds of respondents, Page and Navarick found, "Most atheists express some degree of tentativeness in their beliefs and would be prepared to consider contrary evidence and arguments."[15]

We humans, in this culture, are quick to label people's beliefs, genders, and orientations, along with a plethora of behaviors. Over the last few decades, social scientists have studied and dissected human behavior, categorizing it like geologists label rocks or entomologists label bugs. The researcher's language makes its way into the lives of everyday people who then reduce complex thoughts and behaviors into overly simplified descriptors. Once we've labeled someone, we build a profile, which isn't usually accurate. At best, it defines a very small part of the person's life. At worst, it creates a stereotype of "others," reducing them to less-than-human castaways. An example of this scenario was provided at the end of 2017 when the Trump administration reportedly banned the Centers for Disease Control from using seven words in official documents.[16] These words included *vulnerable*, *diversity*, and *transgender*. The ban was disputed by the CDC director, Brenda Fitzgerald,[17] but the idea that such a ban could happen at the whim of any leader provides a valuable lesson. When a society begins dividing and identifying the population by classifications, it's a very small step toward removing groups altogether. Yet we pass labels around like Tic Tacs. Once people take them, we no longer feel obliged to learn any more about them. We may choose to identify ourselves, however, any way we wish: Christian, believer, agnostic, atheist, or, to use Pew Research's term, religiously unaffiliated. These terms, and how we define them, are really more about our comfort level with ourselves than someone else's assessment.

I've tried to walk the middle ground when people ask me what I believe about God. In all honesty, this started because I didn't want to alienate people who identified as gay Christians and who contacted me about my book. But when confronted on a talk show and asked to state what I really believed, I chose the term Truth Seeker. If God does exist, I believe God absorbs scientific realities. No division exists between faith and science since, theoretically, God created all that is. God is not frightened by diverse expressions of human beings or disgusted by human behavior. God, as I believe him or her or it to be, understands why we do what we do. We're just catching up to understanding it ourselves.

Ethics and morality, which are ingrained in our DNA, regardless of our theological beliefs, are expressed in how we treat people around us. The ultimate praise we can give a supernatural being is to live in absolute authenticity and pursue the passions that drive us. While this view about God is new to me, a former fundamentalist, it was the accepted view in the mid-1800s. People saw no conflict between God and science. According to George Marsden, "Truths of faith and truths of science were complementary in that they dealt with two different realms of human experience."[18] As you'll see later, faith and expressions of faith change with culture and time.

CHAPTER 2

A Question of Faith or Reality

One's first step in wisdom is to question everything–and one's last is to come to terms with everything.

– Georg C. Lichtenberg

Most of us don't start this journey by questioning everything all at once. It starts much smaller than that. We almost never come out of the gate saying of our life, "This is all wrong!" Instead, we try to make it work. That's because we usually believe what's been handed to us as kids. I used to tell my kids all kinds of fabrications to get a response out of them. I was curious to see how they would react when they heard something so outlandish it couldn't possibly be true. In my management book, *Everything I Learned about Management I Learned from Having a Kindergartner,* I tell the story of how I once told my older daughter hot dogs were made from dead dogs. True to her personality, she didn't say anything at the time. I watched the wheels turning in her head behind her eyes while she ate lunch. Years later, I asked her if she believed me. She said she remembered the conversation but didn't believe what I said was true.

Shortly after the hot dog incident, I forgot to get the kids' Easter baskets out of the closet before they woke up. I jumped out of bed to sneak them into their rooms. While I was taking them off the top shelf in the hall closet–fortunately, I had prepared them the night before–my daughter came out of her room. She looked at me pulling down the Easter baskets, made eye contact, and smiled. Then, without missing a beat, she said, "Thank you, Daddy." Suddenly, the Easter bunny was dead.

All the little things add up, drawing us into a new reality. If hot dogs are not really dogs, then what are they? If the Easter bunny isn't real, then what about Santa Claus? What about Jesus? What *is* real? When it comes to religion, our parents don't sit us down and say, "Here are the top twelve religions and this is what each of them believes. Which one would you like to choose?" Instead, we are told that *ours* is the truth, or we're told nothing and our faith is lived out, covertly signaling that it is the only and obvious choice.

When Questions Strike

I remember standing in the pew during worship, watching the pastor cast a demon out of someone during an altar call when I was a teenager. I was caught up in the electricity of the moment. My hands were raised; I was speaking in tongues. And then, the left side of my brain, the analytical part, started asking questions: "Is she for real, that lady up there? And what exactly are you saying? Are you speaking in tongues or just making sounds?" I opened my eyes and looked around. Much of the congregation was in a frenzy, as was the pastor. I was as equally drawn into what was happening as I was taken out of the moment by nagging questions: Why *do* we need to speak in tongues? What is the purpose of that? At that point in my life, I had been to noncharismatic churches only a couple of times. Based on my upbringing, I wasn't even sure noncharismatic people were Christians. *This* is the way it's supposed to be. Or was it?

For decades, I asked these questions in the context of what I believed were givens: God is the God of the Bible; the Bible is true and inerrant; I am inherently sinful and in need of a Savior; if something doesn't work in my life, it's because something is wrong with *me*, not God and the Bible. While I may have had incessant questions, those truths were as self-evident as the sky being blue and just as undeniable.

For me, the old adage about doing the same thing, or asking the same question, and expecting different results was true. I believed that God existed, yet no matter how hard I tried to get rid of my same-sex attractions, I still had them. When Bible memorization, praying, fasting, crying, and pleading didn't change me, I did them all again, mustering up as much sincerity and contriteness as I could, looking for the right combination. Still lacking results, I prayed harder, beat myself up for getting in God's way, and then lived in constant shame for still not getting it right. Eventually, I began crossing the line between reality and insanity.

After *Going Gay* was released, I sat in the chair across from the host of Sacramento's local NPR station for an interview. I remember being especially tired, having completed a weeklong radio tour and feeling raw. Many of the interviewers had asked personal questions I thought I was ready to answer publicly but wasn't. I was in the midst of processing what I felt about God, conversion therapy, and the history I'd been hiding from for nearly twenty years. I had gone into virtual isolation from ministry friends, especially after coming out as gay. I was trying to quietly live my life, though I did so in unconscious shame, feeling like a failed minister. Writing *Going Gay* was as cathartic as it was informational. I was passionate about the message but vulnerable in its delivery.

NPR's morning show host is a seasoned professional. I remembered her as a TV personality on the local news I'd watched while growing up. She does her homework. She had read the book's manuscript from beginning to end. I could see handwritten notes all over her pages, along with sticky notes protruding from all four sides. She had a lot of questions and I felt unusually nervous.

"Did you ever, at any time while you were in the ministry, say to yourself, 'I really *am* gay'?" she asked. I paused to search for an answer. A flood of unexpected emotions came from nowhere. I couldn't find words for them. The brown wall behind her in the sound booth blurred as my mind raced through seven years of ex-gay ministry and six and a half years of marriage. I knew I never said I was gay. I couldn't have. The dichotomous battle between my sexual orientation and my faith raged inside like a civil war. I was trying so hard to keep my world and way of life from falling apart that such a confession never had a chance. The only thing I could admit was that *the Bible had to be right.* That's what I told her. But the emotions her simple question stirred inside stayed with me.

I went home after the interview and thought about that specific question all day. The host had struck the single nerve that caused so much turmoil for decades. My reaction didn't have as much to do with admitting I was gay as it did admitting what I believed about my religion wasn't true. My religion was a systematic machine squeezing the life out of me one dogma at a time. It took control of me without my permission, and I didn't know what was happening. For decades, I never even saw the hold it had on me. Many of us learn to travel the wordmaze of fundamentalism so seamlessly, we don't even notice the inconsistencies between what we say we believe and how we operate in our world. The ubiquitous pro-life position among evangelicals is an example of this mindless acceptance.

On a flight back East a few years ago, I sat next to a political correspondent from the *New York Times*. She had just interviewed Arizona senator John McCain about the upcoming 2016 election, and I was curious to get her inside take on what Republicans were really thinking during the tumultuous and unusual political upheaval caused by then-candidate Donald Trump. "In the five years I've been doing this job," she said, "this is the strangest political climate I've ever seen. Abortion is still one of the top issues for Republicans . . . even gay Republicans," which she claimed were running Washington behind the scenes and everybody knew it.

Abortion became *the* issue among fundamentalist Christians following the Supreme Court's ruling on *Roe v. Wade* in 1973. But not until six years *after* the Supreme Court's decision, in 1979. The mastermind behind pulling in this traditionally uninterested group of voters was political strategist Paul Weyrich. Weyrich "created or co-founded many of the most prominent conservative organizations in the political and religious arenas," according to author Kathy Baldock.[1]

Abortion was a red herring by the Republican Party, which had already been going after evangelicals for votes. In 1976, the Republican Party asserted for the first time, "Our great American Republic was founded on the principle: One nation under God, with liberty and justice for all."[2] And God had been added to the Pledge of Allegiance just twenty-two years earlier in 1954.[3] The ploy to draw fundamentalists into politics did not start because of abortion but because Jimmy Carter, a Democrat, threatened to pull federal funding from Christian schools that did not desegregate. Christians rallied together under the guise of states' rights to make sure they could legally discriminate against African Americans. By 1979, however, Republicans and fundamentalists found a more palpable moral conviction: stopping abortions.[4]

Writer Fred Clark referred to this as "the 'biblical view' that's younger than the Happy Meal."[5] Even *Christianity Today*, a publication founded by Billy Graham and edited by then biblical inerrancy advocate and author Harold Lindsell, published an opinion piece from a conservative evangelical seminary professor that read:

> God does not regard the fetus as a soul, no matter how far gestation has progressed. The Law plainly exacts: 'If a man kills any human life he will be put to death' (Lev. 24:17). But according to Exodus 21:22–24, the destruction of the fetus is not a capital offense... Clearly, then, in contrast to the mother, the fetus is not reckoned as a soul.[6]

Prior to 1979, abortion was virtually ignored by Evangelicals, who believed it was a Catholic issue.[7] Most fundamentalists simply did not involve themselves in politics.[8]

The inconsistencies many of us experience in our mindlessly accepted beliefs are seldom noticeable to us. What we call love or acts of love become inextricably twisted in our need to also be right and uphold *THE TRUTH*. We exchange compassion and empathy for dogma and doctrine. After the horrendous slaughter of forty-nine people at a gay nightclub in Orlando, Florida, in June 2016, I began to notice how quiet the fundamentalist Christian community leaders were. One Sacramento pastor finally made headlines by publicly stating, "The tragedy is that more of them didn't die."[9] Naturally, many in the community, both Christian and non-Christian, were outraged by his statement.

His beliefs, however, follow the natural course of his fundamentalist faith. Antigay sentiment is interpreted in his sacred texts from the Old Testament to the New. Granted, those cultural interpretations are relatively new (within the last hundred years), but the pastor, who almost certainly doesn't know where they came from, is simply following what he believes his theology says to its logical conclusion. His sociopathic exclusion of empathy and humanity has been replaced by a drive for absolute certainty and truth. When I called out this pastor's line of thinking in a *Huffington Post* article, one man responded by saying, "It's not us, that's just what the Bible says." That statement alone should have given him pause. But we become so focused on our beliefs as truth, we lose the ability to think them through.

For those of us who became Christians, the gospel was presented in relatively simple terms: Believe that Jesus Christ, the Son of God, died on a cross for your sins, that he loves you, and that he is coming back for you one day. Voila! You're a Christian. Or are you?

What makes someone a Christian has been a hotly contested debate even as far back as the New Testament itself. Acts 15:1–2a says, "Certain people came down from Judea to Antioch and were teaching the believers: 'Unless you are circumcised, according to the custom taught by Moses, you cannot be saved.' This brought Paul and Barnabas into sharp dispute and debate with them." Sharp disputes and debates continue two-thousand years later. The Church of Christ, for example, believes you must also be baptized to be saved. Mormons believe you must do good works to be saved. The Pentecostals believe you must avoid certain behaviors to keep yourself saved. Catholics believe in praying the rosary and going to confession to be saved, and the Assemblies of God believes you don't have the "full gospel" until you are speaking in tongues. All these beliefs are supported through various Bible passages. Alas, Pew Research counted forty-one thousand Christian denominations worldwide. According to some, you are a Christian only if you subscribe to their beliefs their way. The breaking point comes when we stop looking at the bigger picture and start paying attention to the details.

Rethinking Everything

Many books have been written on biblical fallacies, and many more have been written to explain those fallacies away. Whether we want to believe the Bible is a hoax or the inspired Word of God, plenty of people and lots of information will take us there. But reason, as you'll see, isn't what we base our beliefs on. We are social creatures, driven by the deep values of the societies in which we live and the pressure to conform. Whether we are surrounded by nuns or sailors, social pressure holds sway over what we believe and how we act.

The bigger question is, Who are you? Really. Who are *you*? If you take away the titles–mom, dad, wife, husband, son, daughter, pastor, worship leader–how do you see yourself? Are you the person you want to be? Are you hiding a part of you that you wish you weren't? Do you have doubts about God, faith, religion, sexuality, or politics you've wanted to ask about, but didn't have a place or feel safe enough to do so? If your biggest fears were removed, what would you do differently? If you had the freedom to say, be, or do anything at all, knowing the people you loved the most would still be there for you, how would you live your life? Do you even know what holds you back? Often we don't.

When my younger daughter, G, was around nine or ten years old, she broke out in horrible, burning rashes around her lips from time to time. We kept a good supply of ChapStick around the house for that reason. Being the tenacious soul she is, not to mention sharing her mother's personality traits, G and her mom got into some pretty hefty arguments. One of them happened to be right before I came to pick my daughters up to take them to school one morning.

Caity, my older daughter, sat in the front seat, and G, at first, sat quietly in the back. I was unaware of the argument with their mom that happened a few minutes earlier. "Caity, give me some ChapStick out of your backpack," G ordered. Caity, being the people pleaser she is, started looking through her backpack without saying a word. I looked in the rearview mirror.

"What happened to your ChapStick?" I asked. I was feeling rather perturbed by G's demanding attitude. I had no idea what my question was about to unleash. Seemingly unprovoked, G began a tirade.

"Caitlin," she screamed, "*lied* to Mom and said the ChapStick that was on Mom's bed was hers, so Mom gave it to her and now I don't have *any* ChapStick!" Turning her anger toward Caitlin, she yelled, "*Now give me some chapstick out of your bag*!"

"Wait a minute," Caity said calmly, "that's not at all what happened." I told Caity to stop looking for the ChapStick because I didn't want to reward her sister's bad behavior. So she went on to tell me, "Mom found the ChapStick on the bed. She said she didn't know who it belonged to and asked if it belonged to me. I told her I didn't know. That's when G started screaming at the top of her lungs at Mom, so Mom said she would just keep it." G began sobbing in the backseat of the car, still decrying the injustice of what happened that morning, how she felt her mom took Cait's side, and that she still didn't have any ChapStick.

Since we had a little extra time before school, I dropped Caity off and parked the car. I told G to come sit in the front seat with me so we could talk. As we walked through the events of that morning, I asked her how she felt about what her sister had said. I asked her if she could see the other side of the story and how her behavior might have affected her inability to get what she was asking for. Once she calmed down, we both had an epiphany. Her argument was never about the ChapStick. What she felt was incredible sadness about thinking that her mom liked her sister more than her. Her bitter disappointment came bubbling to the surface and, as she saw it, confirmed that her mother didn't love her the same way. In fact, the ChapStick was nothing more than a symbol of what she felt should have belonged to her but was consistently out of reach.

A couple of years later, after another big fight, G said, "I've realized when Mom asks my forgiveness for something and I don't respond to her, it makes me feel like I have power over her. If I acknowledge it and tell her I forgive her, then I'm giving up control."

Unlike my daughter, we don't often have moments of clarity about what drives our behaviors, thoughts, feelings, and actions. We may even find that we derail our own ambitions because we are so unaware of our emotional deficits, whether they come out as rage, manipulation, or passiveness. But we'll never know until we begin to think and ask, What is our "ChapStick"? What lies beneath the arguments that derail us or keep us from reaching our goals and destiny? Going beyond the why me questions requires reflection and self-awareness. It requires risk, and we have no guarantees as to where we will land. As a lifelong conservative, I certainly never set out to dismantle my belief system. I didn't expect to write about social justice issues for the *Huffington Post*, and to one day be supporting LGBTQ+ causes. To the contrary, I set out to confirm that what I'd been taught was true.

On this journey, you may find that questions have always been lingering in the back of your mind. Perhaps you've avoided those questions for fear of the answers. You may find emotions completely devoid of words but know something isn't right and something needs to change. It's not so much about the answers that we find by asking the questions; it is the courage to ask the questions in the first place. For the questions we ask will ultimately determine our future.

CHAPTER 3

What We Believe

Belief is a wonderful way to pass the time until the facts come in.

– Carl R. White

Abel and I strolled down the sidewalk next to a busy road in our suburban neighborhood having one of our usual conversations about religion and the meaning of life. As on most Sacramento evenings, the setting summer sun brought a cool, brisk delta breeze. We spoke louder than normal to hear each other over the traffic and the wind. "Belief and truth are not the same thing," he shouted to me. We'd been down this road before, both figuratively and literally. The concepts of belief and truth were synonymous in my mind. All truth led to God, and God led to all truth. I *believed* in God because God was *true*. But at least I wasn't the first person in history struggling to separate the two.

When Religion Collides with Reality

In 1610, Galileo published *The Starry Messenger* (or *Sidereus Nuncius*, if you'd prefer the Latin version), identifying observations he'd made regarding the phases of Venus and moons of Jupiter. He subscribed to and promoted the idea that the sun, not the earth, was at the center of the universe. The heliocentric theory, as it's called, was first proposed in 1543 by astronomer Nicolaus Copernicus. Galileo had been using a new telescope he'd built, based on a Dutch model, that allowed him to make his discoveries. But the Catholic Church would have none of that.[1]

A well-known and respected scientist, Galileo had been warned by the church not to proliferate his heretical ideas. Psalm 19:4b–6 *clearly* proved the sun was moving, not the earth:

> In the heavens God has pitched a tent for the sun.
> It is like a bridegroom coming out of his chamber,
> like a champion rejoicing to run his course.
> It rises at one end of the heavens and makes its circuit to the other;
> nothing is deprived of its warmth.

In 1616, Cardinal Robert Bellarmine told Galileo he was on dangerous ground and in a letter said, "I say that, if there were a true demonstration that the sun was in the center of the universe . . . then it would be necessary to use careful consideration in explaining the Scriptures that seemed contrary . . . But I do not think there has been any such demonstration."[2] Convinced that his telescope did indeed offer such a demonstration, Galileo, in 1632, published the *Dialogue Concerning the Two Chief World Systems*, a conversation among three characters over a four-day period, describing how the universe worked. This time, he published his work in Italian and sparked a conversation among the locals.

In response to the controversy Galileo created, the Catholic Church, in 1633, charged him with "vehement suspicion of heresy."[3] Galileo was forced to renounce his belief that the earth revolved around the sun and spent the rest of his life under house arrest. Not until 1992, twenty-three years after photos were taken from the moon, did the Catholic Church finally absolve Galileo and admit it was wrong.

Many of us raised in religious systems have entwined what we *believe* to be true with what is *actually* true. And we'd sooner hold a grudge for the greater part of four centuries than admit we are wrong. The web of self-justification the human brain can spin is truly astounding. Separating truth from belief can be like pulling seeds out of a pomegranate. Ultimately, the pomegranate must be obliterated to get to the seeds.

The way I used to deal with religious truth and belief was to simply toss out the whole argument. I couldn't determine what was what, so I decided none of it mattered. Still, an overwhelming feeling of frustration lingered. It was like a mental game of cat versus laser: just when I thought I had it, my understanding disappeared. I finally accepted that I was gay, but I grew angry at my faith for telling me that I could not be gay and Christian. Like Galileo, I was labeled a heretic. I was forced to choose between going back into the closet and denying what I knew to be true or facing banishment from the Kingdom of God.

Teaching a lesson on belief and perception to a college class one afternoon, I began by asking an existential question created by social psychologist Jonathan Haidt. Was it okay for a family to eat their dog if the dog had been killed by a car? No one saw the family do it, and the dog was already dead. When I asked the students to explain their reactions and thoughts, one student started by saying, "Well, I'm a Christian…" She then shared her perspective as though the qualifier "I'm a Christian" made her answer the correct answer. When another student, who was not a Christian, challenged her, she crossed her arms defensively. I explained that, regardless of her religious beliefs, the question really did not have a right or wrong answer, and she went completely silent. Her *truth*, "I'm a Christian," was just separated from her *belief*, "It is wrong to eat dog."

Perhaps if the family's pet pig was killed by a car she could have started with "I'm a Christian" and then explained that the Old Testament says eating pigs is wrong. Even then, her theological perspective, a belief, wouldn't have gotten her much closer to a definitive answer about right and wrong. The fact that she called on her religious beliefs in the first place, for a nonreligious issue, speaks to the way so many of us inextricably commingle our beliefs and truths, seamlessly sewing our thoughts and feelings into a single reality.

Our brains are like puzzles. We add pieces as we grow up and go through life, creating a picture that makes sense to us. If we remove one piece of the puzzle, the picture is incomplete. Trying to put another piece in the same place is awkward because it creates a different, unfamiliar picture. Furthermore, we begin to question, if that piece of the puzzle doesn't go there, even though it seemed to fit so perfectly and complete the picture, what other pieces are in the wrong places? Is the entire picture wrong? If our mental conflict is not quickly mitigated by strongly held beliefs, our worlds can come completely undone.

Some people who feel uncomfortable or threatened by the articles I write respond in the comment sections with lengthy lists of Bible verses. They use the scriptures to reinforce and justify their feelings and to reright their worlds, which have been shaken with, often, very different viewpoints. I could easily argue the validity of the Bible passages they use, but I cannot argue their interpretations of those scriptures, which are based solely on beliefs. We reach a stalemate based not on arguable perspectives of truth but on belief, which cannot be argued.

Belief can be defined as acceptance, faith, trust, or confidence in something or someone. It may or may not have any truth associated with it. Even the Bible says, "Now faith is confidence in what we hope for and assurance about what we do not see" (Heb. 11:1). In other words, faith is merely belief without any evidence. As noble as having such faith may *seem*, when clear evidence of truth to the contrary presents itself, maintaining that faith makes a person not pious but delusional. In some cases, it makes him or her dangerous.

Belief in Faith

In a delightfully funny one-woman show called *Letting Go of God*, Julia Sweeney shares the story of reconsidering her Catholic faith. At one point, two young Mormon teens show up at her door to tell her they have a message for her from God. Intrigued, Sweeney invites the boys in, which she says made the boys very happy because "I don't think that happens to them too often." After priming her with questions about whether or not she believed that God loved her and whether or not she believed all the people of the earth were brothers and sisters, questions to which she wholeheartedly agreed, they began to tell her the story of their religion.

The boys told her about a man named Lehi who lived in Jerusalem in 600 BCE. They told her that everyone in Jerusalem was evil, so God told Lehi to put his entire family on a boat and God would lead them away from that awful place. "And," they told her, "God did lead them. He led them to America!"

"America?" Sweeney squalled. "From Jerusalem to America . . . by boat? In 600 B.C.?"

"Yes," they confirmed.

The boys went on to tell her how Lehi's group reproduced and multiplied over the next 600 years until two great races were created, the Nephites and the Lamanites. The Nephites were all very good, while the Lamanites were "bad to the bone," said Sweeney. But then, after Jesus was crucified on the cross and rose from the grave, he stopped by America to visit the Nephites on his way to heaven. Once there, he told them if they remained exceptionally good, they would win the war against the evil Lamanites.

"But apparently somebody blew it and the Lamanites were able to kill all of the Nephites," Sweeney said. That is, everyone except for one man named Mormon, who managed to stay alive by hiding in the woods. He made sure to write down everything that happened in reformed Egyptian hieroglyphics, chiseled onto gold plates, which he buried near Palmyra, New York.

Sweeney said she was so into the story, she was sitting on the edge of her seat. She asked what became of the Lamanites and was told they became the Native Americans. "So you believe the Native Americans were descendants from people who were totally evil?" she asked.

"Yes," they confirmed again.

Then they told her about a guy named Joseph Smith who found those buried gold plates in his backyard. At the same time, he found a magic stone and put it into his hat, in which he buried his face. This allowed him to translate those gold plates from reformed Egyptian hieroglyphics into English.

Sweeney said she initially felt superior to the boys and smug in her own faith. But, she said, "The more I thought about it, the more I had to be honest with myself. I mean, if someone came to my door and I was hearing Catholic theology and dogma for the very first time and they said, 'We believe that God impregnated a very young girl without the use of intercourse–and the fact that she was a virgin is maniacally important to us–and she had a baby, and that baby was the Son of God,' I would have thought that was equally ridiculous. I'm just so used to *that* story!"[4]

Sweeney's example poignantly illustrates that what we believe about faith depends on what we were *taught* to believe about our faith. The number of adherents doesn't make the faith any more or any less true. Faith is more about topology, or the relationships between linked elements, than truth. For example, American Christianity has evolved into its own brand. While roughly one-third of the world claims to be Christians,[5] that number also includes 1.1 billion Catholics,[6] over 8 million Jehovah's Witnesses,[7] nearly 16 million Latter Day Saints,[8] and many other groups that evangelicals would consider non-Christians. Additionally, 73 percent of the world's citizens live in countries in which their religious group makes up a majority of the population.[9]

According to the Pew Research Center, "Muslims are a majority in 49 countries, including 19 of the 20 countries in the Middle East and North Africa."[10] Muslims also show the most growth of any religious group. By 2050, Christians and Muslims will make up nearly equal shares of the world's population.[11] The reason the Muslim population is growing so much isn't because of a profoundly successful mission outreach program but simply because Muslims have more babies.

Christians, on the other hand, pour billions of dollars into proselytization programs with very few results. The nonprofit group About Missions found that the annual income for Christians totals around $12.3 trillion. Of that $213 billion goes toward Christian causes. $11.4 billion goes toward foreign missions and 87 percent of that figure goes toward work among Christians, while 12 percent goes toward work of already evangelized non-Christians. Only 1 percent goes toward the unevangelized.[12] But Christians in industrialized nations, where a majority of Christians live, don't produce as many children as Muslims. Research shows that the more people who live in poverty, the higher the fertility rate,[13] and a majority of the Muslim population generally tend to live in poorer, less developed countries.

Religious beliefs hold enormous influence over the cultures and societies in which those beliefs operate, even if the people affected have little more than a nominal connection to the source of those beliefs. Princeton anthropologist Clifford Geertz says, "Sacred symbols function to synthesize a people's ethos—the tone, character, and quality of their life, its moral and aesthetic style and mood."[14]

When Abel's father died in 2014, his mother decided, unilaterally and inexplicably, to have a Catholic funeral. All the kids were shocked since their parents didn't go to church and Abel's siblings identified more as evangelical Christians than Catholics. The day of the funeral was filled with much more pomp and circumstance than could ever be attributed to Abel's family. His mother is a poor Mexican immigrant who lives a simple life on a small piece of property in Palmdale, California. The cathedral was enormous. Large, colorful statues of Jesus and Mary hid in nooks and crannies around the church, which seemed to contain more pews than the small city of Palmdale had residents.

I sat with Abel's family in the front of the church, but I positioned myself off to the side to allow Abel and his siblings to sit together. Abel's immediate family looked lost not simply because of the death of their patriarch but because they clearly didn't know what to do during the service. No one had given them a funeral bulletin. Even then, the bulletin did not state when to stand, when to repeat what was said, or when to kneel. So Abel and his family just sat. At the end of a prayer someone rang some chimes. Abel described the experience as feeling as if he'd just walked into a liquor store with his dad. He couldn't shake the image and smiled broadly every time the chimes went off. He also couldn't shake the feeling that the church provided his family with an Indian minister and, as he put it, "tried to pass him off as a Mexican."

Behind Abel's immediate family sat his extended family, most of whom seemed to know exactly what to do and when. They stood. They repeated. They knelt. Clearly, these were the traditional and faithful Mexican Catholics who attended Mass on more occasions than just Christmas and Easter. Had it not been for the aunts, uncles, and friends, the entire service could have looked like a farce. A Catholic funeral is what was expected. It's what "normal" Mexican immigrants do who were raised in a sociological structure where involvement in Mass is as common as wearing a pink dress to one's own quinceañera. But Catholics aren't the only ones who follow sociological rules.

On a visit to New York City, I stepped off the subway next to the September 11 memorial and right across from St. Paul's Chapel. The church was originally built in 1766. At the time, it was the tallest building in New York's skyline and sat by itself off in a field, away from the growing city. It was the church George Washington visited following his inauguration and during the two years New York was considered the country's capital. Visitors can see the boxed pew where he is believed to have sat. Another box on the other side of the building was created for visiting governors, magistrates, and aristocrats.

The chapel survived the great fire of New York in 1776, following the city's capture by the British during the Revolutionary War. In fact, the church's grounds were where the militia practiced drills to fight the Brits. Over the next two years following the war, as New York's buildings outgrew and overshadowed St. Paul's Chapel, the church continued to play a significant role in the lives of New Yorkers, carrying many of them through the attacks of September 11, 2001.

I stepped inside the double doors to see magnificent arches, grand columns, a podium highlighted with gold overlays, and large windows extending from the sides of the auditorium to the front. On both sides of the chapel 9/11 memorials stood. Boots of rescue workers, still covered in dust, ashes, and debris, were mounted together in one section. Adorning the walls were photos of volunteer doctors, nurses, chiropractors, and masseurs who tended to the workers twenty-four hours a day after the attack. Fire and police departments from all over the country sent patches of their precincts and stations as a show of solidarity. As I made my way to the front, I noticed a middle-aged woman kneeling at the far right of the altar, hands folded, lost in her own prayers and thoughts. The place where I stood that day felt sacred not just because it was a church but because of its place in the community and significance in history.

Religion and religious influence are natural parts of our society. Whether or not we believe in the doctrine and practices of the churches around and within our communities, their influences are felt and we conform. The influence of religious art, values, culture, morality, and behavior, good or bad, becomes indiscernible as to where it ends and our beliefs begin. Many religious symbols and phrases and even religious music can trigger memories or nostalgia, making them feel that much more real and personally relevant.

If I Feel It, It Must Be True!

I grew up with Southern gospel music as the soundtrack to my childhood and attended church with one of America's favorite gospel quartets in the late 60s, so gospel music still resonates with me. I began playing piano at thirteen years old and learned gospel riffs and four-part harmony. In my later teen years, I started playing black gospel music and traveled with a local group. The Mississippi Mass Choir is a channel on my Pandora app. If I'm not listening to books or lectures while lifting weights at the gym, I'm having church on the elliptical. While my beliefs about God have changed significantly, on the occasions I've attended church, I've been brought to the verge of tears by the familiar music, which continues to inspire me and stir my emotions.

Experiential faith, which teaches that a relationship with God is based on experiencing or feeling God, often used as "evidence" of God's existence in the evangelical church, is difficult to deny. That very real feeling of a supernatural presence was one of the most difficult things for me to understand as I began unraveling my Christian experiences. What was it I felt if not God? Where did it come from? How did it happen? For my entire Christian existence, I used that feeling to distinguish my *relationship* from others' *religion*. It not only confirmed that everything I believed about God and the Bible was right, but also kept me from looking anywhere else for answers, even to the detriment of my own mental and physical health.

When it comes to passion, black churches may do it the best, but we white Pentecostals are a close second. Music is a powerful tool for igniting passion. For me, playing the piano, and later the Hammond B3, the organ featured most prominently in black gospel music, came naturally. To this day, I sometimes blast gospel music through my house and fire up my keyboard. I "have church" all by myself. It makes me feel alive and puts me in touch with emotions I sometimes forget to have.

Research shows that music affects the limbic system even in newborn babies.[15] The limbic system is a complex system of nerves and neural connections in the brain that involve moods, instincts, and basic emotions. More than our day-to-day emotions, "music can trigger changes in the major reaction components of emotion, indicating that music can evoke real emotions (not merely subjective feelings)."[16] In other words, music that is especially tied to a deep, core belief system has more of an impact on us than, say, the emotions we feel when we pray or participate in other types of religious activities. Certainly, believers can and do sometimes feel intense emotions when they pray, but the impact of music adds another dimension to that experience. It's not uncommon for some people to turn on praise and worship music during their daily devotions, which helps "put them in the mood."

One woman I know kept and played a cassette tape of my worship music for nearly thirty years! When I found out, I wasn't sure if I was more shocked that she kept my music for thirty years, that she still played it, or that she still had a cassette player. This is an example of someone who was stuck, perhaps even addicted, to an emotion that kept her tied to her belief in God, as well as her connection to me and our past friendship. The good and familiar feelings the music evoked in her kept her from moving forward with her life–to the detriment of her marriage and family. Music often works like glue, melding our thoughts, beliefs, emotions, and feelings into what seems to be one cohesive ball of truth.

George Bernard Shaw famously said, "Emotional excitement reaches men through tea, tobacco, opium, whisky, and religion." Belief researcher Michael Shermer says that feel-good chemical in our brains, dopamine, "may be the most directly related to neural correlates of belief."[17] Researchers at the University of Bristol in England explored the neurochemistry of superstition, magical thinking, and belief in the paranormal. What they found was that people who had high levels of dopamine are "more likely to find significance in coincidences and pick out meaning and patterns where there are none."[18]

Neuroscientist D. F. Swaab says, "Spiritual experiences cause changes in brain activity, which is logical and neither proves nor disproves the existence of God. After all, everything we do, think, and experience provokes such changes."[19] What these experiences do, however, is show us how and where the brain reacts to faith and belief. Swiss neuroscientist Olaf Blanke reported he could produce out-of-body experiences through electrical stimulation of the brain.[20] Depending on how much electrical stimulation was used, study participants would feel as if they were sinking into the bed, falling from a height, or seeing themselves in bed from above.[21] These "spiritual" experiences show how the brain can be manipulated through chemical and electrical impulses. Likewise, Swaab says, "The EEGs of Carmelite nuns have shown marked changes during mystical experiences when they felt they were at one with God. In a state like this, individuals may also feel as if they have found the ultimate truth, lost all sense of time and space, are in harmony with mankind and the universe, and are filled with peace, joy, and unconditional love."[22]

As this research suggests, and as I've often said, we don't read the Bible for guidance but for confirmation. Seldom do you hear of people who prayed about something and ended up doing the opposite of what they were originally going to do. Usually, their prayer leads them right where they were headed in the first place. What we believe about our faith is confirmed through the dopamine reward. Those good-feeling emotions inevitably accompany our new discoveries as we read the Bible, and the emotions we feel when we pray and worship–emotions that feel incredibly real and connected to the Supreme Being we are positive exists. When we get the job we were going for, we attribute it to prayer. When we don't get the job, we attribute it to God's will. Either way, God cannot lose and our faith cannot be shaken. When we believe our faith is true in the first place, everything that happens to us only confirms that what we *believe* about our faith is *true*.

For this reason, most fundamentalist believers have a difficult time wrapping their heads around how some people can leave the faith or have drastic changes in their belief systems. The only way these believers can explain it is that those who leave the faith were deceived by the devil, weren't Christians in the first place, or didn't do it "the right way." The latter are the two most common negative reactions I get when I share my personal experiences with Christians. I'm accused of relying too much on feelings and not understanding the Word of God or being too intellectual and not understanding the relationship I was supposed to have. Since beliefs and experiences are so subjective, however, what these people are really asking is, Why can't you see things *my* way?

Fundamentalism, whether Protestant Christian or Islamic, is a belief system that requires a "strict adherence to any set of basic ideas or principles."[23] Those ideas or principles are usually specific, such as a particular interpretation of the Bible. The argument about the Trinity doctrine, for example, was a contentious debate among both early church founders and early American settlers. It separated the saved from the unsaved, depending on which side of the argument you believed and whom you believed it with. It was semantics to some, perhaps, but a matter of eternal life or death to others. Most people I've met who were not raised in the fundamentalist faith don't seem to carry the same baggage of those of us who were.

Belief is far more than a feeling. It encompasses the entirety of who we are. It's the consciousness of our unconscious. It's the background music to our life stories. It is the silent motivator of our behavior and the advisor of our decisions. Belief, like the strings of a marionette held by a master puppeteer, moves us confidently, courageously, and craftily. Belief is the horse on which we'd bet our lives. We give it power without asking and doubt it only long enough for it to persuade us it's right. When we're living authentically, it shines like a diamond in the sun. When we deny our realities, belief fades the light of our souls to nothingness.

CHAPTER 4

Facts of Faith

A patient pursuit of facts, and cautious combination and comparison of them, is the drudgery to which man is subjected by his Maker, if he wishes to attain sure knowledge.

– Thomas Jefferson

Just over three years after my wife left, I was beginning to think that church was futile and God was simply toying with me. By that time, I contemplated dropping out. However, that would have been a huge life change and it was something I was not ready to do. A boss encouraged me to go back to school to finish my undergraduate degree. Soon, my nights in hotel rooms from traveling with work changed from watching TV to writing papers, studying textbooks, and preparing for exams. Although I wasn't particularly thrilled with the subject matter, I chose business management as a degree since I already conducted management training, and it seemed like the quickest way to finish my education. In hindsight, having school as a focus during this tumultuous period in my life was a blessing in disguise.

If I close my eyes, I can still see the room in the Embassy Suites where I sat with my laptop open, doing research for an assignment. The olive green curtains covered the window in front of me, and the dark brown desk almost swallowed up my laptop in the room, which was dimly lit except for the bright screen. I took a deep breath and let out a long sigh. The depression, normally kept at bay during these times of focus, wouldn't leave me alone on this particular night. I slumped into the leather chair, slightly rolling backward away from the desk. My energy was gone. School didn't matter. My job didn't matter. Nothing seemed to matter, least of all me.

I wondered what my little girls were doing at home. I wondered if they missed me. I wondered if they were being taken care of. I wondered how I got to this place in my life. I was a minister with promise. Everyone said so. I'd directed choirs, I'd worked for Youth for Christ, and I'd been the outreach director at one of the world's largest and most renowned ex-gay ministries. I'd spoken in churches and colleges, been on dozens of radio shows, and appeared on TV. I'd preached, led worship, and committed my life to the ministry. Would I now drift into oblivion, as though I never existed? What had my life been about for all those years, and what happens next? I sat staring into the dark space past the bright computer screen for a few moments. My thoughts turned into mindless, wordless feelings of loneliness and fear.

After another deep breath and another long sigh, I slowly scooted my chair toward the screen to refocus my attention. I placed my hands on the keyboard and then stared at the search bar at the top of the screen before typing something. Whatever I was looking for that night felt as insignificant as I did. But before I could hit enter, I paused and looked at the words. That was not the question I wanted to ask. What I really needed to know was, Where the hell was God? I wanted an explanation for how I got to this place. I wanted to know what all of this meant and if God even existed. I wanted to know if the Bible was true. Below the surface of my faith these doubts had always existed, but I'd never had the impetus to find out the truth. That fateful night changed everything for me. I set out on a journey to uncover the truth behind the faith to which I'd given my life.

Faith for many of us became a mindless form of ritual yet one we allowed to tap into the depths of our emotions. We bowed to it unquestioningly at times when we were the most vulnerable. When we understand what we believe, where our beliefs came from, and how they shaped us, we empower ourselves to choose the type of faith we deem authentic or refuse faith that denies us our humanity.

Compared to other religions, Christianity is a relatively new one and, since its inception, little agreement has been reached about which version of Christianity is the "one true religion." Archaeology provides a rich history of the development of religion with quite a few surprises, especially for those of us from fundamentalist backgrounds indoctrinated in a single story with a single God.[1]

Welcome to the Party

We have a tendency to feel secure in our beliefs if not smug. But celebrating our faith is like showing up to a party that has been going on for thousands of years. We don't know who was there before us, other than rumors, or what the party was like before we arrived. We just assume we're eating the same crackers and drinking the same wine as the other party guests. We assume the rules are the same as they were when the party started and we assume we're carrying on the traditions. But just as a party's vibe is dependent on its guests, religious belief is dependent on those who believe it. A party's trajectory can easily be changed by the extrovert who shows up with jokes or the drunk who vomits on the carpet.

If we think of Christianity and Judaism as a party, there were a lot of guests who took those parties in different directions throughout the millennium (See Appendix A). In fact, we could think of both of those faiths as many parties that eventually became two. Until the faiths were written down with the invention of writing, around five thousand years ago, religious stories and traditions were verbally passed down through generations. Professor William Schniedewind says, "When the Bible became a book, the written word supplanted the living voice of the teacher. Ancient Israelite society was *textualized*. This textualization marked one of the great turning points in human history, namely the movement from an oral culture towards a written culture."[2] And that's when the party started.

Before there were scriptures there were beliefs and stories. These were primitive explanations of life to make sense of what couldn't be understood without access to scientific explanations. Some of those mythologies found their way into Jewish and Christian Bibles, most notably the belief in hell for Christians (See Appendix E). Other mythologies were shared among various religious traditions with similar stories but different names for similar characters. These stories were appropriated into the cultures that utilized them.

According to Professor Edward Greenstein, "There is no such thing as consensus in biblical studies these days."[3] Greenstein says that the Torah–the first five books of the Bible–involve "layers of rewrites, supplements and revisions."[4] German theologian Rainer Albertz says, "The numerous breaks and discrepancies in the texts of the books of Exodus to Deuteronomy make it probable that here various religious traditions of the early period have been compiled and shaped on the basis of the very different interests of rival groups."[5]

Archeological research, in fact, struggles to find any evidence to corroborate most of the Old Testament stories. In 1999, Israeli archaeologist Professor Ze'ev Herzog published an article entitled "The Bible: No Evidence on the Ground." His proclamation was already agreed upon by fellow Israeli archaeologists, but in 2017, "armed with cutting-edge dating and molecular technologies, archaeologists increasingly agree with Herzog that generally, the Bible does not reflect historical truths."[6] This, of course, creates problems for Israelis who, without a written mandate from God, have "questions of identity and 'our right to the land.'"[7]

None of this information disproves God's existence, but it does raise questions about the way we, as evangelicals, believe in God. Researchers without an evangelical or fundamentalist perspective, nor a need to prove or disprove any theological point of view, see Bible stories quite differently based on the physical evidence. If the Jewish texts show evidence of rewrites and changes, then what does that do to our version of the Christian God?

Who is God?

The God I believed existed was very much like my mother. She is a gentle soul who has pearls of wisdom, a servant's heart, and a seemingly endless supply of patience. I never presumed God to be mad at me. Rather, I saw him looking down on me with pity and frequent disappointment. I imagined God's deep sighs of frustration at my inability to pull it together, but I always knew he loved me. I sometimes wondered why this ancient God put up with humans for so long. I was aware of his character in the Old Testament, which was often less than flattering, but I dismissed the inconsistencies. My version of God was kind to me and someone I desperately needed to help me make sense of my mental confusion as a gay kid growing up in a Christian home.

Had I lived even two thousand years earlier, however, the concept of a personal God likely would have been foreign to me (See Appendix B). Most of the major religions of today, which sifted out of the beliefs of smaller tribes, came to believe in a single deity, which became progressively more personal.

God, or Yahweh as the ancient Hebrews came to know him, developed from the once widely-held practice of polytheism among the Jews. In fact, this God once had a wife named Asherah who was worshipped alongside Yahweh.[8] But what's most interesting is the sanitized version of this God that eventually developed into the God Christians worship today.

Before modern times, people never drew pictures of themselves sitting in Yahweh's lap or created memes where Yahweh picked them up and carried them across the shore because they were too tired to walk. If there was a single set of footprints, there was also likely to be a body where the second set of footprints stopped. The traits of the Old Testament God relate more to someone with a narcissistic personality disorder than a sanctified version of the Dalai Lama. Someone with this condition requires constant attention and adulation, has unreasonable expectations, lacks empathy, disregards the feelings of others, and shows arrogant behaviors and attitudes.[9] Looking at just a few of the Ten Commandments tells us a lot about how ancient Israel saw its God.

1. *Thou shalt have no other gods before me* (Exod. 20:3). This commandment denotes a God obsessed with control who refuses to share the spotlight even with "false gods." It's also telling about the era that other gods were even mentioned.

2. *Thou shalt not make unto thee any graven image, or any likeness of any thing that is in heaven above, or that is in the earth beneath, or that is in the water under the earth. Thou shalt not bow down thyself*

to them, nor serve them: for I the Lord thy God am a jealous God, visiting the iniquity of the fathers upon the children unto the third and fourth generation of them that hate me (Exod. 20:4–5). Here we see a deity, threatened by his own creation, who describes himself as such a jealous God that he would punish innocent children generations later out of spite toward the person who disregarded his demand. Michael Shermer says that commandment "might explain the genocides, wars, conquests, and mass exterminations commanded by the deity of the Old Testament" and that Yahweh comes across like more of a Greek god "and much like an adolescent who lacks the wisdom to control his passions."[10]

3. *Thou shalt not take the name of the Lord thy God in vain, for the Lord will not hold him guiltless who takes his name in vain* (Exod. 20:7). Yahweh, the supreme being who created and holds all power over heaven and earth, threatens his small creation for what would amount to a meaningless curse–except that, it appears, his ego is wounded.

4. *Thou shalt not kill* (Exod 20:13). The irony of this commandment couldn't possibly have been lost on the Israelites. In fact, as Shermer points out, as soon as Moses came down from the mountaintop, he smashed the first set of stone tablets in anger and then ordered the Levites, by the will of God, to kill every man and his brother, his companion, and his neighbor (Exod. 32:27–28) to the tune of three thousand of their own people! When, in Numbers 31:7–18, the Israelites killed the Midianite men and pillaged their town, Moses chastised them for not also killing the women.

Historians and literarians have concluded that the Old Testament is one of the most violent and immoral books ever written, with many of the atrocities ordered, unleashed, or approved of by Yahweh. In addition to describing numerous wars and monstrosities, such as the flood that killed innocent men, women, and children, it demonstrates abject disregard of most sentient life. Deuteronomy, for example, says if a man has sex with an animal, both he and the animal are to be put to death, as if the animal had given consent. Or if a man gets caught raping a virgin girl, he's required to pay her father money and they are considered married. The girl has no say in this arrangement. This God is in stark contrast to the Christian God of love and Mercy.

How God Became a Christian

God's transformation from Yahweh to Jesus happened over the span of several hundred years (See Appendix C). Changes can be seen in the rewrites of Hebrew texts, along with the addition of poetic literature at the same time the world's population developed more of a universal consciousness. The landscape had changed between Genesis and Matthew when Jesus appeared. People and, by extension, their views were more evolved about life, politics, relationships, and who God was. Some denied that a deity in a single form existed and placed the onus solely on humans. Humans saw the divine by how they themselves interacted with and treated each other, as well as the world around them and its creatures.[12] A global softening occurred, and its effects can be seen historically in literature and artifacts of the period, including those related to Christianity.

How Jesus Became God

A version of Jesus as a deity began to emerge in the second half of the first century (See Appendix D). Paul's spiritualized version of Jesus clearly does not mirror the Jesus written about in the gospels. At no time in the first three gospels did Jesus ever claim to be God. Only in the book of John–written toward the end of the first century, following the writing of the other three gospels and *after* the writings of Paul–do we see a theological supposition for Jesus as God.

Additionally, the New Testament is rife with contradictions not only among the gospels themselves but between the gospels and what Paul taught about Jesus. These discrepancies have played into the hands of theologians who create doctrines, pastors who speak for God, and politicians who make policies based on their personal or denominational religious beliefs. Here are just a few of those contradictions:

- Salvation is by faith alone (Eph.2:8–9).
  Salvation is by faith and works (James 2:14).

- Salvation is through belief in Jesus alone (Acts 16:31).
  Belief must accompany baptism for salvation (Mark 16:16).

- All who call on the Lord will be saved (Rom.10:13).
  Only those predestined will be saved (Acts 13:48).

- Backsliders are condemned (2 Pet. 2:20).
  Backsliders are still saved (John 10:27–29).

- We must fight against the wicked powers of the world (Eph. 6:11–13). God ordained the powers of the world and we will be judged if we resist (Rom. 13:1-2).

Fundamentalism has created lucrative careers for apologists and televangelists who mitigate these discrepancies. And I have to admit, I was quick to dismiss many more of the discrepancies I discovered. After decades of indoctrination, discrepancy explanations are as natural to me as reading the verses themselves. For example, in John 1:29, John the Baptist recognizes Jesus as "the Lamb of God who takes away the sins of the world." But in Matthew 11:3, John the Baptist sends his disciples to ask Jesus, "Are you the one who is to come, or should we expect someone else?" Changing the order of these events and taking into account other versions of the synoptic gospels, one can piece together a story that makes theological sense and fits a doctrinal motivation (the inerrancy of scriptures). But on their own, which is how the gospels were written and how audiences would have heard them, one must acknowledge the Gospels' inconsistencies and at least question if a divinely purposed uniformity ever existed.

When certain scriptures don't work for us at all, we either dismiss them or create elaborate explanations. Divorce, for example, is permitted when one partner is unfaithful, according to Matthew 5:32, and divorce is wrong for any reason at all, as stated in Mark 10:11–12. Much of the church would cease to exist in America today if churches didn't allow divorced ministers and laypeople to serve. Thus, exceptions have been made and most Christians, even fundamentalist ones, overlook or justify these clear passages.

The Birth of American Evangelical Christianity

Evangelical Christianity, despite the claim from most evangelical leaders, has not existed since the beginning of Christ. Evangelical Christianity began to emerge in the 1730s.[13] It was and remains primarily a North American phenomenon that came from a confluence of Pietism, Puritanism, and Presbyterianism as an outgrowth of the Protestant Reformation of the sixteenth century.[14] By this time, much of Christianity's history already belonged to and was ensconced in the Catholic Church.

Evangelical Christianity and its theology emphasized a personal experience with God. Harkening back to the early days of Pauline Christianity, allegory allowed for Spirit-inspired scriptural interpretation and emotive experiences uncommon in churches framed in liturgy and doctrine. Evangelical Christianity initially settled on the American landscape with other Christian churches and denominations. But in the early part of the twentieth century, evangelicals divided into two groups: modernists and fundamentalists.[15] The modernists focused on social issues, such as poverty, injustice, inequality, and hunger, easily incorporating science and belief in God. Fundamentalists, on the other hand, focused on repenting, soul saving, and appeasing an angry God. Science was at odds with their literal understanding of the Bible.

Christian Fundamentalism in the Spotlight

Fundamentalists and their theology first came to national attention in the 1925 Scopes Monkey Trial. The State of Tennessee sued substitute teacher John Scopes for teaching evolution in a public school, which was a violation of state law. In reality, Scopes was a willful pawn used by attorney Clarence Darrow to bring the modernist-fundamentalist debate into the public spotlight. While Scopes lost the trial for violating the law (a verdict later overturned on a technicality), public opinion was swayed in favor of science and modernist Christianity, relegating fundamentalists into the political and cultural background.[16]

When Evangelicals Got Political

For many years, fundamentalism stayed primarily consigned to the South. But between 1910 and 1970, Southerners began moving West in search of jobs. By the 1960s, more Southerners were living in California than in Arkansas. "Love, Christian fellowship, communalism, belief in miracles, experiential faith, the expectation of Christ's return: these were merely the outlying pillars of the Jesus Movement's faith that circled around the center column of belief in the fundamental importance of evangelism," according to historian Darren Dochuk.[17] Southerners began building some of the first megachurches in Southern California and found political allies in politicians such as California governor Ronald Reagan. In the late 1960s, when SIECUS, the Sexuality Information and Education Council of the United States, began to provide sex education to high schools in Anaheim, California, it riled a new and what became a very powerful and vast force of evangelical parents who discovered they had a voice.[18]

Nevertheless, many fundamentalists were leery of involving themselves in politics. With the civil rights movement, however, private Christian schools were threatened with losing federal funding because of their refusal to integrate. That's when political strategist Paul Weyrich stepped in:

> [W]hat galvanized the Christian community was not abortion, school prayer, or the ERA [Equal Rights Amendment]. I am living witness to that because I was trying to get those people interested in those issues and I utterly failed. What changed their minds was Jimmy Carter's intervention against the Christian schools, trying to deny them tax-exempt status on the basis of so-called de facto segregation.[19]

In 1978, one year before launching a political attack against Jimmy Carter in favor of a Ronald Regan presidency, over two hundred evangelical leaders met as a sign of solidarity to create and sign what became known as the 1978 Chicago Statement on Biblical Inerrancy. It was the first time in Christian history that a group had come together to agree that the biblical canon, in its current form, was inerrant.[20] Harold Lindsell, editor of *Christianity Today* at the time, released his book *The Battle for the Bible* in the same year, declaring in it that if the scriptures were not inerrant, then Christianity would have no foundation upon which to stand.[21] The statement of inerrancy united fundamentalist Christians in ideology but divided them in implementation.

Eight years following the signed statement, evangelicals met to decide on a common mission addressing cultural and political issues of the day. Participant and theologian Kenneth Kantzer described the meeting this way:

> No one seemed to agree with anybody. Every issue became a battleground. All were committed to an inerrant Bible and accepted it as their final guide on matters of faith and practice. To many, radical disagreement as to how the Bible should be interpreted and applied seemed to pose a flat contradiction to their united commitment to an inerrant Bible. If all really accepted the Bible as their guide for life, how could they disagree so as to what is required of them?[22]

As theologian John McDermott points out, "[I]n practice, no one is entirely a fundamentalist, nor would it be possible to be one. There are so many contradictions in the details in the biblical stories that a fundamentalist approach is always a selective approach deciding which parts of the Bible to take literally."[23]

With the growth of Jerry Falwell's Moral Majority and newly realized political power, evangelicals helped unseat Jimmy Carter, who had been demonized as "an enemy of the family and 'traditional' values."[24] Their first president, Ronald Reagan, would be elected in 1980, despite the fact that he had been divorced and remarried, a theological disparity to most evangelicals at the time. But biblical morality came back into play in 1998 when Democratic president Bill Clinton's affair became public. Evangelicals, such as televangelist Pat Robertson, called for Clinton's impeachment calling, him "debauched, debased, and defamed."[25] When polled in 2011, 30 percent of white evangelicals believed that elected officials who committed an immoral act in their personal lives could still behave ethically and fulfill their duties, but by 2016, with their chosen candidate, Donald Trump, headed into the White House, that number had jumped to 72 percent.[26] Professor Kevin Kruse, in his book *One Nation Under God: How Corporate America Invented Christian America*, provides evidence that conservative politics has had its eye on evangelical Christians for political purposes since the 1940s.[27] Thanks to powerful Christian media moguls such as Jerry Falwell, Sr., Pat Robertson, and James Dobson and conservative political strategists such as the belated Paul Weyrich, millions of followers are convinced that their brand of Christianity is and always has been the God-ordained, unadulterated, biblically sanctioned truth.

Christianity has been a mixture of concepts since its inception. The concept of who Jesus was and what he stood for has morphed over time. Claudia Setzer notes, "The images of Jesus throughout history are as varied as the people who have embraced him."[28] Reza Aslan points out, "People don't derive their values from their religion—they bring their values to their religion."[29] While evangelical Christianity started out with the ideological intent of maintaining a high moral ground and a personal relationship with God, it has gone the way of the many versions before it, becoming mired in the fight for political and religious power.

Likewise, its stance on biblical inerrancy and authority grew out of a need to unite its membership and provide its political and religious leaders with divine authority. Evangelicals have given the Bible equal footing with God himself. The strict interpretation and unwillingness to think differently have wrapped God tightly in a box, united Christianity with conservative politics, and cordoned off a large segment of the population as enemies of God. In truth, there is no war on Christianity, as 70.6 percent of the United States identify as Christians.[30] To the contrary, the perceived "war" is a backlash against fundamentalist theology, which is based on nothing more than a misguided belief that the fundamentalist version of Christianity is the "only one." Historically speaking, it's not. Evangelical Christianity is simply another Christian experience, tailored and homogenized to fit within the culture that is uniquely American.

PART II

Rethinking Reality

CHAPTER 5

Truth

You take a knee for the Lord and you stand for the flag.

– Kellyanne Conway

Finding a self-identified conservative, evangelical Christian in the United States these days whose version of Christianity doesn't mirror the American dream, or more closely the GOP platform, is virtually impossible. A disagreement on gun laws, an argument in favor of affirmative action, or a vote toward marriage equality is the same as an assault on the Almighty himself. The Bible doesn't say anything about gun control. It doesn't address education rights or procorporate values. A solid argument can be made that it doesn't even say anything about homosexual relationships, a concept not identified until the late 1800s. (The term homosexual is not found in scriptures until 1946.[1]) So how did God become a Republican?

On February 28, 2018, the body of Billy Graham lay in honor in the nation's Capitol Rotunda, where only three other civilians have ever been placed. Two of them were officers who died in the line of duty protecting the Capitol from an armed assailant, and the other was Rosa Parks, a civil rights icon.[2] Billy Graham's legacy, however, was that of "America's pastor."[3] Graham became the self-appointed "pastor to the presidents," which ranged from Harry Truman to Barrack Obama.[4] To the religious right, Graham had earned his spot in the Rotunda for his "godly" influence on the nation. At first glance, Graham's message of salvation was always on point. He stayed in his lane, serving both Republican and Democratic presidents. He seldom strayed into politics, except for his endorsement of Richard Nixon, which he publically regretted.[45] But his legacy was anything but pure gospel.

As far back as the 1950s, Graham was an anticommunist, a trait he shared with Richard Nixon. He talked political strategy with Nixon and was in favor of crashing the North Korean economy for US national interest.[6] He was recorded at the White House in 1972 making anti-Semitic remarks. "A lot of Jews are great friends of mine," he said. "They swarm around me and are friendly to me. Because they know that I am friendly to Israel and so forth. But they don't know how I really feel about what they're doing to this country, and I have no power and no way to handle them."[7] Graham complained that Jews had a stranglehold on American media and would take the country "down the drain." He apologized for his comments at a 2002 crusade.[8]

A supporter of Martin Luther King, Graham bailed King out of jail in Albany, Georgia in 1957,[9] however, he wrote a letter to King telling him he thought the civil rights movement was moving too fast and King should "put the brakes on a little bit."[10] Following the delivery of King's famous "I have a dream" speech, Graham said, "Only when Christ comes again will the little white children of Alabama walk hand in hand with little black children."[11] Just months after the passage of the Civil Rights Act in 1965, at an Alabama crusade Graham proudly spoke about the Confederate flag and his heritage as a grandson of two rebel soldiers. Once again, Graham apologized many years later, both for his comments and for his lack of more involvement in the civil rights movement, specifically expressing regret for not attending the March on Selma.[12]

The problem is not that Graham had shortcomings. It's that Graham, like today's religious leaders, became so caught up in the passion of his political party's agenda that his message became indistinguishable from God's message. Right or wrong, Graham laid the foundation for the evangelical theocracy that has slowly encompassed conservative American politics. Frank Schaeffer, a former family friend of the Grahams and once considered conservative Christian royalty, wrote, "[Billy Graham] shaped an evangelical movement that then became as political as he was in his Nixon-supporting years and unlike Billy, this movement never repented of trading Jesus for politics."[13] To the contrary, Schaeffer goes on to write, "Billy Graham's veneer of pious civility is long gone from the white evangelical movement. It's been replaced by Billy Graham's own worst inner demons that he repented of after he'd become Nixon's confidant."[14]

Whether or not this was Graham's intention is unknown. His son and successor, Franklin Graham, has taken his father's theology to the extreme. Franklin, in 2011, jumped on the "birther movement," claiming Obama was not born in the United States, and even back then was ready to get behind a Donald Trump presidency.[15] Franklin's chant for political power has led him to defend Donald Trump's affairs[16] and support his antihuman policies. For example, Franklin is the president and CEO of Samaritan's Purse, an organization whose mission is to, according to its website, help "victims of war, poverty, natural disasters, disease, and famine."[17] But Franklin said that helping immigrants from war-torn countries is "not a Bible issue."[18] However, the Bible is very clear on this issue, unlike abortion, gun control, and nationalism, and states in one of many verses on the topic, "When a foreigner resides among you in your land, do not mistreat them. The foreigner residing among you must be treated as your native-born. Love them as yourself, for you were foreigners in Egypt" (Lev. 19:33–34).

Evangelical Christianity has created a Republican Jesus whose political ideologies are just as unapproachable as its theological ones. Political inerrancy doesn't allow for compromise or even discussion over matters deemed settled by God's word, whether or not the topic can even be found in God's word. Religious documents are held up as evidence and read in a way that reinforces and confirms these political ideologies indeed come from the Lord. This is not new.

In 1860, Rev. James Thornwell wrote in favor of slavery, "The parties in this conflict are not merely Abolitionists and slaveholders, they are Atheists, Socialists, Communists, Red Republicans, Jacobins on the one side and the friends of order and regulated freedom on the other."[19] One hundred years later, in 1960, Bob Jones, Sr., preached in favor of segregation, "When you run into conflict with God's established order racially, you have trouble. You produce destruction and trouble, and this nation is in the greatest danger it has ever been in its history."[20] Both preachers found truth in a version of God common to their cultures and upbringing.

American Christians have been conditioned to believe that without their version of God in control at the highest levels of the land and leading the nation to repentance, death and destruction are the only possible outcomes. Rev. Jerry Falwell, following the September 11 attacks on the World Trade Center in 2001, said, "What we saw on Tuesday, as terrible as it is, could be minuscule if in fact God continues to lift the curtain and allow the enemies of America to give us probably what we deserve." He blamed, among others, "the pagans and the abortionists and the feminists and the gays and the lesbians who are actively trying to make that an alternative lifestyle."[21] Falwell believed that faith and obedience to his view of God was the only thing keeping America safe. His view, and that of the evangelical Christian establishment, doesn't add up.

Researcher Gregory S. Paul analyzed, in detail, seventeen First World democracies to find out how they scored on twenty-five indicators, including social health, homicides, incarceration, poverty, abortions, and corruption. The United States was not only the most religious but also the most dysfunctional. Paul found the United States to have the highest religiosity but the lowest societal health.[22] The country has the highest homicide rates, highest gun violence of developed nations,[23] highest incarceration rates, and highest abortion rates.[24] Yet the United States boasts the largest concentration of Christians in the world.[25] If Republican Christianity were the answer (as opposed to any one of the other forty-one thousand versions), it seems there would be less division, more order, and more peace. When it comes to developed nations, other countries rank higher than "God-fearing Americans" on issues of social concern.

Of the 70.6 percent of Christians in the United States, only 25.4 percent identify as evangelicals.[26] Though a minority, evangelical Christians have gained unprecedented influence in national politics. Consequently, nationalism, capitalism, and anti-immigration have become synonymous with prayer, Bible reading, and church attendance. Political culture has not just *influenced* faith; it has *become* faith. American evangelicals move between their faith and political belief systems so seamlessly the two become virtually indistinguishable. If one is attacked, so is the other.

So what can we make of God? What is the truth about the Supreme Being? As stated earlier, "The images of Jesus throughout history are as varied as the people who have embraced him."[27] Indeed, a quick Google search on "depictions of Jesus around the world" produces an interesting array of physical characteristics, which, not surprisingly, resemble those of the cultures in which Jesus is portrayed. The same could be said of Buddha, Allah, Brahman, or any god of the twelve major world religions. Whatever truth exists about God comes not from the outside but from within.

A God Who Needs No Introduction

When I was a toddler, one of the babies in our apartment building died. I was acutely aware he wasn't coming back, as my father tells it. "Where did the baby go?" I asked my parents.

"He went to be with Jesus," they told me.

As we knelt down to do our prayers that night, I said, "Don't ask Jesus to watch over me anymore."

I was raised to believe that no matter what happened, everything was within the will of God. One way or another, things would work out. And going to heaven was better than being on earth. But the duplicity was glaring, even to a child. "Why not just kill ourselves?" I often wondered. Every funeral seemed to be a horribly sad occasion, and I went to a lot of them when I was a kid. Most of my father's siblings died during my childhood. Despite the faith I was taught, I saw and found no comfort in death.

I remember listening to my wailing grandmother after another child of hers had died. Amid emotional songs and shouts of praise, the gospel was preached. Toward the end of the funeral, ushers invited the grieving loved ones to walk up and view the body for the last time. I was around seven years old and petrified. I decided, instead, to make a beeline for a hallway off to the side. It seemed like a good place to wait until the funeral was over. The minutes ticked by as I waited for my parents to come and get me, but they never did. I finally decided to venture out and find them. One hallway led to another, none of which led to my parents. Then I turned a corner and ran right into the coffin containing my aunt. I was traumatized. I feared hospitals and death well into my adult life. The smell of that particular funeral home, indescribable to this day, stays with me.

These types of experiences, which were a mixture of anxiety and fear, comfort, love, faith, doctrine, and dogma, built the foundation of my belief in God. I accepted the "truth" about God, despite my naturally analytical brain, but much more was happening in those formative years. Values were placed on certain ideologies. Funerals were homegoings. Church was where God met with us through worship. Swearing made God unhappy. If I didn't believe in or follow God, I would go to hell.

When I became an adult, especially during my time as a conversion therapy leader, politics became as much a part of my spiritual consciousness as Bible memorization. Growing up in the 1970s and '80s at the height of televangelism under the influences of Jerry Falwell, the preaching of Jimmy Swaggart, and the mystical words of knowledge by Pat Robertson infused in me a specific brand of faith. My truth and personal confession of faith from the ages of fifteen to forty, revolved like a Chicago turnstile around *that* version of God, the inerrant Bible, and my troubled reality. That God had always been there. I knew him intimately. He needed no introduction.

Truth

I received a call at work early one morning telling me that my younger daughter, only eighteen-months-old at the time, had cut off the tip of her finger. She had been standing in the bathroom doorway, unbeknownst to her aunt, who shut the door on her hand. An ambulance was called and my daughter was taken to the emergency room. As soon as I got the news I rushed to the hospital, where I found my little girl writhing in pain. I experienced one of the most helpless feelings I'd had as a parent. My daughter screeched at the top of her lungs and there was nothing I could do to make her pain go away. The doctor came into her room and explained to her mother and me that he needed to give her a shot in the wound to numb the pain so he could sew the tip of her little finger back on with stitches that went through her fingernail. As horrifying as that sounded, I knew that's what needed to happen. So I lay across my daughter's chest and held her hand still while the doctor poked the needle into her wound. Fortunately, the anesthesia worked fast, and my daughter was exhausted from the crying. She fell asleep just as the doctor finished the procedure.

That trip to the hospital was the first time I came face to face with my soon-to-be-ex-wife's new boyfriend. My parents were there, too, as were my in-laws. We all saw him. Emotions were raw and some tense moments occurred between my ex and me. By the time the ordeal was over and we all went our separate ways, I was exhausted. I woke up the next day feeling as if someone had taken a sledgehammer to my back. However, I knew my little girl would be okay because I, too, had cut off the tip of my finger in a car door when I was four years old, and it was sewn back on. Were it not for the scar on my finger and the story my parents have had to repeat more than once, I would have never known it happened.

When truth confronts us, it's difficult to deny. Unlike my feelings of same-sex attraction, which I could stuff down and lie to myself and others about, divorce documents telling me my marriage was over and seeing my wife with another man was an inescapable reality. Life wasn't going to turn out the way I'd planned and there was nothing I, or my incessant prayers, could do about it. The proof stood in front of me. Even if I walked away, it still existed. Untouched and unbothered by my denial, the devastating effects of my divorce were unstoppable. No faith was required, just a willingness to face it.

Truth is the uncompromising, unobstructed acceptance of reality. Does God still live in that reality? Perhaps a better question is, Can the God we believe in survive that reality? We cannot pray away bad financial situations or bad relationships, especially when we created them. And we usually don't get to choose or change the consequences of those truths. As Oprah-esque as it sounds, truth really is individual and personal. My truth, like my version of God, may be different from your truth simply because my perception of reality is different from yours.

For example, in 2012, country singer Randy Travis crashed his car on the side of the road near Tioga, Texas. He then got out of his car and walked into the local convenience store–naked. An employee there called the police, who picked up Travis and put him in the squad car. The video of that arrest was released in 2017 and embarrassed Travis and his family because it depicted a clearly altered Travis making death threats to police officers. The exchange was laced with expletives from Travis, whose public persona is that of a humble, church-going Southern gentleman. Upon the release of the video, Travis's lawyer released a statement stating Travis had apologized to the officers for those statements, which were made after a horrific accident and severe head injury. The lawyer reminded the public that Travis would be remembered as someone who "lived his life as an ambassador of goodwill, tolerance and acceptance."[28]

Randy Travis's reality and thus his truth were different in those hours with the police officers. Whatever the reason–drugs, alcohol, or a bump on the head–walking around naked and threatening the lives of cops seemed like perfectly reasonable behavior to him at the time. He was living in his truth and responding accordingly. The officers gently and respectfully engaged with Travis, even offering to take him to the hospital, which he declined. Travis was convinced he was fine and his arrest was unwarranted.

Truth is always subjective because it always depends on our interpretation, whether we are chemically altered, we grew up in a cult, or were immersed in our own culture. We are shaped and formed by the society in which we live, which sometimes contradicts our personal truth by asking us to conform. Whether or not we embrace our truth depends largely on us and what we're willing to risk. Humans are, by nature, complex and diverse beings. Internal and external pressures drive us through our biology, our neurology, and a host of other underlying, often imperceivable influences. No matter what anyone tells you, there is no such thing as *the* truth when it comes to existential matters. Denying truth does not negate it, but simply creates a momentarily safe bubble to make us feel better in the short term.

Living in Truth

One day, Abel and I jumped on a bus near our hotel room in New York City. I'd never been on a New York bus before. I recommend it as one of the more culturally inclusive experiences a person can have in New York City, next to riding the subway. Unfamiliar with the cost, Abel grabbed a handful of coins out of his messenger bag and passed them to me.

With coins spilling over the side of my clutched palm, I asked the bus driver how much it cost for two tickets. With a stereotypical New York accent she loudly rattled off the price list while I started dropping coins in the meter as she drove the bus to the next stop. I couldn't remember if she said the cost was $2.50 each or $1.25. Nevertheless, I shoved coins into the slot until something dinged. I looked up at the driver.

"Well, did you put all the money in there or not?" she yelled at me.

I had no idea how much money I put in the meter. I assumed there was a ticker going somewhere and she would tell me when I was done.

"Yes. Yes, I did," I said without any confidence at all.

The driver glared at me as if I were trying to pull one over on her and handed me two tickets. I made my way to the back of the bus where Abel was, feeling like I was about to get in trouble. As I walked I stared back at the seasoned New York riders who knew, clearly, I wasn't from there. I shoved the rest of the coins in my pocket and sat down.

At the next stop an elderly woman stepped onto the bus. She looked like she was in her late sixties and she had long, disheveled gray hair. She was around five feet, four inches tall and had bushy gray eyebrows. Her nose was long and her eyes were close together. She wore a long blue denim skirt with a white and blue long-sleeved blouse. Her teeth were very large and very crooked. She got on the bus talking and never stopped. I had the feeling I'd seen her somewhere before. She was a caricature of someone I'd seen in a sitcom or someone who played character roles in movies. Perhaps it was just her uncanny resemblance to the crazy cat lady on *The Simpsons* that made her seem familiar.

I've seen people like her before, but they were not quite as animated. These are the people who stand out from everyone else because of their physical traits, personality characteristics, or both. They have refused to or simply can't conform. They are misfits. Yet most tend to find their niches or a social group in which they live. They make life fit their reality rather than conforming to everyone else's view around them. They seem to have accomplished what many of us "normal people" can't: radical self-acceptance. They own their truth and it shows.

If it were not for social norms, how many more of us would also be caricatures? I wonder what we would do or say or how we might act differently. If we had the opportunity, how many of us would dress differently, express ourselves more honestly, or just detach from the world in which we find ourselves?

Discovering my truth, as I chronicled in *Going Gay*, was a long, arduous process. Even after the book was published, I wondered what was next. Having the story out there didn't make acceptance of my truth any easier. In some ways it made it harder. I had to face up to what I'd written about. I had to dive deeper into areas of shame I'd worked so hard to avoid for all those decades. I felt life was passing by too fast and I'd just started living.

Truth outside of faith becomes less controllable. You no longer have quick and easy explanations for everything. When you find that empty parking space next to the front door of the mall, it's as much of a random chance it was before, but now you recognize it as a random chance, not a divine intervention. You also recognize much bigger truths: poverty is a problem around the world that can't be prayed away, as are disease, brutality, and war. Children go hungry every night in America, and unless we do something besides worship louder in the pew the problem is not going to be solved. "Thoughts and prayers" is a meaningless statement to victims of school massacres. The petty things we asked God to do for us, like getting us a good price on a new television or helping our sports team to win, suddenly become insignificant. Our truth is that we are part of a much bigger living, interconnected sentient organism that needs all of us to help keep it alive and healthy.

Humans aren't the only ones who discover deeper truths. Our cat, Sam, loved playing with lasers as a kitten, as most cats do. He could play for hours frantically chasing the laser up the wall, down the hall, and virtually anywhere else it went. As Sam grew older, however, he became less interested in capturing the laser and more interested in just watching it move. If it stood still long enough, he might muster the energy to go over and check it out, but that became less and less likely. And then one day, years later, as the laser flickered across the floor, Sam looked up. He suddenly realized the laser came from a source. He pawed the hand of the person holding it. He looked at it from several angles–front to back and side to side–noticing the button that turned the light on and off. The mystery of the laser had been solved.

Sam turned from believing that the light was some kind of mystery bug that could one day be caught to seeing the truth that the light was emanating from a device that was being controlled. Of course, that he figured it out certainly didn't help me sleep any better at night. But it does illustrate the point that truth is not elusive. It's not hidden. However, it does require thought and contemplation. Finding truth requires us to look at things differently, with purpose and without fear. We have to look up, examine our surroundings, and question whether what we believe is really true, if there is evidence, or if there is another explanation. Does our "truth" liberate or shackle us? Does it lead to freedom or more hiding? Does it help us think more clearly or cloud the issues? Is it based solely in our beliefs or in our reality?

CHAPTER 6

The Conflicted Brain

A great part of my life's work has been spent to destroy my own illusions and those of humankind.

– Sigmund Freud

Standing around the office one day, my coworkers and I somehow got onto the topic of bacon. I've always been a fan. Most vegetarians and vegans I know confess the same thing, even years after crossing over to plant-based eating. I casually mentioned to my office mates that, although I do love bacon, neuroscience has shown that pigs, like dogs, have a capacity for emotions that is very similar to humans. "Bacon isn't quite as enjoyable with that knowledge," I confessed.

"My grandparents raised pigs on their farm for food," someone said. "Before the pigs were butchered, the pigs knew what was going to happen. They would often wet themselves because they were so terrified." And with that last statement, I stopped eating bacon. (Side note: After learning that cows and chickens also experience emotions like humans and struggle to survive in slaughterhouses, I became a vegan.)

What occurred to me in that moment is called cognitive dissonance. I had two opposing thoughts: "I love bacon," and, "It's cruel to kill pigs for food, especially if pigs express the same emotions as humans." Could I continue to eat bacon while thinking about a terrified pig about to be slaughtered? If I eat it in my sanitized kitchen, it's certainly easier not to think about where the bacon came from. On the other hand, now that I know that pigs are terrified to die, just like humans, I have to work a lot harder to get the image out of my head. I was placed in a mental dilemma. (And now, so are you.)

Cognitive Dissonance

Cognitive dissonance is simply a state of being for humans. Our brains naturally and cleverly cover, disguise, defend, and deny mental conflict. Whether it's taking, or should I say *stealing*, office supplies from work, justifying our saying hurtful words to a spouse, not telling the store clerk we got back too much change, or praying to a God we're not even sure exists, cognitive dissonance fills our lives every day. Like mentally dismissing the image of a pig in a slaughterhouse, we justify our behaviors and swallow our doubts to do the best we can to continue living our lives without disruption. Mental conflict appears when the dissonance gets too loud and we find we can no longer ignore its insistence in the background.

In 2010, at the Center for Cognitive Studies at Tufts University, researchers Daniel Dennett and Linda LaScola studied pastors who no longer believed in God. One of their subjects, called Adam, was a forty-three-year-old worship leader at a Church of Christ congregation in South Carolina. He was a conservative Christian who attended a conservative college, eventually earning a master's degree in religion. When he was confronted with mental conflict in college he said,

> OK, here's what Biblical scholars are saying, and there's some questions over here, but I just trust God, and know he's guiding me, and I'm learning this so I can be a minister and help people. When I was working with people, it was a lot more practically focused on, "OK, here's what the Bible says, how do we live it out? How do we encourage

> other people? What's the whole evangelistic side of Christianity? How can we win more people into Christ?" I mean you're sincere; that's what your goal is. You don't want anybody to miss out and to go to hell.[1]

But his hunger for knowledge eventually led him to rethink his beliefs about God. A Christian apologetic book he read began to change his mind. The purpose of the book was to answer the criticisms non-Christians have about the faith. Adam wanted to become a more skilled apologist, able to answer the skeptics intelligently. Instead, Adam said, "If God is God, he's big enough; he can handle any questions I've got. Well, he didn't. He didn't measure up! I always thought there was absolute truth out there. Now I'm a lot more relativistic."[2] Adam estimated he watched, read, or listened to about sixty videos, books, and podcasts that year. As much as he wanted to believe he was right about his faith, he said he had to confess that some of the atheist debaters made points he couldn't argue against. To keep his mind open and listen, he faced his cognitive dissonance head-on and came out the other side as a nonbeliever himself.

Yet Adam stayed in his position as a worship leader in the ministry. He struggled to give up the rich community his life as a minister provided him. "You have great friends who are close; you can depend on them. When there's hard times, financially, emotionally, whatever, you've got a support group," he said.[3] He feared that leaving his position would have a detrimental effect on his family, still strong believers, and members of the congregation. At the same time, he thinks people could benefit if they face reality, "It'd be good for people to grow up and to think things through at least. If they decide to keep their faith, that's fine. But if they don't, let's be real about it."[4] Adam wonders if it is better to leave people in their ignorance, if Christianity isn't true, or encourage them to question it themselves. In the meantime, he chose to continue working for the church and keeping his family in that position. Not everyone, however, has the luxury of making those decisions.

I'm contacted on a fairly regular basis by men who have been married thirty, forty, fifty years or more who are struggling with their sexual orientation. They often have grown kids and sometimes grandkids. Their sex lives with their spouses have been nonexistent for years. Either the relationship is cold and distant or the spouses have become comfortable, platonic friends. The mental discord these men experience has been described as simmering water that's coming to the surface. They don't think they can keep it from boiling over and by the time they contact me, they feel like they are about to explode. These men feel very alone, yet some hold high positions within their communities, businesses, or churches. Some are pastors. They know that to admit they are gay would likely have devastating social, relational, and even financial consequences. Some write, "I've never told a soul about this before" or "I can't believe I'm writing this down. If anyone ever found out, my life would be over." Their conflict is bigger than a struggle over sexual orientation; it's a struggle over self-identity, a belief system that doesn't match their realities, and an overarching view of whether or not God even loves them. Sadly, I almost never get a return email when I respond to the most desperate pleas for help.

In my work with survivors of conversion therapy, and people struggling to reconcile their faith and sexuality, I see a running theme. Their questions, which often start over a conflict regarding their conservative, literal beliefs about the Bible, expand to questions about whether or not any of the Bible is true and, sometimes, even if God exists. Their spouses often begin to question the same issues. Many of those who confess their sexual orientation to their pastors and church leaders suddenly find themselves on the outside of once-vibrant social circles. They are asked to step down as deacons, pastors, and worship leaders. As Mark Twain famously said, "A man is accepted into a church for what he believes and he is turned out for what he knows." These men, their wives, and their children sometimes become fodder for church gossip. In many cases, incredulously, wives are blamed for the husbands' homosexuality.

The realization that their belief system isn't working as designed sends these men into a mental tailspin. When they followed the rules and *appeared* to be the upstanding family men that was expected of them, they found favor, position, and sometimes power. But that lasted only while they swallowed their doubts, kept secrets, and put on the friendly faces others wanted to see. It's not that they didn't have doubts before, or that they suddenly turned gay. They were always gay. The marital struggles were always real, no matter how attractive or together the couple seemed. But when the secret comes out, even if it had only been thinly veiled or rumored to be true, false ideals are suddenly exposed. What was *supposed* to have worked–prayer, Bible reading, accountability, confession, and forgiveness–didn't. Over time, the mind can no longer make excuses or cover up reality. Reality festers like an infection. It needs attention before it goes septic. But that seldom happens at first. Instead, many of us spiral into self-justification, denial, and willful blindness to our doubts.

Self-Justification

What causes mental conflict for one person may not affect another. How we live for years, or our entire lives, with mental conflict depends a lot on how our brains work: what we perceive to be mental conflict, what we don't, and what we can live with are very individual. But how we justify our decisions and behaviors is remarkably similar.

Bernard Lawrence Madoff founded a securities investment firm in 1960. He remained the chairman of that firm until December 11, 2008, when he was arrested for what became known as the world's biggest Ponzi scheme, involving more than $65 billion. According to reports, he confessed to his sons that the asset management unit of his firm was "one big lie." The US Securities and Exchange Commission had investigated Madoff's firm many times before but never discovered Madoff's secret. Madoff later confessed guilt to eleven federal felonies, stating he began the scheme in the early 1990s, but investigators believe he actually began the fraud in the mid-1980s, with evidence suggesting it may have begun as far back as the 1970s.[5]

How could Madoff sit on that information for so many years and not experience tremendous guilt? Cognitive dissonance researchers Carol Tavris and Elliot Aronson explain:

> Self-justification has costs and benefits. By itself, it's not necessarily a bad thing. It lets us sleep at night. Without it, we would prolong the awful pangs of embarrassment. We would torture ourselves with regret over the road not taken or over how badly we navigated the road we did take. We would agonize in the aftermath of almost every decision: Did we do the right thing, marry the right person, buy the right house, choose the best car, enter the right career? Yet, mindless

> self-justification, like quicksand, can draw us deeper into disaster. It blocks our ability to even see our errors, let alone correct them. It distorts reality, keeps us from getting all the information we need and assessing issues clearly.[36]

While Madoff's case may involve a more sinister psychological anomaly, his self-justification for continuing with the scheme and bilking billions of dollars from investors is an extreme version of how our brains sometimes keep us mentally trapped for years. Once the God component gets added, self-justification can be a death sentence.

If the social pressure we feel from our families and churches isn't enough to make us stay the course, we often have the nagging feeling that if we even *try* to look at things differently, God is hanging over us like the proverbial Catholic schoolmarm, ready to swat us with a wooden ruler. We must look straight ahead, work through the answers on our own tests, and dare not ask a friend for help–not because our friend wouldn't give it to us but because asking for help is a sign of weakness, a crack in the armour of faith. We don't want our friends to be disappointed in us, but more importantly, we don't want to do anything to put our own eternal lives in jeopardy. So we tell ourselves to buck up. God has a plan. We don't have to understand but just trust him. If God's plan is in conflict with what we think, then we clearly don't understand what the Word of God is saying. And if we dare speak up, multitudes of people are there to remind us we are doing something wrong!

But when we step back and look at the mental acrobatics we go through to keep the faith, it seems almost, dare I say, cultlike. Are we drinking the Kool-Aid because we are forced to do so? Is *God* really the one driving us to keep the purity of the scriptures intact? What is the mental image that causes us to continue enduring our deepest struggles? What exactly continues to push us to make our faith work–and work in the way we believe it should?

As an outspoken critic of politics, a writer on sexuality, and a skeptic of religion–topics most people consider sacred and off limits for a civil discussion–I attract what my friend and fellow author Bill Prickett calls "Holy Trollers." He categorizes them as biblical literalists, prophets of doom, concerned evangelists, defenders of faith, and biblical ninjas. Some are put off by the titles of my articles and leave long rebuttals without reading what I've written. Others respond with long diatribes about my biblical ineptness. Some post strings of Bible verses, sometimes related to the topic and sometimes not. My favorite was the guy who said, "You insulted the Pope" (because I said the pope has no formal education in human sexuality) "and now you're asking people to think for themselves. I don't even think you're a Christian!" On the few times I've tried to engage with these people to find out what they hoped to accomplish, I've only been met with more Bible verses and occasional pseudoscientific references or anecdotal stories to "prove" I'm wrong. "Just because you are a failed ex-gay doesn't mean God is incapable. Look at this person," many people have written.

Our differences are not likely due to a lack of intelligence on anyone's part. That's the easy answer, isn't it? "You're stupid"–end of discussion. We feel confident and self-justified in our assessment and we move on with our lives and beliefs intact. If we are convinced that certain people are stupid and incapable of having reasonable conversations, we can more quickly dismiss them and never even consider what they have to say. Or worse, we believe stupid people don't deserve to be heard. They are not like the rest of us. They should be silenced. Whether we have extreme religious beliefs or extreme religious doubts, our belief system works the same: we self-justify our answers and push away contradictory claims either in favor of or against what we want or need to believe.

The Things We Do for Love

In 2016, a well-known gospel singer gave a sermon to her congregation in which she spoke about the "perverse" spirit of homosexuality. She had recently recorded a song for a movie about to hit theaters when the video of her sermon got out. Her appearances on television were cancelled, and she quickly drew ire from the entertainment industry. The situation went from bad to worse for this singer, who seemingly didn't have a friend in the world, except, perhaps, from one unlikely source.

I had written an article to address the situation, and it was placed in the Black Voices section of the *Huffington Post*. Twitter lit up and commenters were quick to debate my words. Within a couple of hours, I received a private message from someone telling me how the singer came through for him at a time when he needed help the most. He was once gay and transgender, but thanks to the singer, his life had changed. I wanted to know more about his story. I clicked on his social media page and was instantly struck by the disparities. The name was genderless and the preferred pronouns were gender neutral: they, their. The social media page belied the confident heterosexual who had emailed me.

I responded by telling him that I thought it was great he was standing up for his friend and that I didn't think the singer intentionally spoke hate. He thanked me and asked if I would write a story to put her in a better light. It was clear to me he felt indebted to her and that her influence had made a huge difference in his life. But research shows that transgender people don't suddenly get over gender dysphoria and gay people don't suddenly become straight. I wanted to know more about him. Through a series of email exchanges I asked him several questions, beginning with what drew him to the singer's church.

"I was going through some problems at the time so my friend invited me to visit the church. I was gay and transgender, but God was just so powerful I joined the church that night," he said. And then he used a word I knew well. "God gave me deliverance." *Deliverance*–the magic destiny fundamentalists strive to reach and a word that evokes shouts of praise and dances of joy.

I asked if he still considered himself gay or transgender, and he responded by saying he no longer uses labels for himself. So I asked more direct questions. "Do the members of the church believe you are no longer gay?" He responded by sending a list of Bible verses. So I asked again, "When you use the word *deliverance* at church, are you speaking it the way the members of your church hear it?" More importantly, I asked, "Do they know what you are *truly* thinking and feeling?"

He avoided answering the question by providing more scriptures and telling me that the Bible speaks clearly for itself. Having interviewed many "ex-gays" and written many stories on the topic, I heard exactly what he *wasn't* saying.

Our sense of self-justification is strong and often propelled by the "truth" we need to believe to maintain the ideologies we think are vital to life. Whatever this young man felt or thought in the still hours of the night–and he admitted to "same-sex" and "gender temptations"–were pushed aside in favor of a life more closely aligned with who he felt he needed to be. He belongs to a community that offers him acceptance, but only as long as he conforms to the social norms expected of him. He certainly didn't see it that way. He didn't want to. Yet, by his answers, I could tell he was willing to give up a significant portion of who he is to stay in fellowship. To him, the word *deliverance* means an ongoing fight against the internal person he is. To his pastor and members of his congregation, it means he is no longer gay or transgender, that God, through the Holy Spirit, has changed him and made him straight. It's in this young man's best interest at this point in his life to push the discrepancy between the definitions to the back of his mind and stay plugged into his community. That's what most of us do.

We are wired for community and belonging, and nothing is inherently wrong with adjusting or controlling our behaviors to maintain our connections. We adjust them naturally when we're with our grandparents as opposed to our friends, our coworkers, or our spouses. The dangerous conflict happens when we start acting like someone we're not for the sole purpose of love and acceptance. Over time this is what creates cognitive dissonance. When the dissonance between who we are pretending to be or what we pretend to believe and who we really are or what we really believe gets too strong, we begin struggling to find a sense of reality. Letting go of the reality, which is usually attached to community, is nearly impossible because of the high price we will pay. So most of us stay in mental conflict for years. Some develop addictions, and some lead separate lives where they have an outlet to feel more comfortable being who they are.

Clarence Busch was the catalyst for the creation of Mothers Against Drunk Driving, or MADD, an organization that fights to end drunk driving. Candace Lightner founded the organization after Busch struck and killed Lightner's thirteen-year-old daughter who had been walking on the side of the road, in a hit and run. Busch already had four drunk driving citations prior to striking Lightner's daughter, spending only two and a half years in jails, work camps and a halfway house for the incident.[7] Thanks to MADD, a minimum drinking age was established nationwide, as well as stiffer penalties for drunk drivers everywhere. Besides Busch's penchant for alcohol and driving drunk–he received two more convictions of drunk driving after being released from prison–the public knew little about him. And despite the fact that a made-for-TV movie about his life depicted him as an out-of-control drunk with a fearful, submissive wife, Busch was a church-going, God-fearing, closeted alcoholic.

Our families were friends through our Assemblies of God church. Clarence Busch was an active member of the church, along with his wife and kids, whom I knew from the youth group. Our families had spent time together at each other's homes, church functions, and occasionally restaurants. My family was shocked, along with his wife and kids, to learn the depth and devastation of his addiction. Drinking alcohol wasn't an acceptable practice in our church. Anyone who drank was suspected of not being saved. A Christian struggling with alcoholism was unfathomable. So rather than get help, Busch hid his problem from his family, his friends, and his church.

We learned later that he would tell fellow Sunday morning ushers that he was going outside for a security check of the cars in the parking lot but instead would sit in his car and drink. Busch compartmentalized his Christian faith and his alcoholism, keeping the two lives separate. He operated in a way that kept his community at arm's length for fear of rejection, keeping up the appearance that everything worked for him despite the mental conflict. Though he believed in deliverance, or at least said he did, his reality was quite different. He couldn't separate what he believed to be true about God and how it all worked for him personally.

The mental conflicts we face often put us in uncomfortable positions. We don't ask for these conflicts. Quite frankly, we'd rather they didn't exist. For several years after my divorce I thought I would have much rather stayed married and kept up the facade than feel like a total failure and suffer the embarrassment of thinking I was the only one who couldn't make my ex-gay life work. In hindsight, of course, the divorce was the best thing that happened to me. I'm loved and in love with my spouse. I no longer suffer from health issues or mental anguish. I have a robust group of friends, live a comfortable life, and have found my voice. Mental conflict, however, was only the beginning of the journey.

CHAPTER 7

Rethinking Me

Freeing yourself was one thing; claiming ownership of that freed self was another.
– Toni Morrison

Seldom do we take time for reflection when life is going well. We have no reason to second-guess our decisions or question our motives when things are working to our advantage. We squeeze ourselves into Christian explanations for a sometimes very un-Christian existence. But phrases like "God won't give us more than we can bear" and "All things work together for good" can become fodder for a mental firestorm. During my divorce, I could think of no logical reason for my Christian family to be torn apart. The anguish and self-loathing of my existence at that time was contrary to the "abundant life" I'd so adamantly preached. I knew something had to give soon. Unwittingly, I'd started a journey toward self-awareness, not knowing where it would lead or how long it would take.

Self-Awareness

Self-awareness takes inventory of our feelings, thoughts, emotions, and beliefs as well as the consequences or surroundings of the life we've created. Perhaps that seems like an odd statement. Many of us feel more like passive participants or maybe even victims of our circumstances. Mentally processing life as happening *to* us is easier than thinking about being responsible for what it's become.

I don't mean to suggest that we screw up our lives on purpose. We tend to follow our belief road map very closely, particularly as it relates to core values, and then make life-altering decisions, such as whom we marry, where we work, how we vote, where we go to church, and where and how we spend our money. Acting on our beliefs is the consequence for believing, and often the catalyst for change. When the consequences don't turn out the way we think they should, we are compelled to take a closer look.

Self-Belief

"This is going to sound a little weird coming from me," my high-school-freshman daughter said while looking at my old high-school photos at her grandmother's house, "but you were kinda cute." I glanced at a picture. I was a scrawny kid with ridiculously thick, curly dark brown hair. I realized she was right, at least compared to the pop music icons of *her* day. They also have no muscles and hair that is either uncombed or has unmanageable cowlicks going in opposite directions. (I have the latter.) I'd learned to lower my expectations whenever one of my daughters, at that age, pointed out a "good-looking man." Clearly, we had different criteria–perhaps as it should be.

No matter what I looked like, high school was miserable for me. I carried so much shame about who I was as a gay kid. Nothing anyone said or did could have changed my view. I learned to perform musically to find praise and acceptance, but even that didn't change how I felt about myself.

Outside influences on what we think of ourselves are one facet, but internal influences are another. I've known plenty of people who were abused as kids, grew up poor, or struggled to fit in yet somehow didn't struggle with their self-worth. I, on the other hand, who grew up in a relatively good family, struggled intensely to recognize my own value. Some days I still can't seem to find the internal fortitude to pull myself together. The reason some of us struggle is not so much about *why* we believe the way we do about ourselves but *what* we believe about ourselves and the way it manifests. We can't always change the why, but we can change the what.

Self-Compassion

At a mindfulness conference I attended, the facilitator asked the attendees to write down what they would say to a friend who had just lost his job. People shared their responses, which included encouragement, support, and empathy. The facilitator then asked the audience to write down what they would say to themselves if they had just lost a job. The tone changed. Comments were much harsher; people expressed impatience and even disappointment at the sense of failure.

Why don't we offer the same compassion to ourselves that we offer others? The pain we feel is often deeper as participants in such a situation than observers. Yet we don't feel we deserve to be comforted or to experience the same peace we wish for others. A general lack of compassion is part of our Western culture, and the lack of compassion we have for ourselves can be astounding.

Dove soap company conducted an interesting experiment in France. It asked women to write down their body flaws and then hired actresses to say those words to a friend in a crowded cafe within earshot of the person who wrote them. The women who wrote the words chastised some of the actresses for saying such horrible things to their friends. Other women became tearful upon hearing their inner thoughts voiced aloud as criticisms toward other equally beautiful women. They labeled the words as "mean" and even "schoolyard bullying."[1]

The idea of self-compassion sounds like letting ourselves off the hook or giving ourselves excuses. But growing research shows that just the opposite is true. Researcher Kristin Neff says, "Self-compassionate people set high standards for themselves, but they aren't as upset when they don't meet their goals. Instead, they're more likely to set new goals for themselves after failure rather than wallowing in feelings of frustration and disappointment." Neff says that people who have the ability to show self-compassion tend to have healthier behaviors overall, such as sticking to weight loss goals and taking care of themselves.[2]

If you grew up in a church that preached Christ is everything and you are nothing, you likely internalized a sense of unworthiness. If love was withheld by parents, friends, or pastors because you didn't measure up to the ideals of the faith, self-compassion is a concept almost completely outside the realm of comprehension. The outcome is often a lack of patience with ourselves, self-loathing, and an underlying feeling that we deserve all the bad things that happen to us. Furthermore, when we begin to question the faith, we sometimes feel an overwhelming sense of shame for even asking questions. Much of this happens unconsciously, and it's difficult to label these feelings as a problem with self-esteem or a lack of self-compassion.

Vyckie Garrison escaped the Quiverfull movement, a fundamentalist cultlike practice to which the infamous reality TV stars the Duggars, of *19 Kids and Counting*, adhere. Quiverfull contains many of the beliefs found in fundamentalist Christianity, such as the husband being the authority of the house and all the standard tenets of the faith, but they also don't believe in birth control. Women should have as many babies as they can and their children, warriors for God, must help create a theistic dominion in the government. That seemed to work for a few years for Vyckie–until she had a complete emotional breakdown. But because of the indoctrination of her faith, Vyckie had a difficult time identifying what she was feeling:

> The signs of emotional abuse include put downs, shaming, and guilt-tripping. Well, this is something my husband would never do... there really was no need since I was already fully aware of my inherently sinful nature, my "desperately wicked heart." He didn't need to remind me that even my very best efforts were like filthy rags in comparison to God's holiness.
>
> Plus, I knew that as a woman, I was particularly susceptible to deception by Satan. How many times, when we were discussing an important decision, had my husband said to me, "What you are suggesting *sounds* reasonable, but how do I know that Satan isn't using you to deceive me?"
>
> Well, according to the Bible, it was very likely that Satan WAS using me. "And Adam was not the one deceived; it was the woman

> who was deceived and became a sinner. But women will be saved through child-bearing—if they continue in faith, love and holiness with propriety" (1 Timothy 2:14–15). As a good Christian woman, the last thing I wanted was to be accused of having a "Jezebel Spirit!" Jezebel is the bossy, bold and dominating woman, who "wears the pants" in the family, and in the Bible account, things ended badly for her."[3]

Coming to terms with what we believe about ourselves and how we got there can be excruciating. Sometimes we feel stupid for believing something for so long that wasn't true or embarrassed for not seeing it earlier. Self-compassion can be difficult to muster, particularly if we want to crawl under a rock. Many of us have been told, "Just get over it," or "Don't feel that way." We've been told to suck it up and get on with our lives. Perhaps we've even said this to ourselves. I know I did. The hollow feeling that follows comes from the self-asked, "What's wrong with you?"

Victim or Survivor?

I chose early on to become a survivor of ex-gay therapy instead of a victim. I certainly don't want to diminish the effects of conversion or reparative therapy. They are real and in many cases severe. Some people have committed suicide because they felt they could never be "normal." Religious abuse from authority is common, particularly in fundamentalist organizations that stress the role of hierarchy and conforming roles. I've heard horrific stories of mental and physical torture, humiliation, and exclusion by victims who couldn't perform for their religious communities. Choosing to be a survivor released me from the control of my experiences, though it did not deny the experiences themselves or the emotions that accompanied them.

Being victimized is not the same as being a victim. I felt victimized by the entire fundamentalist movement, though unwittingly on the adherents' part. I was led to believe things about myself that were not true. I made important decisions based on those beliefs and spent years of my life living a lie. Perhaps more tragically, I led others astray, telling them they could become what I believed God wanted for them. Decades later, some of the people to whom I ministered and I were all in the same boat, trying to unravel the lies and figure out who we were.

In the "detox" process of addressing past abuses, we must focus on how those abuses made us feel and not rehash what was done to us. If we wallow in the abuse, we continue to be victimized, thus giving abusers even more of our time and energy. I've met a lot of people through the years who get addicted to the feeling of victimhood. They use the attention they receive because of their abuses to validate themselves as human beings. They unconsciously fear that if they don't have problems in their lives, which in many cases defined them for years, no one will pay attention to them. In a distorted way, they believe they will lose their value and purpose.

I received a call one day from a well-established author who finally decided to write her personal story about being married to a gay man for over twenty-five years. For forty-five minutes her tone vacillated from that of an objective journalist to a jilted wife. "I want to give this story the fair attention to detail it deserves," she'd say, followed by, "I fucking hate him!" Her rampage included how she'd lost her church, her children, and her home. "He couldn't even be honest with me about how many times he cheated! I did everything for that man." The bitterness of her sorrow was deep. My heart broke with hers.

Sadly, she confessed, I was the first person to whom she ever told her story. Her church told her the reason her husband was gay was that she wasn't a good enough wife and didn't try hard enough. She was told to get him involved in an ex-gay ministry, but that only drove his deceptive behavior further underground. With his church behind him, his wife became the perfect scapegoat, one he could easily throw away when he was ready to move on.

She had every reason to be angry. She had been shamed into silence. She believed that she wasn't good enough for her husband and that something was wrong with her spirituality. She threw herself into writing books while maintaining shallow friendships and keeping others at bay. She believed her lot in life was to embody all the abuses heaped on her by her ex-husband, friends, pastor, and fellow church members.

Our current state, as miserable as it may be, is a comfortable place to hang out because we know it well. We create a symbiotic relationship with pain.

We let it define us, and it provides the warmth of a familiar, worn-out blanket or an old pair of shoes. "If it ain't broke, why fix it?" our subconscious asks. "Besides," we usually go on to reason, "I'm just not worth anyone's time and investment to help me figure out this problem." But we don't suffer completely alone. We drag other people down with us by complaining, making negative comments, and pointing out their flaws. If our pain doesn't keep us mixed up in other people's drama, we create our own.

Abel, who worked with mentally disabled adults, said he had one client who mastered the art of emotional manipulation. His job was to help his clients become more self-sufficient. If he said something to this particular client like, "You can buckle yourself up in the car, Lydia; you know how," she would respond with a light and airy, "Okay, Abel, I'll do it, as long as you don't care that I do it wrong and get hurt really bad if we get into a car accident." The goal of responses like this is to deflect what we're really feeling, which may be pain, sadness, and insecurity. We want people to feel those negative feelings with us. When they don't, we emotionally manipulate our words so they do.

For someone who feels like a victim, self-compassion requires concerted effort to stop the negative self-talk and to start saying positive things about ourselves. I use the word *saying* as opposed to *believing* because before we can believe positive things about ourselves, we have to hear them.

In the height of my anxiety as a young adult, I met with a counselor who believed that the only problem I had was self-talk. "Look in the mirror every morning when you get up," he said, "and say to yourself 'I love you.'" His magic formula sounded ridiculous, but the anxiety I experienced was intense and I was willing to try anything to make it go away.

I vividly remember the first time I climbed out of bed, walked into the bathroom, and looked in the mirror after that counseling session. I was startled by what stared back at me. It wasn't the mussed, curly brown hair or the scrawny, nearly meatless body I didn't like; I hated the person who occupied that body. I hated him with a passion. He disgusted me. I saw someone who was worthless, a complete failure. I couldn't face him. I quickly turned away from the mirror to avoid eye contact. A feeling of intense sadness washed over me as I looked down. That exercise served as a reminder of why I didn't deserve help or attention or healing. Rather than start my day with a boost of self-confidence and compassion, I retreated into a mental spin of self-doubt and self-loathing. I did what I've seen a lot of broken people do through the years. I couldn't find the courage to face myself and I cut off the positive message of others who tried to help me. I dismissed their kind words, changed the subject, or avoided conversations about me altogether. It was easier to focus on others than on me because any conversations about me ultimately led to an evening of self-berating and depression.

Getting to self-compassion isn't easy, especially when we can't or refuse to listen to ourselves or others tell us anything different than what we already believe. We have to first identify what we honestly feel because our feelings, like physical symptoms of an illness, tell us what's really going on.

What Do I Really Feel?

All my life I followed the rules. I was taught that if I was obedient–to God, to my parents, to authority–the feelings would follow. So, despite how I truly felt about something, I told other people and *myself* that I felt the way I was *supposed* to feel. I did this for so long that at forty-something years old, I lied to my boyfriend about how I felt about him. I didn't want to lose the security of our relationship, even though I wasn't necessarily happy.

Brené Brown, in her book *Rising Strong*, says that our bodies tell us when we're not honest.[4] For me, the intense anxiety gave it away. I refused to acknowledge what was happening to me because I didn't want to accept the truth. The fake-it-till-you-make-it theology I was raised on caused me to believe that if I just "did the right thing" and held out long enough, God would intervene and fix me. I heard preachers talk about how too many Christians missed their blessings because they gave up just as God was about to do something in their lives. Our circumstances don't always have perceptible, logical reasons. So we make the pieces fit neatly into our personal narratives. We assign "God's plan" or some greater good to make our circumstances make sense, even if they make sense only to us.

Sometimes our commitments come at a high cost, as was the case with my friend Abby, whom I met through a social media group. Abby's parents were flower children of the 1960s. Given the liberal environment in which she was raised, she was highly unlikely to become a fundamentalist Christian, but when she heard the gospel message, it all made sense to her. As a young adult, she threw herself into church and Bible studies and surrounded herself with Christian friends. Her pot-smoking days were behind her. She found incredible joy in working with young people, sharing her story of change and helping others face the difficulties of life by submitting themselves to God. Soon, Abby met Seth through the youth ministry and the two hit it off.

Similar to Abby, Seth was a child of the '60s with parents who embodied the culture, beliefs, and political leanings of the young people at that time. Unlike Abby, however, Seth dabbled a little too much in experimentation and became addicted to drugs. He was in and out of rehab for several years until he, too, found Jesus and committed his life to God.

As far as Abby was concerned, Seth embodied the transforming power of Christ. They spent hours working together in the youth group where Seth frequently preached. Abby watched adoringly. When Seth proposed, she jumped at the opportunity to join their lives together. It seemed like a match made in heaven.

Seth and Abby married and started having children immediately. But Seth's behavior became erratic. They changed churches frequently because Seth's brand of Christianity was too legalistic even for fellow fundamentalists. His messages left young people confused, parents outraged, and pastors dumbfounded. Abby stuck by her man, though their life wasn't turning out the way she imagined. She prayed that God would change him while she submitted to his leadership, the way the Bible taught her.

As the years ticked by, Seth's behavior became abusive. He claimed he was casting demons out of his children when he spanked them. Abby intervened when she knew about it, but Seth more frequently carried out his devious activities when she was at work or the children were home alone with him after school.

Seth's old habits returned. He smoked marijuana, got drunk and drifted off into altered states of consciousness, all while professing his faith and preaching his version of fundamentalism to anyone who would listen. After years of Seth's abuse and bizarre behavior, Abby filed for divorce.

"People told me not to marry him," she confessed, "but I thought I could change him." She searched for meaning through all the chaos, believing that

God had a purpose. "I prayed about everything that was happening. I believed I was supposed to stay in the relationship because it was the right thing to do. I knew how God felt about divorce." She had put up with missing money, Seth's inability to keep jobs and the craziness that followed his addictive behaviors, but once he started abusing the kids, she knew it was time to call it quits.

The sense of relief Abby felt by simply acknowledging what was really going on was huge. She was facing the first hurdle of reality, that things were not changing and no amount of prayer was going to fix him. She needed to move on with her life and protect her kids. They'd spent too many years being emotionally abused by their father already.

Hiding, dismissing, and ignoring our realities holds us emotionally captive. I'd spent years maintaining a wall of protection from the glares and judgments of people within my church community. Those protections included nearly every deceptive behavior my community found unacceptable. Consequently, the mesh of my self-esteem was stretched, ripped, torn, burned, and in some places completely annihilated. Like Abby, when I finally acknowledged my situation, I felt angry, raw, exposed, and sad, but the train wreck was finally over. All that was left was the cleanup.

What Are My Self Protections?

I stood just inside the door of the old shed in my parents' backyard as a young teenager. I could feel the early evening summer breeze blowing against my tear-stained cheeks. I don't remember what happened this time, but I vividly remember the familiar feeling of failure that sent me back to the shed. It was my hideaway, my go-to spot where no one would think to look. There, I'd often close my eyes and imagine disappearing into nothingness. I would simply cease to exist. The feelings of loneliness, fear, and anxiety would disappear, too.

In my family, my father often berated us as a means of discipline. It was the way he was raised, too. Abuse is the gift that keeps on giving, and our family was no exception. My sister's way of dealing with it was to lash back at our father, while I internalized every word. Even years later, after he had apologized and asked for forgiveness, the self-loathing continued and was reinforced by a theology of shame. The intense self-hatred I carried most of my life kept me from feeling I was ever good enough. The first time I heard Abel say to me in the middle of a disagreement, "You don't even look like you care," my heart sank. I did care. I desperately cared, but the overwhelming feeling at that moment was the one that told me I didn't deserve to be loved. His statement was a familiar one. I'd heard it from my wife. Back then, I felt cornered: she had pushed me to the brink and I had no choice but to detach from her.

We can handle our pain in a plethora of ways, from inane escape through television and video games to the more detrimental methods of alcohol, drugs, and risky sexual behaviors. Whether we internalize our pain or attack others, the outcomes look the same. Cutting, for example, is a relatively recent phenomenon on the rise among teens. It's how some of them deal with emotional conflict and depression. Cutting is both an inward and outward expression of pain that scars teens and their families. It often takes the person's mind off of the emotional pain to focus on the physical discomfort. Other ways of handling pain include the use of defensive words, defensive behaviors, or silence.

My younger daughter's occasional rants would be easier to dismiss if her words didn't come with so much truth. I can acknowledge the truths when she's talking about other people, but they're painful to hear when she's talking about me. "You know, you could be friendlier when the waitress takes our order," she's told me on several occasions. I consider myself quite friendly toward service people. I realize they have a difficult job, one I most certainly could not do with the grace many of them display. But my face doesn't show it. I believe it's colloquially described as a resting bitch face. I have to make a conscious effort to smile, or I come across as angry. That's what my daughter tells me, anyway. I don't like hearing those things about myself.

Learning that I focus too much on money, that I dismiss her or other people's feelings, or that I complain too much makes me feel defensive. Rather than being outright combative, though, I sulk and just stop talking. My self-protection is the same as it was when I was a kid, minus the shed. Depending on the severity of the conflict, I want to disappear. I don't want to deal with the problem. Hearing that I have flaws feels like a personal attack. To comfort myself, I usually eat, watch television, or clean. My escape is disconnection and isolation until I can either process what was said or push it out of my mind completely.

Self-protections may be subtle, or they may have profound impacts on our lives, as they did in Teretia's case. Teretia grew up in northern Chicago in a middle-class home, but her parents struggled with their finances because of her dad's drinking. Alcohol consumption was a badge of honor to her father, despite the detrimental effects on his family. Teretia wasn't even sure he saw the problem. Both parents worked, at least when her dad could find and keep a job for any length of time. His frequent outbursts were often directed at her, and Teretia wasn't the kind of person to take them quietly. Vulnerability was seen as weakness. She learned to fight outburst with outburst, and no matter how much her heart broke, she knew she could never let her father see her cry.

Teretia went to college on the East Coast, where she met her future husband at a church in their small college town. He was generally unaware of her past. Though she admitted she had a difficult relationship with her parents and had even been sexually abused as a child, he had no idea how her experiences would so deeply change their relationship.

Shortly after their marriage, depression set in for Teretia. Her love for her husband turned to anger, particularly when it came to establishing the pecking order. She wasn't buying the church's "husband is the head of the household" rhetoric. It seemed good in theory as she listened in the pew, but it wasn't going to fly in practice. Whenever arguments arose, Teretia pulled out all the stops. She hit below the belt and made sure to expose any and every vulnerability her young husband had. When he confronted her about her tactics, she denied all responsibility and blamed him for the outcome of the argument. "Well, if you hadn't said . . . " or "If you only did . . . " were her go-to phrases. She couldn't acknowledge any of her own faults or her contribution to problems in the relationship because any vulnerability, she was convinced, left her unprotected. Their marriage collapsed just three years in.

Self-protection for Teretia involved a lot of blaming and argument redirecting, according to her ex-husband. When he brought up her disinterest in sex, she yelled at him for not helping in the kitchen. "Had I known the impact of the sexual abuse, we could have dealt with it," he said, "but she refused to acknowledge any of it, and our fights were just pointless."

The difficulty with self-protection is finding balance. We can't let everyone back into our lives who have hurt us in the past, but we can't cut everyone out either. Teretia's husband was eager to help her, but he, too, verbally lashed out at his wife in anger. She created an emotional catch-22 in their relationship. She struck first to keep from getting struck, and when her partner struck back out of hurt and anger, she took it as confirmation that she was in danger and needed protection from him. Her form of self-protection was well practiced and carried her through several relationships. How can we navigate and dismantle self-protections when they have become such a part of our lives?

In the early days after the release of *Going Gay*, I was contacted by people who felt I needed encouragement. Often they had only read an article or blog they'd stumbled across online. They would write to say they were concerned about my mental or spiritual well-being. Most of the time they missed the point of the article entirely, believing that they knew what was better for me. People who place themselves in our lives to help us become more like them by defining our lives for us have an ulterior motive, which more often than not is to keep us trapped in the religious dogma we so desperately desire to escape. People who truly care for us have no agenda, and we can usually feel the difference.

In the movie *Saved!* the main character, Mary, played by Jena Malone, suddenly finds herself in an unexpected situation. A devout Christian attending a Christian high school, Mary gets pregnant by her barely closeted gay boyfriend. When her equally devout friends see Mary pulling away from them and they have no idea why, they stage a "spiritual intervention." Mary is accosted on the street by her friends in one of the most hilarious scenes in the movie. They throw her into a van and begin performing an exorcism. Mary refuses, gets out of the van, and argues with her hyperspiritual friends. The scene culminates with her friend Hillary, played by Mandy Moore, throwing a Bible and hitting Mary between the shoulders with it while shouting, "I am filled with Christ's love!" All the while, Mary finds herself getting closer to her friends' archnemeses, two misfits who don't measure up to anyone's standard of spirituality but exemplify the love and acceptance Mary needs most.

Sometimes we find love and grace in unusual and unexpected places. One of the biggest surprises I discovered, for instance, came when I met gay people face to face. After years of being told how awful and demonic this group was, I found sincere, loving, kind, and accepting people. They had no ulterior motives.

Despite the many years I'd been warned that "those people," agents of Satan, wanted to drag others into the "gay lifestyle," they were incredibly accepting of anyone, even this Republican-leaning, struggling evangelical Christian. One benefit of leaving the church for me, in fact, was gaining the ability to release people to be who they are. When I stopped separating sinners from saints, a huge burden I didn't even know I carried fell off my shoulders. The people in whom we confide not only encourage us to be our authentic selves but also celebrate us when we are.

Stop

I sat on my new therapist's green leather couch at our very first session, staring at a man I didn't know. Somehow he was going to help me sort out all my issues and ambivalent feelings: fear, depression, my role as a dad, my relationship to God, and, mostly, my intense self-hatred. I'd been on the couches of so many counselors, therapists, pastors, and even a couple of psychiatrists before–too many to count, actually. I wondered what was going to make this time any different. If anything, my situation was much worse. I was older, more confused, and responsible for more people than just me. Somehow I found the courage to try therapy again. Perhaps I was more desperate. I felt sick to my stomach.

The scrambled thoughts in my brain were no less confused, and when he asked how he could help, I vomited a tumultuous string of disjointed, anxiety-filled phrases. He calmly and compassionately held up his hand. "Take a breath, Tim," he said. "Let's pause here for a moment."

That pause was a small but powerful flash of silence in a tornado of chaos. I exhaled. My shoulders dropped. When my words and explanations ceased their distraction, I felt what they were trying to say. I was deeply afraid of abandonment, of rejection, and facing the lies I told myself to make my life work. I suddenly knew what was different about this time. I stopped. I stopped running. Stopped fighting. Stopped denying. I was ready to face the hideous person I didn't want to see in the mirror. He turned out to be that little boy hiding by the shed, afraid to be seen while hoping someone would find him. He needed me as much as I needed him.

A journey into ourselves is as much about taking back our lives as finding out who we really are. The process is sometimes as unpleasant as it is incredible, frightening as it is freeing, and troubling as it is satisfying, but it is a journey with glorious rewards nonetheless.

PART III

Making Sense

CHAPTER 8

Angry

Not all monsters look like monsters. Some carry their monstrosity inside.
– Fredrik Backman

Mike Ralston didn't grow up in the fundamentalist faith but became a Christian as a troubled teen at a time when evangelicalism was popular in the 1970s and '80s. "I listened to Christian radio night after night, and the pastor on the show talked about having a father," Mike told me. "As an adopted kid, what he said very much appealed to me. I embraced it and then I threw myself in headlong. I read the Bible, went to Bible studies, and it really shaped my life as a young man. I was in it 110 percent, sold out, and stayed committed for thirty years."

Mike said he had questions early on when he experienced what felt like spiritual highs that were unrelated to his religious life. "In my midtwenties, I went to bounty hunter school and had what felt like spiritual experiences, or at least very similar experiences to what I'd had in church." But Mike pushed the similarities to the back of his mind. A decade later, while working with the prison population as a deputy sheriff, he said questions arose again. "I met so many people in the jails who said they were Jesus or the Christ or the devil, but no one ever claimed to be Muhammad or Buddha." Working with people on what Mike called "the gritty side of life" was in sharp contrast to his "sterile experiences" in church. "My faith wasn't really holding up to the realities beyond the church walls," he said.

Another decade later, when his father got sick, Mike said, "I was praying for help. I wasn't asking for some big miracle; I just needed help with one thing, which seemed easy enough, but there was no answer. I wondered why it was so difficult. I went through the usual mental explanations Christians go through, thinking maybe it was a test from God, or there was some other higher purpose. After a while, I was just so worn down and exhausted." Yet his main questions revolved largely around the Bible itself. "I'd read it, studied it, and had it tattooed on my body," Mike said, "but it wasn't delivering what I believed it said it was supposed to deliver. I was tired of no answer as an answer. At some point you kind of have to ask yourself, is this really working?"

Mike began studying the origins of his faith and didn't like what he found. He said, "I felt lied to. Emotionally, I felt tricked. I'm a cop. I take reports and look for evidence. When I gather information, I know how to do it. I've been trained to do it. Yet I believed these stories without any evidence at the time. I just felt like I'd been fooled, and I was angry."[1]

Angry at a God Who Doesn't Exist

I could relate to Mike's story on so many levels. When the blinders came off my own eyes I felt as if I'd been cheated on in a marriage. The person I trusted and thought loved me turned out to be someone else completely. I felt stupid. I felt like everyone knew about it but me. Like Mike, I'd given decades of my life to this person, rejected who I was, and dismissed my own feelings. The weight of this revelation was so heavy that the word *God* triggered a look of disgust on my face, a look I was completely unaware of, until a therapist told me about it. She assured me it was invisible only to me.

I wanted someone to be held accountable for all those wasted years. I knew that person, or persona, was the version of God I had imagined, but he was absent. I'd been in love with a fictional character constructed out of information that had been fed to me. I'd built a life on an imaginary deity who came with everything but a face. But that's what I needed–I needed to see a face. I needed to confront that face. I needed to see it express shame, embarrassment, and sadness. I needed that face to apologize to me. I was angry at a God who didn't exist.

But my feelings were not uncommon. Religious trauma therapist Dr. Marlene Winell, says:

> [R]eligious indoctrination can be hugely damaging, and making the break from an authoritarian kind of religion can definitely be traumatic. It involves a complete upheaval of a person's construction of reality, including the self, other people, life, the future, everything. People unfamiliar with it, including therapists, have trouble appreciating the sheer terror it can create and the recovery needed.[2]

My life, like Mike's, had been in upheaval. The very foundation was shattered and I felt alone and exposed. I had more questions than answers. Compounding my discomfort was the realization that wanting to believe is what kept the belief alive. In some ways, losing my faith was like getting caught stealing from the cookie jar. I had to admit I took part in my own deception, though I was looking for someone, anyone, to blame.

When we've been shaken to the core, anger is a natural defensive and distracting response. Anger stands out like an open wound that is ugly and repulsive. Our anger either turns toward the people or symbols that represent the version of God we now despise or is directed toward ourselves. Reba Riley, author of *Post-Traumatic Church Syndrome*, says,

> [Post-Traumatic Church Syndrome] presents as a severe, negative–almost allergic–reaction to inflexible doctrine, outright abuse of spiritual power, dogma and (often) praise bands and preachers. Internal symptoms include but are not limited to: withdrawal from all things religious, failure to believe in anything, depression, anxiety, anger, grief, loss of identity, despair, moral confusion, and, most notably, the loss of desire/inability to darken the door of a place of worship.[3]

This kind of anger turned inward ravishes the soul from the inside out. All the negativity we feel toward our nonexistent deity can quickly tear us apart, making us feel stupid, broken, worthless, shameful, and perhaps disposable. Those thoughts can ferment, becoming part of our core and replacing the religion we now despise.

"In some ways," Mike said, thinking about the years he stayed involved in church, "I wanted to be lied to. I wanted to believe the message. It was so difficult to realize it was my fault and that no one really lied to me; I wanted to hear it. I bought into it as a kid thinking it was going to answer all of my problems."

Flipping the switch

Mike's life changed when his actions and attitudes were finally called out by people who knew him well. "That was a wake-up call," he said, "which helped me see what I was doing to myself and others." He left the recovery-from-religion group he started and spent some time alone. Having this time of self-contemplation helped him realize how ingrained the binary thinking of good and evil or right and wrong had become in him. "These ideas have been around a long time," he said, "and my fight was against this absolute, exclusive way of seeing the world. Once I started to see beyond that, the anger began to dissipate."

Mike said he realized that after spending three decades in one way of life, he was going to need several more years to see life differently. "Anger subsided when I realized I *was* angry and there *was* a loss," he said. A large part of dealing with his anger has simply been unraveling and unloading his past. These days, Mike spends more time alone in contemplation, as well as spending time with his family and doing the things he enjoys. Though his marriage got rocky, he said coming through the other side of his anger helped him become a better husband and father.

Anger can be directed at more than just our version of God. We may get angry if we feel we wasted our time or energy. We may feel that we let our dreams or ambitions go because they weren't "godly." Maybe we stayed in an abusive relationship, feeling that's what we were called by God to do, or we're angry that we ever married the person in the first place. We may also have a deep sensation that life didn't turn out the way we wanted, or we're just unhappy. Whatever the catalyst for the anger, its impact may be the very thing needed to move us toward freedom.

Anger Can Be Good, Too

After struggling with my own anger for quite some time, I became frustrated with the lack of movement. Anger served no discernable purpose, yet it consumed me. That's when a friend reminded me that if it weren't for anger, some things would never get done. Most people affected by oppression do nothing to stop it. Slavery began in 1619 in the United States and lasted until 1865. Women didn't get the right to vote until 1920. In our society, marches and demonstrations are often the first expression of anger and a call for change. Those with the fortitude and ability channel their raw emotion into productive outcomes. As anger is the catalyst for social change, it can also be the incentive we need for personal change. Oliver Emberton said, "If you're not pissing someone off, you probably aren't doing something important."[4]

In *Anger Management for Dummies*, Drs. Charles Elliott and Laura Smith say that anger is a built-in resource and we should think of it as a birthright. They say, "The *motion* part of *emotion* has to do with motivating behavior."[5] They explain that anger protects us from harm by providing a fight-or-flight response, which is designed to help us survive. Additionally, they say, anger is the antidote to impotence. In other words, rather than lacking power and ability or feeling weak and inadequate, anger infuses us "with a sense of empowerment, a feeling of strength, confidence, and competence. You're standing straight up to the frustrations and conflicts you've been avoiding. Anger is a can-do emotion: 'I can fix this problem,' 'I can make a difference here.'"[6]

But how and where we direct that anger is just as important. I had a Facebook friend who spewed anger at his former faith through cynical jokes and blasphemous memes. He bragged about losing friends who couldn't handle his sense of humor. It didn't take much to set him off. When he was challenged, he posted tirades on his Facebook wall. While I could appreciate where he was coming from, watching the debacle from the outside made me cringe. He pushed people away who were unwilling to go down that negative path with him. In instances like this, we can easily move from victims to victimizers.

When my children were younger and I first began dating men, I wore my heart on my sleeve. I was so convinced that I wasn't worthy of anyone's love that every time a date didn't work out, I internalized that the problem was me. If I wasn't sulking on my bed because "Mr. Right" didn't call me back, I was being short with my kids, showing anger at every little thing that didn't go my way, and throwing temper tantrums over the smallest inconveniences. I'd spend countless hours thinking about what I had done wrong and what I needed to change. The anger and depression spiraled around me like an other-dimensional tornado. Inevitably, however, my thoughts took me to what really made me angry: I didn't know what to do next.

You Have a Right to be Mad

After we've screamed, yelled, cried, and allowed anger to have its way with us, it's our turn to take control of *it*. Anger, like any other emotion, is not linear. It's not a one-time feeling that happens and we just deal with it and move on. When we've been hurt, especially over a long period of time, anger keeps coming back. Eventually, the pain does lessen and we're able to learn and grow from it, but the interim is what often keeps us trapped.

My friend and author John Smid told the story of going to see a therapist when he first started to face the pain of what all his years in ex-gay ministry did to his life. "Who are you angry with?" The therapist asked him. At first, John said he wasn't angry with anyone. He wasn't able to pinpoint exactly what happened and certainly didn't know whom to blame. But the next time he saw the therapist, he'd had a chance to process his feelings.

"I think I'm angry at the former ministry leaders," John told the therapist.

"Great," the counselor said. He placed a chair in front of John. "Now, what would you say to them if they were here?"

A burst of fury welled up within him. He'd been holding back all the pain, hurt, anger, and frustration for years. A string of curse words flew from his mouth as the representation of mistrust, lost years, and inconsolable sadness he felt. It was the first time John felt the freedom to say what he'd been feeling and put into words what he'd been thinking.

Let It Out

We seldom have the opportunity to address those who have hurt us, especially when the pain doesn't come from a person as much as it comes from a system of beliefs. More often, we have difficulty putting words to the feelings we haven't yet identified and find ourselves in a cauldron of emotional stupor that may last for years. Perhaps the thoughts and behaviors we've learned as a way to cope are not even conscious ones.

Since our beliefs have unconsciously guided our decisions, we tend to focus our anger on the people with whom we surrounded ourselves because of those beliefs. In other words, it's much easier to blame ministry leaders than it is to blame the beliefs themselves, which were represented by those leaders. Our beliefs are ideologies silently guiding us and telling us what to think, what to do, and how to act.

Whether you yell at a chair in front of you, as John did, write down your feelings, or talk to a friend or a therapist, spend some time reflecting on what you actually feel and get it out. Talk about it. Listen to it. You may even be surprised to find out what's there. Anger is a secondary emotion triggered by fear, hurt, or self-protection and can be difficult to look behind. We often rely on those angry feelings to keep us emotionally safe. What's more, we use them to manipulate others into doing what we want, or simply staying away. Laying down our anger can unleash a flood of sadness, feelings of loss, or intense pain.

The phrase "letting go of anger" never sat well with me. I always saw that phrase as another way of saying "Don't feel that way." The real challenge is looking at the anger. Why do I feel angry? What sets me off? Or as my therapist often asks me, "Can you hold on to that feeling and describe it?" I hate when he does that.

Sitting still, thinking about our anger, and feeling it can't be done in a single session. Anger covers up vulnerable emotions like feeling abandoned, deceived, or cheated. Intense anger becomes a wall of defense used to keep people away and protect our fragile emotions. Anger justifies how we treat others. It relieves our conscience after we lash out and say hurtful things.

I described my marriage as I remembered it in *Going Gay*. My ex-wife didn't read the book because she was afraid of being hurt by what I had written. Her sister filled her in on some of the details, and my ex-wife had a reason for concern. We had been divorced for nearly twelve years by the time *Going Gay* was published, and, even though we had both moved on, I still felt a tremendous amount of anger toward her. I used my anger as a defense because of the hurt I felt about her leaving me. But the anger also kept me from gaining perspective and feeling compassion toward her. Ultimately, it kept me from moving on emotionally, hurting my relationship with her and our kids, even after it became just an underlying, unresolved feeling of discontentment. Subsequently, I interviewed her for an article I wrote for the *Good Men Project* about her experience in our marriage, and I saw, for the first time, her perspective on what it was like to be married to someone in ex-gay ministry. It wasn't exactly a garden of roses for her either, and the kind of relationship we had when we were married made a lot more sense. I had to accept more of the blame than I was able to accept at the time I wrote the book.

Anger isn't always identifiable. It doesn't always feel like rage. It can be masked as ambivalence or distrust or disrespect. It comes out in cynical or biting comments or, in my Facebook friend's case, nasty humor. There is no easy or simple way to identify anger or "let it go." We must examine why we're angry, look at what sets us off, and hold it and describe it. That's not going to happen by counting to ten, or going for one walk around the block.

Feel It

The problem, as Brené Brown points out in her book *The Gifts of Imperfection*, is "We cannot selectively numb emotions. When we numb the painful emotions, we also numb the positive emotions."[7] And we Americans are notorious for numbing our feelings. In fact, a 2005 report said, "About 130 million Americans swallow, inject, inhale, infuse, spray, and pat on prescribed medications every month." The report said, Americans buy much more medicine per person than residents of any other country.[8] A 2014 report showed that nineteen out of every one thousand Americans reported using amphetamines, and Americans came in at number one for drug overdoses at 139.1 fatal overdoses per one million people.[9]

And if we're not doing drugs, we spend an inordinate amount of time watching television: five hours a day per capita on average, more than any other country in the world.[10] We find an incredible number of activities to distract ourselves, from playing games on our phones to scrolling through social media and from shopping to eating. Avoiding our feelings has become a national pastime all its own.

Validate It

Author Matthew Paul Turner says, "Healing comes only when we learn or relearn how to be angry, then learn how to not feel guilty becoming angry, then learn how to not run away after becoming angry, and then learn how to let go of that anger and move on."[11] Unfortunately, we're often quick to dismiss the emotion as silly and unreasonable. "Perhaps I'm overreacting," we tell ourselves and push the feelings back down. Instead, validate yourself. Validate your anger and validate the feelings that cause the anger. You're not crazy; you're human.

Many of us from fundamentalist backgrounds were taught to simply submit and trust God. We were taught that our anger wasn't just or fair. In some cases we were taught that the emotion of anger itself was a sin. Validating our anger acknowledges to ourselves that it exists. We can finally call out the proverbial elephant in the room instead of trying to ignore it. What's more, we don't need the approval or affirmation of anyone else. Self-validation gives back the control we lost and puts healing and wholeness back in our own hands. Psychologist Karyn Hall says, "Validating your thoughts and emotions will help you calm yourself and manage your emotions more effectively. Validating yourself will help you accept and better understand yourself, which leads to a stronger identity and better skills at managing intense emotions. Self-validation helps you find wisdom."[12]

Hall says it's important to be present when we feel our emotions. Don't drift off into daydreams or get ahead of the anger. Facing them and feeling them, she says, "allows emotions to pass and helps build resiliency."[13] And that resiliency, or the repetition of working through our emotions like working out at the gym builds emotional strength. We may not gain control of our feelings, but we can control how and when we respond to them, regaining a sense of control over our lives.

Secondly, Hall suggests reflecting on your anger as a way to accurately label it. "Reflecting means observing and describing," she says.[14] Think about how it makes you feel physically. Where in your body do you tense up? Can you define how it started or where it came from? Do certain places, people, or even words or phrases cause you to tense up?

About three years into our relationship, I agreed to go to various churches with Abel to see if we could find a place we both felt comfortable. I knew we had hurdles right from the beginning: he came from a Presbyterian background and I was Pentecostal. He listened to "white" worship music, and I, choirs with the word mass in front of them. He wanted to go to church, and I didn't. Still, the idea of finding a community again sounded appealing. So when a coworker invited him to her community church, which met at a local school, Abel enthusiastically agreed to go. To be clear, Abel approaches all of life with enthusiasm. I've introduced him as my Mexican SpongeBob, to which I am his irascible Squidward.

We arrived late, partially because we got lost looking for the school and partially because I was stalling. Naturally, we ended up sitting where most latecomers sit, the front row. The church had a Pentecostal flair to it, hampered only by its single guitar worship team and mediocre singers. I didn't know any of the words to the songs, but the three-chord melodies weren't that difficult to figure out. The biggest obstacle was my lackluster will to be there. I spent most of the worship time staring at the elementary artwork that adorned the walls of, clearly, the school's lunchroom. The church had hung large banners in strategic places with single-word distractors, such as Emmanuel, to try and hide the fact we were sitting in a cafeteria. The smell of discarded milk and old books belied the simple Christian décor.

I smiled politely when the pastor told us to greet three people and tell them how happy we were to see them. But as someone who suffers from face blindness, I had no idea if I'd met them before or not. Furthermore, I didn't care. Since Abel, on the other hand, talks to everyone as if he or she were his elementary school chum, it wasn't long before a crowd surrounded us, warmly welcoming us to their humble congregation.

We settled into our chairs for the usual announcements, reminders, and recognitions, and then the pastor began to preach. He was an Indian man who moved to the United States and became an Assemblies of God minister. I was never clear how he got here or why, but his delivery came with all the luster of pastors from my youth. I knew the cadence, I knew where he was going, and I knew he expected verbal responses from his audience. A few of the faithful wholeheartedly obliged. Increasingly, I felt uneasy. At the risk of being too conspicuous, Abel and I typed notes to each other on our phones and passed them back and forth during the sermon. But toward the conclusion of the sermon, Abel was drawn into the stories of unsubstantiated miracles told with Trinity Broadcasting Network theatrics. It's not that he believed them; he responds the same way to Harry Potter movies and repeats of *Modern Family*. He just really loves a good story. I, on the other hand, grew angrier at each wild tale and outlandish statement. To make matters worse, the pastor went well over his time, one of my biggest pet peeves. I felt a rage swell inside of me. After fidgeting for several minutes in my squeaky metal chair I told Abel, "I'll meet you in the car," and I left.

When church finally ended, Abel went to find his coworker and tell her how much he appreciated the invitation. In the meantime, I was sitting in the car, fuming from the service, impatient with Abel's socialization, furious at the pastor I'd never met before, and now, sweltering from the hot afternoon sun. Abel finally made it back to the car, feeling rejuvenated and happy to have seen his friend, while I sat quietly in the driver's seat. I had the car on and in gear before he ever climbed in. Well aware of my sometimes overly negative disposition, I asked Abel what he thought of the service.

"It was great!" he said, not surprisingly. But Abel is a thinker. I knew more was going on in his head, and I was eager to hear him rip the pastor to shreds so I could justify my own feelings.

"What did you think of the pastor?" I asked.

"I thought he was a good speaker and really interesting," he said.

That's it? I can't remember if I said that aloud or not. I just remember the hammer never came down any further from Abel's perspective. Rather than waiting for Abel to ask what I thought, I went off about the pastor. I was incensed that he made people stay late. "That's disrespectful," I sputtered. "And his story...that was just...bullshit," I said. I rattled on about how uncomfortable I felt there, how manipulative the pastor was, and how he used every platitude, and every worn-out cliché I'd ever heard.

"Wow," Abel said. "He really got to you. I didn't get that at all. I didn't take every word of his sermon as truth; I just heard it as inspirational." He went on to ask me questions about where those strong emotions came from, questions I couldn't answer in the moment but did spend time reflecting on in the years that followed.

I was an avid fan of Jimmy Swaggart as a kid and young adult. His sermons and the way he could turn a phrase sent chills down my spine–it was so artful and passionate. I emulated his style when I preached, which I'm sure looked awkward on me. I believed what he said. I was convinced it was true. I was convinced it was fact. Now, I was convinced it was malicious.

Coming to terms with my sexual orientation had turned the tables and I was now on the other end of Christian fundamentalists' scriptural ire. I enjoyed the passion of "truth" until it was directed at me. That day the pastor and his style reminded me of all the other pastors and church leaders who turned their backs on me with absolute resolve. They truly believed I'd chosen to be the way I was and I could do something about it. They never asked me. To the contrary, they simply cut me off while spouting ideas and ideals I knew were wrong. I also knew that the miracles of which this pastor spoke simply were not true. There was no evidence to back up his words. The stories were so outlandish a journalist couldn't have passed them up if there was any way to prove them true. But the congregation, listening to his saga, went along with them. They believed. They *wanted* to believe. I simply couldn't do that anymore. The pastor's passion was a passion I'd lost and one I could never go back to even if I wanted.

I needed years to unpack what I was feeling and to recognize my triggers. Anger, sadness, feelings of loss, loneliness, and disappointment–all those feelings simply came out as anger. As I addressed each of them and the nuanced ways they influenced my thinking, actions, and relationships, my anger subsided.

Karyn Hall also says that "radical genuineness" is a critical step toward self-validation. Own the fact that at times you have impulsive thoughts, petulant attitudes, or underlying grievances that, as yet, have no resolution. "An important distinction is that who you are is different from what you do," Hall says. "You are not your behavior, yet changing some of your behaviors may alleviate some of your suffering."[15]

Face It

I was on a mission to get fat after my wife left. Other than work, I didn't have any outlets. I'd been skinny all my life. I'd battled depression and anxiety while trying to make sense of my world. By my late thirties, though, I'd filled out and was still trying to make my world make sense. It never did. Perhaps out of boredom, desperation, or just plain giving up, I wanted to see exactly how fat I could get.

Mind you, I have a swimmer's body and I'm small boned. Genetics are on my side when it comes to looking toned. To get fat, at least at that age, I had to put some serious work into it. But with the lack of any real direction in my life, I was dedicated to my new goal. I'd spend hours watching television with Hostess products in one hand and the remote in the other. On the weekends, I'd get off the couch long enough to drive to McDonald's and get a double Big Mac combo meal with a large Coke. During this same time I realized I no longer had to wait for someone's birthday for birthday cake. I could stop by the local grocery store at virtually any time, which is often what I did, and purchase an entire "single-serving" quarter-sheet chocolate cake with buttercream frosting. That was my favorite. The biggest challenge was hiding it from the kids. I had no intention of sharing. I went down this path for several years, culminating in a top weight of 199 pounds. To this day, I'm a little disappointed I was never able to reach 200. I'd like to think I'm an overachiever at everything I do, but my body simply wouldn't budge.

I'd been diagnosed with ulcerative colitis twenty years earlier, and the symptoms were out of control during this period. My doctor prescribed medication often used for cancer patients as a form of chemotherapy to try to manage the symptoms. (I wouldn't find out how powerful and harmful the drug was until several years later.) My still relatively young body managed to stave off symptoms of diabetes and high cholesterol. Prozac managed the rest.

Fortunately, the very first guy I dated had a penchant for older men. He was completing his doctoral program in physical therapy and was the exact image you'd expect to see on a billboard advertising sports medicine doctors. In his spare time, he taught spin classes at his gym and invited me to work out with him. The only thing I knew about gyms before this is that they were often connected to grocery stores, which sold cake, and surrounded by fast-food chains in parking lots I frequented.

I was ready for a change in my life. I was tired of being tired and depressed. An added incentive was that this very attractive and smart young man showed interest in me and told me I had value. Though the relationship ultimately didn't work out, his words of encouragement helped me start digging up from the bottom.

Within a few short months, I'd dropped fifty pounds–again, thanks in part to genetics. I changed my diet, cutting out the carbs and most sugars that triggered the ulcerative colitis. The symptoms disappeared and I stopped taking the medication. I joined a gym and started working out every day. I stopped taking Prozac. Eventually, I started going to therapy to face my feelings. In hindsight, I probably could have been the subject of my new love's thesis–or at least a before-and-after model for the successful practice he opened after he graduated from college.

I'd like to say my feelings of anger went away as I gained control of my body, but in truth, I really started to feel angry *after* I got my health back. The distraction of food and the consequences it wreaked on me were gone. It was like being invited to a party with my worst enemy and suddenly finding that no one was left in the room but us–not even a cake. And that's when things got real.

CHAPTER 9

Guilty

Guilt is a useless feeling. It's never enough to make you change direction–only enough to paralyze you and make you . . . well, useless.

– Daniel and Dina Nayeri

I was baptized at around sixteen years old in a small Assemblies of God church within a short walking distance from my parents' house. The church was my first spiritual home after making my own decision to commit my life to Christ. At the end of one Sunday evening service, those of us getting baptized were asked to go behind the sanctuary platform and up the stairs into a small changing room. Our clothes had long sleeves and full-length pants so we could retain a sense of modesty while being dunked in the makeshift hot tub built into the sanctuary platform.

My heart raced as my turn came to go into the tank. The youth pastor, Kyle, had been chosen to baptize me since we worked so closely together in the youth group. The senior pastor hovered above us on the sanctuary platform performing his duties as the MC. He also asked questions of each person getting baptized, some personal and others about professions of faith.

When I finally made my way into the tepid water, the pastor asked me what I planned to do with my life.

"Go into the ministry," I said with certainty. The audience applauded. I had earned a reputation as an anointed musician, and my proclamation proved, in all our minds, I was dutifully answering the call of God.

"Praise God," the pastor responded to my answer. "Have you been witnessing for the Lord?" he asked.

"Yes," I said a little less confidently.

"How many people have you led to the Lord?"

That was a question I wished he hadn't asked. I suddenly felt exposed. In truth, I *did* talk to my high-school friend–I only had one–about Jesus, and another friend from the youth group and I led him in a coercive prayer of salvation. But I wasn't sure I could add him to my tally of souls saved. So I answered, "I don't know," sounding more like a three-year-old who was asked to guess his mom's friend's age. The congregation quietly snickered. With that, I was told to profess my faith and I was baptized in the name of the Father, the Son, and the Holy Ghost.

Remembering how many people we'd led to the Lord as fundamentalists, at least at that time, was as important as an alcoholic knowing how long she'd been sober. Witnessing, or sharing the faith, was just one of the guilt-inducing activities expected of members of the church. As an introvert, I had a difficult time talking to anyone about anything, let alone talking about Jesus. In a sense, I took the easy way out. Becoming a minister brought sinners to me. I was usually the one sitting behind the piano, and they knew where to find me when they were ready.

One researcher found through a convenience sample of one hundred people, categorized as fundamentalist Protestant, liberal Protestant, Catholic, personal faith, and unknown, that fundamentalist Protestants experienced fear at a higher rate than people of all other religious affiliations. While fundamentalist Protestants experienced feelings of guilt at a rate only slightly higher than liberal Protestants, those feelings of guilt were significantly higher than for other religious affiliations. Researcher James Kennedy says, "Based on personal observations of fundamentalist religions, [C.B.] Strozier suggested that people who are attracted to fundamentalism tend to have high guilt, and then develop reduced guilt about past (pre-conversion) behavior and increased guilt and fear about current behavior and thought."[1]

Kennedy notes that "religious fear and guilt contribute to suppressing a positive relationship between religious faith and well-being."[2] In other words, the more important a person's religion is to him, the more his reported experience of well-being is hindered by feelings of guilt and fear.

Psychologist Susan Krauss Whitbourne says that guilt is an emotion that falls in the "sad" category "that people experience because they're convinced they've caused harm."[3] She outlines five main reasons we feel guilty: we did something wrong, we didn't do something we wanted to do, we *thought* we did something wrong, we didn't do enough to help someone, and we are doing better than someone else. These cover the gamut of religious guilt, especially where Bible verses are readily available so someone can tell you exactly why you *should* feel guilty.

As a minister, I often heard and quoted the scripture "Therefore, there is now no condemnation for those who are in Christ Jesus" (Rom. 8:1). That's what I said, but the undercurrent of guilt I saw and felt in church could be debilitating, especially for a gay person. Any religion built on commandments, whether we're told to love one another or abstain from premarital sex, causes guilt. We're either not doing what we're told, doing something we're told not to do, or thinking something we're not supposed to think.

The Bible is rife with warnings about "those people" who do xyz and aren't welcome in the kingdom of heaven. Praying and repenting may bring temporary relief, but we can easily get caught up in mind games when the feelings to do xyz come back or, God forbid, we do it again. Then we wonder if our repentance was effective, if we really meant it, or if we're just too bad to be saved. We learn to live with the cognitive dissonance, especially if we were raised in fundamentalism.

The struggle with guilt moves to the background over time, and, for some, can become an identity. "But for the grace of God," we say, or "I'm still keeping on." Guilt and struggle become our constant companion, as even the Apostle Paul wrote,

> We know that the law is spiritual; but I am unspiritual, sold as a slave to sin. I do not understand what I do. For what I want to do I do not do, but what I hate I do. And if I do what I do not want to do, I agree that the law is good. As it is, it is no longer I myself who do it, but it is sin living in me. For I know that good itself does not dwell in me, that is, in my sinful nature. For I have the desire to do what is good, but I cannot carry it out. For I do not do the good I want to do, but the evil I do not want to do—this I keep on doing. Now if I do what I do not want to do, it is no longer I who do it, but it is sin living in me that does it" (Romans 7:14–20).

As good as it feels to believe in an ideology that we are dirty rotten sinners whom God has graciously forgiven, it doesn't do much to empower us toward authentic living. Guilt can plague our minds to the point that our behaviors simply get buried.

Keith was a young divorced man I met through my church's men's group. He worked at a tech company and helped me buy some equipment when I was building a music studio several years ago. As we worked together, I got to know Keith and his story. He exhibited an upbeat though quiet persona at church. He was a smart guy who was always willing to help anyone. But the story behind the smile was very different. He struggled with infidelity. The guilt he felt for losing his family consumed him. He couldn't figure out what drove him to do what he did. He prayed, sought counseling, and stayed close to the men's group, but he felt he was constantly losing the battle. After years of praying and confessing, Keith learned to put on a happy face, maintain his friendships, and just stop talking about his problems. He wasn't alone.

As a minister, I encountered many stories like Keith's. I've met men who were sexually abusing children, beating their spouses, secretly drinking, struggling with an addiction to pornography, or just masturbating too much. In some of those cases, psychological problems were clearly going unaddressed. In most cases, these men had confessed their struggles to pastors or friends, only to find that their problems continued. Most churches are grievously uneducated when it comes to handling the serious problems of abuse and addiction. Pithy answers often do more harm than good. Where some could stop, they did. Others melted into guilt and despair.

Of course, men aren't the only ones who struggle. Women, already feeling social pressure to work and take care of their children, their home, and their men, struggle with similar issues related to sexuality. Sheila, a relatively new convert at a Bible study I attended decades ago, met a young man in the same Bible study to whom she found herself attracted. When one thing led to another, they ended up in a sexual tryst about which both felt horribly guilty. He decided to confess his part of the sin to the Bible study group while she was there–apparently without telling her he was planning to do so. Most of us listened with interest, and a little envy, to the sordid details. Sheila was so overcome with shame, she broke down sobbing and confessed she was the one he slept with. You could almost hear the collective silent gasp and slut-shaming when the object of the man's attention turned out to be a Christian woman within our group and not some girl he met at a local bar.

The guilt we feel isn't just self-induced but also comes, if not overtly then certainly covertly, from the social pressure we feel from the groups of which we are a part. Religious social norms can take the form of expected speech, church attendance, social activity, and conformance to ideas of theology and politics. A group of researchers found, for example, that someone who may have no problem smoking cigarettes alone was less likely to smoke around her social group.[4] The behavior didn't stop; the smoking just took place away from the group. In other words, the individual didn't change being, believing, or acting as who she was, but social pressure changed her public behavior. Social conformity, a powerful motivator, becomes so ingrained in us we don't realize it is there. Yet the nagging feelings of failure for not meeting social expectations may continue to produce guilt even after we leave the social group.

It's Not You, God; It's Me

Before we go too far down this road of blaming all our psychological discomfort on our chosen deity, we must answer the chicken-or egg-question. Did our religion and perception of God cause guilt? Or did we bring the guilt into our relationship or perception of God? One meta-analysis, by researchers

Charles Hackney and Glenn Sanders, looked for correlations between psychological adjustment and religiosity. Hundreds of studies on the topic have produced vastly different results. Some claim religious involvement creates a more well-rounded, psychologically healthy individual. Other studies show an adverse correlation between religion and mental health. Some studies have shown no correlation at all. Hackney and Sanders took a different approach, stating, "Religion is a multifaceted construct and it is possible that different aspects of religiosity are differentially related to mental health.[5] In other words, our perception of God, our motivation for involvement with our specific religion or denomination, and our psychological makeup are just some of the factors that determine whether religion positively or negatively impacts our lives. In addition, what, if any, mental health issues did we bring into our religion or perception of God to begin with? Did we already have a mood disorder, such as depression, anxiety, or guilt? How we perceived the outcome and perhaps dissatisfaction of our faith is a mixture of all these factors and more.

Those of us from the fundamentalist side of the house were taught, believed, and felt that God was a person with whom we were in a relationship. Due to the nature of the interaction between the seen world and the unseen, our interaction with the person of God was one-sided. God, we believed, spoke to us through his word, church leaders, and friends. We may have even believed we heard that still, small voice, which gave us direction or confirmed that he loved us. Whatever experiences we had, as with any other relationship, depended on how we perceived them. Our emotional well-being was a significant part of that perception, and perception is all we have to go on when developing any relationship. I learned this the hard way a few years ago.

Texting is my preferred method of communication. I hate talking on the phone. But conversational texting almost always requires a relationship with the person on the other side of the phone for it to be effective. Otherwise, misunderstandings are too easy, and conversations quickly get awkward. Such was the case with a long-lost relative I found on Facebook.

Because my father had so many siblings, I did not know most of my aunts and uncles. There were large age differences between many of them and my father. My grandmother was married at thirteen and started spitting out kids soon after. My father was fourth from the last, and many died before I met them. However, Rymels are prolific. One of my uncles, Sam, was married seven times. He never divorced; he just left one wife and married another. Strangely, he had three daughters by three wives and gave all his daughters the same name. None of them knew each other existed. While I know we have family all over the country, I don't know much more about them or even how we're related. So when I stumbled across someone with the same last name, I quickly and foolishly asked him to be a Facebook friend.

One late Friday afternoon, Abel and I were headed to my parent's house for dinner. My sister was visiting from back East, and I was excited to connect this person to our family. My sister is much better at our family's genealogy than I am, so I thought she might help put the pieces together. After chitchatting via instant messaging with our long-lost relative during the drive over (I was in the passenger's seat), I told my family whom I found and was talking to online. I asked if anyone knew of him. After a few guesses and several questions, we finally figured out how we were related. He didn't live very far away, and I suggested we should get together at some point and learn more about each other. Enthusiastically, he agreed. The conversation continued as my family and I sat down to eat, but I began focusing on my sister and taking longer to respond to any messages. I handed my phone to my sister so she could chat with our newfound relative for a while, and then she handed it back to me. When he seemed confused by the change of direction in the conversation, I told him the last question wasn't from me but my sister. Then things got weird.

"I don't appreciate that at all," he messaged me. "I need to know who I'm talking to and I don't like people playing games with me." I apologized and said there was no intended deception, but he wouldn't let it go. Eventually, I put my phone down, only to find a barrage of odd and ominous messages later. He accused us of gossiping about family members we didn't know. Later, I responded by apologizing again and telling him I was going to visit with my family for the rest of the evening and wouldn't be online. Needless to say, I didn't pursue a closer relationship with this person.

I made a lot of assumptions about him because we shared the same last name. But I didn't know him. I never heard the inflections in his voice when he talked. I didn't know anything else about him besides his affinity for animals, which I discovered on his social media profile. His pictures looked kind enough, but that was all I had to rely on to put together who I thought this person was. The rest of my perception of him, good or bad, was all on me. Similarly, our perceptions of God are who we believe him to be based in part on our own personalities. Social influences, doctrinal ideologies, and mental health also factor into this ethereal relationship. For that matter, even how we hear the Bible read to us or read the Bible to ourselves helps determine how we perceive the voice of God.

Guilt Is Guilt

For some, particularly those who suffer from obsessive-compulsive disorder (OCD), guilt and the feelings that accompany it can become all-consuming. Fundamentalist theology focuses on controlling our thoughts and actions. Of course, when our thoughts are biologically imposed, they can be impossible to control. For example, a boost in sex hormone levels at the age of puberty induces sexual thoughts and biological reactions. While Jesus said, "But I tell you that anyone who looks at a woman lustfully has already committed adultery with her in his heart" (Matt. 5:28), just "looking" is the best-case scenario for a thirteen-year-old boy. Some people are consumed with guilt for merely being human. Not all guilt is bad, but unresolved guilt can become obsessive or even toxic.

Dr. Art Markman says, " Guilt is a valuable emotion, because it helps to maintain your ties to the people in your community. It provides a painful consequence for actions that would weaken the groups that you belong to."[6] Certainly we *should* feel guilty in some instances. If we are rude to someone for no reason, hurt someone's feelings intentionally, or take something that doesn't belong to us, then our conscience is there to guide us to do better. A society cannot survive when it is full of individuals acting on impulses for their own benefit. Guilt becomes toxic, however, when it isn't settled. When a person's day-to-day activities are interrupted because of guilt, relationships are incapacitated, or other negative behaviors become apparent, guilt has become a problem.

Psychotherapist Karl Melvin says that people who suffer extreme guilt become afraid to take risks, censor themselves so they become less natural and less impulsive, become overly agreeable, worry more about what others think of them, obsessively replay events in their heads, try to read the minds of others, and can often come across as intense individuals who take life too seriously.[7] Life coaches and couples counselors Marlene and Bob Neufeld, say,

> Guilt is often toxic. It may seem that it is there to help us change, but it doesn't often actually cause real lasting change. It more often causes self-doubt, self-recrimination, and self-judgment. It reduces self-esteem and self-confidence. Over and over again, we see how toxic guilt paralyzes our clients. It tricks us into thinking that we're dealing with our mistakes when all we are doing is feeling bad about them.[8]

For those of us from religious backgrounds, guilt may be the constant thought that we're bad for leaving our faith or changing the way we think about faith. It may be the incessant fear that we're wrong or that we're not teaching our children the "right way." It may come from outside sources, such as parents, church members, pastors, or coworkers. We may have heard from fellow congregants that the reason we are sick, having financial difficulties, going through a divorce, and so on, is because we are not obedient to God the way they think we should. Whatever the cause, allowing our guilt to consume us serves no purpose whatsoever.

Dealing with Guilt

We had just completed a cheer competition with my girls when they were around eight and ten, and stopped at a local fast-food restaurant on our way out of town. Cheer competitions, particularly those held in schools around the region, required long days and seldom provided any food to eat on the premises. We were usually starving and cranky by the time they were over, the girls more so if they didn't manage to win first place. On this particular occasion, my younger daughter, G, kept hanging on to me while we waited in line. I was feeling a bit annoyed. Then she put her hands in mine, stood on top of my feet, and started leaning back and forth. After she did this repeatedly, I let go of her hands, causing her to fall to the floor on her back. I can still see the expression on her face. She sheepishly looked around to see if anyone had seen what happened, and tears welled up in her eyes from embarrassment. I apologized profusely, but she ran to her mom, throwing her arms around her mom's waist. It's a moment as a dad I wish I could take back. She wasn't physically hurt, but I still feel guilty about the pain I caused her that day. What was my motive? I've asked myself. Why did I let go of her hands? It's true I wasn't in a great mood, but even then, I wouldn't have hurt my daughter on purpose. I know that. So why do I remember the incident and the feelings that accompany it so vividly?

I have never told that story to anyone. That's likely the reason it's lingered nearly a decade after it happened. Guilt doesn't go away on its own. It comes up when we're standing in line at the bank, when we find ourselves in similar situations with other people, or when we lie down at night faced with the silence of our own bedrooms. How we resolve it depends on how willing we are to face our guilt, talk about it, and apologize when necessary.

Religious guilt is no different. If, like me, you simply left your church one day without warning and never went back, you may feel you have unresolved relationships or loose ends that were never tied up. The best way of dealing with our guilt is to talk about what makes us feel guilty. See a therapist if necessary. We have to accept our situations for what they were, including any extenuating circumstances at the time. My irritability isn't an excuse for letting go of my daughter's hands, but I likely wouldn't have let go if I wasn't feeling irritable. Most importantly, radical acceptance of the past is the healthiest step we can take for ourselves and the people around us.

CHAPTER 10

Shameful

Shame corrodes the very part of us that believes we are capable of change.

– Brené Brown

My wife and I sat on lawn chairs just outside the back door of our beautiful beachfront property. The gorgeous dark wood trim and custom wood ceilings offset the massive windows surrounding the house. We could hear the ocean waves crashing against the shore and smell salt water in the coastal breeze. We had just closed escrow on the property and it was finally ours. Next door to us, and attached to the house, was a bustling coffee shop with beautiful marble counters accented with black and white subway tiles. We could have coffee anytime we wanted. That's when it hit me. Why was the coffee shop attached to our house, and why didn't I own it? The real-estate agent, who was mysteriously standing in the living room, previously unnoticed, said, "Oh, you can purchase the coffee shop if you want."

The house was expensive enough, so I tepidly asked, "How much more a month would that be?"

"Thirty dollars a month," she replied.

"I'll pay half!" my wife shot back, now sitting on a couch near one of the large windows.

"I can afford thirty dollars a month," I told the agent. I didn't believe my wife would pay her half. Besides, what was a little extra money when we're talking about our dream home?

And then I woke up.

A number of things were odd about that dream. For one, I've never wanted to live in a beach house. I was born near Monterey Bay, California and lived there as a child. My fondest memory was shivering in the fog and being forced to eat a picnic lunch on a sand dune while trying to keep our blanket from blowing across the highway. Secondly, I wouldn't buy a house with a coffee shop attached. A dedicated coffee room sounds delightful, but it wouldn't be shared with the public. Thirdly, and most poignantly, I was married to my ex-wife. My "normal," in my own dream, was a lie.

I distinctly remember having the same feeling in this dream I felt when I was married to my wife. An emotional wall divided us. She was my friend, but any relationship beyond that was always forced. I acted the way I needed to act, performing for acceptance and intimacy. My entire life had been a performance. But as in the dream, I didn't know my life wasn't real. My actions brought superficial love and acceptance. I was unaware of the loneliness left inside. Like a performer who finishes his award-winning act only to end up alone in a dimly lit hotel room at the end of the day, I was left with my own thoughts in the middle of the night.

"I Will Always Love You If . . ."

Religious affiliation is often a series of performances, some of which are conscious to us and others of which are not. Don't swear, don't drink, don't talk about your sexual feelings. Always be patient with your kids. Don't speak unkindly to your spouse. Wear your Sunday best to church and never, ever let anyone know about the horrible argument you had with your family on the way there. Don't let anyone know if you're having financial problems and always pay your tithes–or act like you do even if you don't. Keep your doubts to yourself or expect a lecture from fellow church members about why you are wrong. If you find out your kid is gay or your spouse has substance abuse problems, you have two options: exploit the person to prove your spiritual commitment or quietly love them and keep family issues to yourself.

Many of us have been so programmed with a fake-it-'till-you-make-it theology that we can't stop faking it. We feel an unbearable amount of intrinsic pressure to continue looking, acting, and playing the part of a good Christian. Even after stepping away from the faith, we may not be able to see ourselves separately from the one-person play we've created. The lies about who we are and what we believe are sometimes so deep, we don't recognize them as lies. Our feelings, often in the form of depression and anxiety, belie our thoughts and actions. This is the shame that follows us after we start to rethink what we once believed to be true. Shame is "a painful feeling of humiliation or distress caused by the consciousness of wrong or foolish behavior," according to Google. It's the feeling that we're not acting the way we're *supposed to*, even though we don't necessarily believe, consciously, that what we're doing is wrong. We simply don't know how to accept the fact that we are wholly human and embrace it.

Shame on You

One of the articles I wrote for the *Huffington Post* around the time of the 2016 election was a piece called "An Open Letter to the GOP: 'We Are You.'" In it I said, "You can shake your heads in disdain and point your judgmental fingers in distaste when you see [LGBTQ+ people] on TV, in pride parades, or Democratic rallies. But remember, the ones you won't see are the ones sitting next to you at church, speaking at your podiums and on your couches. But they're there. They've always been there. We are you, too."[1]

The same could be said for virtually any group of people anywhere. We belong to all kinds of social groups and clubs, some of which may contradict what we say we believe. Affiliation with a group may have no bearing on what a person says he or she values deeply. Yet religious shame can cause some people to hide their behavior for social reasons. We happily attend our groups physically but often feel we don't truly belong there.

I had just finished my speech at a small progressive church when an older woman in the audience raised her hand. "Will you talk about the damage caused by conversion therapy?" she asked. I paused briefly. My mind raced through a series of stories I'd heard from men and women I'd interviewed. People had been mentally abused, physically tortured, excommunicated from their congregations, and cut off from their own families and friends. They had lost spouses, children, and jobs. They had been ridiculed from pulpits and expelled from the only communities they had ever known.

Then there was my own story. Sometimes, to this day, when I step on a stage, I feel something is intrinsically wrong with me. It's a message that was reinforced throughout my life in church teachings, societal examples, and the continued nagging feeling that I am just not "normal." I'm keenly aware that despite how much I look and act like a straight man, I'm not like the heterosexual men in the society in which I grew up or even among my church peers who also married and raised families. I could never hold a traditional job as a minister, and my family is not like everyone else's. I will never be the person I spent most of my life trying to be, and I wonder if that sense of shame will always exist.

I answered the woman's question with statistics, research, and cerebral sterility, maintaining my composure and emotional distance. I was careful to quote the numbers as accurately as I could remember, but before I could cite the proper sources, she interrupted me: "You mean you don't think we should ban conversion therapy for minors?" She was incensed. I was taken aback, trying to understand where her frustration was coming from.

"Of course we should ban conversion therapy for minors," I retorted, but let's understand what the numbers actually tell us." She had thrown me off my game and I was backtracking. This really should have been the easiest question I answered all night. It wasn't; it was personal. To adequately answer her question, I needed to be vulnerable, which I wasn't ready to do.

For those of us raised with clearly defined roles around gender, spirituality, religious activity, speech, relationships, and culturally acceptable behaviors, shame can run deep. We may feel we haven't measured up while thinking everyone else has. Rather than talk about our perceived shortcomings, we hide them. We are embarrassed by our own thoughts. Consequently, a lot of people in our social circles walk around with smiles, and we all feel we are the only ones with problems. The end result is a lot of lonely people feeling ashamed and embarrassed, working hard to pretend they are something they're not.

As a young minister, I attended and even led my fair share of singles classes. We may have called the class "single and fabulous," but whatever spin we put on it, it was still a class of misfits in the corporate church. These were the people who didn't fit the church's ideal of the married couple with children (those are the families the pastor is speaking to in nearly every sermon), so they didn't get to join the rest of the church in couples retreats, Valentine's Day dinners, and church date nights.

We on the ministry staff liked to pat ourselves on the back for making a place for these poor souls, but the church was hardly a safe place for them. A scarlet letter was emblazoned across their foreheads. We just didn't talk about it. Single people didn't talk about it either. They attended the class as a function of their faith and because it was their primary source of human interaction. I was keenly aware of all this when I eventually became one of them.

A tremendous amount of shame comes from not fitting into the society in which we belong. Marketing companies caught on to this idea decades ago when they started advertising clothes, washing machines, hair products, and cars. When the ideal life was created by advertisers, it included being white and middle class, and having the latest amenities.

In 2009, Chris Rock produced the documentary *Good Hair*. He uncovered, or at least explained, the $9 billion industry created to help African American women's hair look more like white women's hair, using hair extensions, toxic relaxers, and time-consuming hair treatments. However, the idea that "white hair" is normal and desired goes back before the civil rights movement took hold. An experiment by Kenneth Clark presented young black children with a choice between a doll that looked like them and a white doll.[2] These children consistently chose to play with the white doll. Clark's experiment was used to persuade the court toward desegregation, explaining that these children felt inferior because of racial stereotypes. Interestingly enough, the scenario was reproduced in 2005 with the same results.[3]

Kitchens, Medicine, Peanut Butter, and Normal

In our house, we've always had a space in the kitchen cabinet dedicated to medicine. It's where you go to find vitamins, bandages, thermometers, antacids, and the like. As my kids were growing up, quickly caring for minor scrapes and burns in the kitchen, where we were more likely to be, was a lot more convenient than rummaging through an overly crowded bathroom shelf. After our kitchen was remodeled, we found we had a lot more spaces than things to put in them. One of those spaces has a three-tier lazy Susan in a corner cabinet. It initially held nothing but a bottle of Tylenol. Then we somehow managed to stuff in two full shelves of bandages, fiber pills, allergy medicine, prescriptions for everyone, including the dog, and two half-empty jars of peanut butter. Those went on the third tier by themselves.

The peanut butter first landed in the pantry after the remodel, which *seemed* logical, but as I was making my daughter's sandwiches for school, I soon realized everything was conveniently located except the peanut butter. It was "over there." Way over there. I'm a man who firmly believes everything has its place, and if my friends voted who among us would be most likely to store his peanut butter away from other related items, I would not be on that list. However, when school lunches are too often a late-night afterthought, a parent goes for convenience over structure. Soon, the peanut butter found a new home in a neighborhood of neti pots, antiseptic ointment, and B12 vitamins.

One day I was struck by the epiphany that this had become our new normal, and it made me smile. So I posted this question on Facebook among my friends: "Does anyone else keep peanut butter in their kitchen medicine cabinet?" The first response questioned why we had a medicine cabinet in our kitchen, followed by a barrage of responses like "No, we keep our medicine next to the microwave in our bedroom" and "No, but I don't keep peanut butter in the bathroom either." Most people, however, confessed that while they did not necessarily keep peanut butter with their medicine–though one other person did–they did indeed keep medicine in their kitchen cupboards, and it was likely mixed with food items or kitchen tools. What appeared to be a fun little quirk for our family ended up being a rather common experience for a lot of people. It turns out we were pretty normal after all.

As Patsy Clairmont famously said, "Normal is just a setting on your dryer." While humans are homogeneous, meaning we tend to gravitate toward people who look like us and hold similar values, vast differences beyond hair and eye color remain. Intelligence levels, sexual orientation, genders beyond male and female, races, personalities, family backgrounds, and DNA are just a few of those differences. What is considered normal is what our society–church, politicians, advertisers, family, and friends–tells us is normal. While who we are may appear to fall out of line with those in our immediate social circle, that doesn't mean we are not a normal variation of our fellow human beings. In fact, as I stated earlier, we are probably just like those in our social circle; it's just that no one is talking. For this reason, I'm an advocate for sharing our stories in as many situations as we can. Not everyone is a writer or a speaker or even has a platform, but everyone has a sphere of influence. Everyone has people he or she can reach that no one else can.

Shame's Antidote

I was nervously approached by a young man after I had talked about conversion therapy at a conference. "I just want to say thank you for your apology to those of us who went through conversion therapy," he said. "I know you didn't do anything to me personally, but it was still good to hear someone say 'I'm sorry.'" He went on to tell me that while he was involved in conversion therapy, his church offered a nurturing environment, a place to live, and even a job. But when he began to have doubts and struggles, the people he had grown to love and trust quickly threw him out of his home, his job, and his church. "It was difficult to even go to the store without seeing someone from the church," he said. "If they didn't ignore me completely, they made sure to tell me I was a sinner."

I listened intently, filled with incredulousness, anger, and compassion. How he survived all of that without getting addicted to drugs or committing suicide was a miracle in itself. Like the rest of us, he desperately wanted to fit in with his community and would have given anything to have "normal" feelings and lived a "normal" life. He was, instead, deemed sinful, broken, and wrong. He was ostracized and left without family, his friends, or a place to belong. I couldn't help but hug him, if for nothing more than a small consolatory gesture for all he'd experienced. More than that, I hugged him to thank him for feeling safe enough to share his story with me.

A few months later I received an email from him. He'd beautifully written his story in vivid imagery, capturing the emotions he'd expressed to me when we first met. I asked if I could publish his story on my blog, which he agreed to let me do. I began hearing from others who related to the story he told. They came from similar small towns with similar family backgrounds and, like this young man, had been ostracized from their churches, families, and friends for expressing their deepest thoughts and feelings. All of this grew from one person willing to tell his story.

Telling our stories one time doesn't suddenly make the pain go away. Even after speaking for a few years and sharing my own story, deeper feelings I didn't know existed were uncovered. In some ways, it's gotten harder. At the same time, exposing the wounds allows them to heal. When I share my story I'm making a conscious effort to tell other people, "You're not alone. I'm with you on this journey, too." While we may express it differently, our humanity is a shared experience.

As human beings, we love success stories. Why? Because no matter what facade we show to everyone else, a good success story makes our problems seem a little smaller, even if no one else is aware of them. We all secretly need the inspiration of others to keep us going. A success story, however, doesn't necessarily have a resolution.

We like happy, Hollywood endings, though most stories don't end that way. If they did, Hollywood wouldn't seem so magical. Then again, Hollywood movies have a long history of only leading us up to the point where the prince and the princess fall in love and get married, criminals are identified and arrested, or the mystery is solved. Seldom do movies go on to show couples fighting over who forgot to put the cap back on the toothpaste, one person resentfully cleaning out the litter box, or an entire family mindlessly watching television just to avoid speaking with each other. But in those spaces is where life happens.

CHAPTER 11

Depressed

He was . . . a melancholy-looking man. He had the appearance of one who has searched for the leak in life's gas-pipe with a lighted candle.

– P. G. Wodehouse

Not much says "you're unlovable the way you are" like conversion therapy. It starts with the premise that gay people are broken and defines everything else about them in terms of their brokenness. I've met many gay men and women who, decades later, still struggle to find their value even after accepting their sexuality, getting married, and raising families. Our sexuality, like our personalities, our eye color, and our skin color, is an inherent part of who we are. Beyond the horrific ways people and organizations try to extract it, their message has told generations of people, "You are not acceptable to God." Those of us raised in religious environments, who did nothing but exist, internalized the message from an early age that something is desperately wrong with us. Many of us became perfectionists, or developed obsessive-compulsive disorders, and when all else didn't work, we compartmentalized our lives. We got so good at unconscious self-berating, it became like automated, self-sufficient software running in the back of our minds–like antivirus protection but inculcating harmful viruses into our thinking.

Debraun is someone I've known for a long time. The relationship he has with mutual friends keeps us connected. He has a good heart, but that's not what most people see. He's rough around the edges, he constantly rubs people the wrong way, and most of what he says is in the form of a complaint. He's also a bit of a conspiracy theorist. He'll argue vehemently with people who disagree with him, though he offers little more defense for his perspective than condescending laughter, eye rolls, and looks of superiority. I have to remind myself he has a good heart and try to avoid conversations on anything important.

Debraun didn't have a great childhood. His father and siblings excluded him from their activities when they weren't making fun of him. He grew up to become an amazing artist in his own right, though his health eventually put an end to a promising career. As a father, he's hypercritical of his kids, believing his advice is *always* what's best for them. He has a way of telling stories so he comes out on top. When the protagonists in his stories don't follow his advice, they inevitably suffer for it, not the least of which is getting a Debraun-styled I-told-you-so.

Unfortunately, Debraun has lived his life this way for many years. It's left him fairly secluded with only a few friends he sees rarely. He's resigned himself to his lot in life without much enthusiasm. He doesn't say it, but Debraun doesn't believe his life will get any better, and he doesn't have any desire to change the outcome. Those who choose to simply accept their fate find themselves in a lonely place with little hope.

Psychologist Stacey Freedenthal says this kind of self-hatred almost always comes from childhood: "Children believe what they hear from others. If a parent tells a child that she is good for nothing or can't do anything right, then that becomes the truth in the child's mind." Once the belief is in place, it's very difficult to get rid of because thoughts and beliefs, like behavior, are physical attributes of our brains. In a catch-22, we reinforce neural pathways in our brains by telling ourselves we are not valued or important and then interpret cues from others or our circumstances as reiterating the initial premise.

The Chair

In the corner of my house sits a brown leather recliner. It's really a leftover piece of furniture we didn't know what to do with after we remodeled our home. But it seems perfect in this corner. It sits right next to a wall of windows with a clear view of the sky and overlooking nearly the entire backyard. It's mostly used as a ladder or jump-off point by Sam, our cat, to get his fat body to the window ledge where his food bowl is. That's the best place we could find to keep the dog out of it. Because of its location, the chair looks more like a scratching post than a piece of furniture. Sam meows at passersby for a lift to his bowl. When that doesn't work, he climbs up the chair, digging his front paws into the seat and dragging his perfectly capable back legs with him. The chair is also a place where I sometimes sit to write, contemplate, and cry.

Staring out the back window into a vast, empty sky isn't therapy for me, but this place seems to resonate with feelings of hopeless resolve in my darkest depression. Words to describe the feelings are elusive. At those times, a deep sense of sadness consumes and obliterates my intellect. The slightest insinuation that I've said the wrong thing in the wrong way during those times is enough to start the self-flogging: "How can anyone possibly love you? You're a nuisance. You're not worth anyone's time and energy."

I'm enamored with death. During depressive episodes I'll spend hours reading stories of people who have died or committed suicide. When I'm in that state, I envy the idea that they don't feel any emotional pain–or any pain at all. I wonder what it's like not to feel. Sometimes I lie in bed imagining what it would be like to take my last breath and sleep forever without dreams or thoughts.

To an outsider, I seem to feel despair without reason. And despite all that's wrong with the world, I have nothing to be sad about. But depression doesn't always make sense. Sometimes it is a chemical imbalance (as in my case), sometimes it is situational, and sometimes it stems from experiences and feelings implanted before we were consciously aware of them. Overcoming it is a work in progress.

Depression like mine is sometimes debilitating. It can last weeks or months, derailing the best-laid plans. Articles I want to write become little more than titles. All my ideas suddenly sound stupid, or the work feels so overwhelming I believe it can't be done. Interaction with people is uncomfortable and frightening. And of course, after years of involvement with fundamentalism, I sometimes hear that voice in my head that says, "You're depressed because you're running from God." Logically, I know that's not true. I struggled with the same depth of depression as a Christian. I'm in a much better place now, making huge strides toward healing and going long stretches with depression under control. Nevertheless, that familiar voice persists.

Approximately 7 percent of the adult US population deals with major depressive disorder.[2] Depression often coexists with anxiety disorders, OCD, eating disorders, sleep disorders, and a host of physical ailments including headaches and chronic pain. Statistics don't differentiate between Christians and non-Christians when it comes to depression, but given the barrage of messages most of us received from ideological pure pastors about how we should pray harder and trust Jesus more, it makes logical sense that many more of us would struggle with depression, anxiety, and other stress-induced maladies.

In hyperreligious settings, depression and anxiety are often treated like spiritual problems. On the Focus on the Family website, an article written by a fundamentalist medical doctor says, "The tendency toward depression or alcoholism is not a sin; giving in to them, however, is a sin."[3] The fact that alcoholism is listed alongside depression is telling. People do not wake up as alcoholics, though they very well may wake up depressed. Though the article does state that depression can have a physical cause, the number one suggestion for dealing with it is to read your Bible and pray, followed by thanking God "for loving you and bringing you through the bout of depression."[4] I pity that man's patients.

Similarly, an article on Pat Robertson's Christian Broadcasting Network website suggests that if you struggle with depression, the first thing you should do is "ask God right now to forgive you for your sins and to come and rule in your life."[5] Again, in passing statements, the site says depression can be caused by physical conditions and suggests a visit to a medical doctor may be in order. However, the article reminds the reader, "God can heal any physical problem, including one that causes, or is caused by, depression."[6] Scriptures are conveniently hyperlinked. One is Psalm 103:3, which says, "He forgives all my sins and heals all my diseases." The other is Matthew 8:16-17, which tells how Jesus cast out demons and healed the sick.

When Robin Williams committed suicide in 2014, Christian media lit up, declaring that Williams had succumbed to the devil. "It's with great sadness that I am about to say this: Maybe Robin Williams is in Hell."[7] Another blogger wrote, "This tragic outcome of Robin Williams' life demonstrated that no matter how talented and influential one is, if they lack a sound spiritual foundation in Jesus Christ, they will perish and end up in eternal hell."[8] Multiple problems with these statements show up here, but one glaring oversight is that suicide does not discriminate between Christians and non-Christians. As it turned out, Williams's widow, Susan Schneider, revealed two years later that Williams had been diagnosed with a debilitating brain disorder called Lewy Body Dementia.[9] The progressive disease left him incapable of thinking clearly, and he didn't have long to live. Schneider described Williams as the "bravest man I've ever known."[10]

No single solution exists for depression. Depression is a complex psychological and physiological disease. Some of those affected will spend lifetimes on antidepressants, while others will find solace in strong social networks. Research shows that those who do best combine ongoing psychotherapy with other forms of treatment, such as medication or exercise, and a support system.

The most difficult aspect of depression for many of us is simply finding the internal fortitude to do something about it. Depression screams at us to give up, call it quits, and confess that all the negative thoughts and emotions we feel about ourselves are true. Depression is not likely to go away on its own, but acknowledging and admitting it is a part of our lives helps us make peace with it.

The Tale of a Leash

I have a dog named Habib (pronounced Ha-beeb). We usually just call him 'Bib (Beeb). He's a little brown terrier mix I rescued from a shelter when he was a puppy. I'm not a biologist, but I'm convinced he is made mostly of tension and bundled nerves. Abel thinks Habib looks and acts uncannily similar to the squirrel in the movie *Ice Age*. He's a quirky little guy whose personality vacillates between that of a frightened chihuahua and that of an over-confident but caged German shepherd. I'm fairly certain, if we could test him, he would lie somewhere on the autism scale.

Training 'Bib has produced challenges of its own. Typically, if you point to an object in the presence of a dog (or even a baby), it looks with delight in the direction you're pointing. This is documented in a number of behavioral journals. It's a rather basic animal behavior. But then there's Habib. Pointing to anything while making eye contact causes him to drop to the floor like a scolded puppy. No amount of positive reinforcement has changed this frustrating behavior, which he brought with him to our home. He is incapable of learning anything if pointing–or accusatory judgment, as he sees it–is involved. Nevertheless, he and I have developed a mutually beneficial relationship. It's probably not what either of us had in mind as master-dog relationships go, and it took a solid seven years to get it, but it works for us.

I began taking Habib for morning walks while I was recovering from a head injury, at which point I'd been banished from most daily activities. Going for walks was a welcome change, though I have to admit, doing so outside wasn't my first choice. Habib was ecstatic. As soon as I got out of bed, 'Bib knew what was coming next. He danced around my legs while I brushed my teeth, spun in circles while I groggily put on my clothes, and jumped on and off the bed or climbed clumsily onto my lap. I was afraid if I made eye contact, he'd wet himself with excitement. So I played it cool. The sight of his harness and the clatter of his leash had him bouncing toward the door while I was still trying to remember if I had put on both socks. As soon as we stepped outside the door, Habib, an unexpectedly stalwart little guy, started dragging me down the street at a surprisingly swift pace. I bounced behind him like a partially deflated helium balloon tied to the back of his chain. Our walks weren't nearly as relaxing as I'd first envisioned.

I explained my situation with Habib to my parents one day, who occasionally watch him when I'm out of town, and my father pulled out the retractable leash they use. "Here, take this," he said. "See if that works any better."

It was revolutionary and allows me to ease into the walk. Habib now runs ahead of me or lingers behind while I keep an even pace. I get to wake up more slowly and listen to my favorite authors and podcasts. When other people or dogs walk by, I hold my thumb on the button, which locks the leash in place and keeps Habib next to me. "Brilliant!" I thought. "Wish I'd invented this."

For the most part, Habib navigates the neighborhood with ease. In our neighborhood, stop signs, street signs, electrical boxes, and fire hydrants are scattered around people's front yards. This requires Habib to be aware of his surroundings while darting up and down, back and forth across lawns and landscapes. He is surprisingly good at turning, dodging, and backtracking to avoid getting his long leash wrapped around a pole. But we have our days.

When Habib gets his nose set on something in front of him, he goes for it with the kind of tenacity that defines him as a terrier. While I continue to move forward he stands focused. He forgets for the moment that he is tethered to a long string to which I, just a short ten feet away, am holding onto with a death grip. If Habib stops and isn't monitoring the tension in his line, he and I are both met with a startling yank. That *should* be his cue to get back on track. But Habib's natural inclination is to pull in the opposite direction. If I yank harder, he digs his paws into the ground and pulls himself backward. And true to form, when I say his name and point in the direction he needs to go to untangle himself, he drops to the ground and rolls onto his back. Counterproductive and very unhelpful.

With a leash in one hand and a large water bottle in the other, I sometimes walk to him and use my foot to pick him up and then nudge him in the right direction. With ears down and puppy dog eyes up, he digs in harder. More pointing, this time with expletives, causes more dropping to the ground. We get nowhere. I sigh heavily. I can clearly see a resolution, but he refuses to move. "Dumbass," I mutter. But then, between more leash yanking, pushing with my foot, and louder expletives, I manage to get Habib past his obstacle and back on track. I quickly look at my surroundings and give a nod of apology for my language to the family with school children getting into the minivan across the street, and Habib and I are on our way.

One day I began paying particular attention to the way Habib navigated his surroundings with leash in tow. I watched his movements, the way he weaved in and out of signs and poles and bounced around shrubs and trees. Then, he got stuck. This time, I stopped. I didn't offer any direction; I just looked at him and waited to see what he would do. Habib looked at me, wagging his tail in embarrassment, if that's a thing, and turned around. A few seconds later, he walked toward the pole and then around the opposite side, releasing the tension on his leash, and went back down the path he was headed. He was calm and onto the next olfactory adventure that presented itself in that morning's journey.

Perhaps I was more awake that morning, or more likely I just forgot my headphones on the bathroom counter, but I thought about how I deal with obstacles in my own life. Rather than working with frustration, pain, depression, or anxiety, humans resist it. We metaphorically pull the leash in the opposite direction by numbing the pain, denying its existence, and convincing ourselves it's something else. We try to escape its grip by pulling harder on the harness.

Going *toward* the pain seems counterintuitive. Just like Habib who couldn't figure out why my pushing him in the direction of the problem would resolve anything, we simply try to run harder in the opposite direction, believing that if we just go fast enough, pull hard enough, or resist long enough, we'll be free. In fact, as Habib demonstrated, if running in the opposite direction can't help, the only other option is to roll over onto our backs and give up. And some jerk shouting at us–and pointing at who knows what–only makes the problem worse. "It simply can't be done," we tell ourselves in resignation.

There is a huge difference between giving up and letting go. Giving up is resigning in defeat, while letting go is full awareness, acknowledgment, and embracement of our realities. When Habib stopped, and appeared to think for a moment–though I cannot vouch for anything that actually went through his head–he made the decision to move toward the object that ensnared him. It stopped him in his tracks, but he wasn't flustered. He was still wagging his tail. He made eye contact with me. He released the tension on his own leash by voluntarily moving toward the object. Esoterically speaking, he accepted and acknowledged the position he was in. He didn't let it get him down or throw his paws up in frustration because his entire morning walk was ruined. He simply faced the problem, addressed it, and went about his business.

Our ongoing struggles can easily make us want to give up. Why bother doing anything if we can't be consistent? Why bother with relationships if we can't stay connected? Some days depression is my reality. I have a spouse who is more aware of the effects of it than anyone, and who stands beside me and helps me live as consistent of a life as possible with it. He doesn't pretend it's not there, and he most certainly doesn't make excuses for me. It is the reality of our lives, and oddly and counterintuitively, acknowledging that releases the tension of the depression, and provides a firm foundation from which to move forward.

CHAPTER 12

Who Am I Now?

The closer you come to knowing that you alone create the world of your experience, the more vital it becomes for you to discover just who is doing the creating.

– Eric Micha'el Leventhal

Tony is a good friend of mine who, like me, spent the first half of his life in ministry. It wasn't a change of heart that caused him to leave his job but the frustration of the day-to-day problems that began to wear him down. "People are just petty," he told me one day over coffee. "I had a vision in my head about ministry that never seemed to materialize. For the first several years I stayed focused on the good I felt I was doing by meeting with families, praying for people, and leading Bible studies. But then I just started to see things differently." Tony worked at several churches, thinking the next one would be different because the pastor or a ministry leader or family that caused problems wouldn't be there. "I started to think there was something wrong with me," he confessed bitterly.

After moving his family to different churches, both in and out of his denomination, and relocating around the country several times, he decided he didn't want to do it anymore. "I prayed God would release me, though

I honestly had no idea what I would do for a living." His wife, Tony said, graciously gave him space to figure out his next move.

Moving on after life in the ministry can be difficult. Dr. Marlene Winell says,

> For most people, the religious environment was a one-stop-shop for meeting all their major needs–social support, a coherent world-view, meaning and direction in life, structured activities, and emotional/spiritual satisfaction. Leaving the fold means multiple losses, including the loss of friends and family support at a crucial time of personal transition. Consequently, it is a very lonely "stressful life event."[1]

Psychologist James Moyer adds, "The psychological effects of having left fundamentalism often persist long after the time of one's actual departure. Many former fundamentalists experience chronic dissatisfaction and difficulty finding direction for their lives."[2] What does a former church leader do when his or her entire life has been in the church? More than a job, ministry is a lifestyle. It doesn't have set hours. Nor does the minister ever truly leave work at the office. You're at a loss. You sense a void and have a haunting feeling you should be doing something more important with your life. Secular jobs may pay the bills, but they don't generally provide purpose and meaning to those of us answering a higher call.

What's more, if your beliefs have changed, your decision to leave brings a sense of finality. Abel has jokingly told me I should call *The 700 Club* and say I've repented and I'm straight. He thinks it would be a good way to earn some extra cash, as such a confession would hurl me into the limelight of ex-gay ministry once again. It's a story hosts would love to tell their donors. But the thought sickens me. I can't imagine going back into any closet where I can't be honest about who I am and what I believe. Once we come to a new sense of reality and authenticity, we're left with the question, Where do we go from here?

To start, taking care of our mental and physical health is the most important step when facing an existential crisis. We have a difficult time making rational decisions or thinking clearly when our minds or bodies are experiencing pain. One of the first questions I ask my daughters when they call me upset is, "Have you eaten today?" Nine times out of ten the answer is no. Their blood sugar levels have dropped, they have headaches, and whatever is bothering them is severely magnified by their bodies' lack of nutrients. Similarly, when I'm contacted through my website by married gay men who don't know what to do, I provide links to therapists and support organizations before I ever talk about how they can educate themselves and their spouses on the issues. Physical exercise releases a cornucopia of natural pharmaceuticals in the brain that help give us perspective. With our mental and physical health in check, we're in a better position to find our passions.

Finding Passion

After spending over two decades making music, leading Bible studies, and attending church practically every time the door was open, I found more free time on my hands than I knew what to do with. I wasn't productive. I was filled with shame and could barely look people in the eye. I'd given up looking for passion and, at the time, was content disappearing into the background in my secular job. Slowly, as I faced my demons, the desire to do something important came back. However, I didn't know what that was. There isn't a huge market for gospel singers outside of church.

Getting me to step outside my comfort zone took a lot of encouragement from others. I was still a raging, nondrinking conservative whose crowd was definitely not in the local gay bar. But I learned from Bible school that a person can always find his crowd. So that's what I did. I created a Meetup group of conservative gay men, most of whom had been married and most of whom were older than me. While that served a need for a short time, and Abel and I made a few friends from that group, I was still changing, rethinking, and figuring out what I wanted to do.

It's easy to get discouraged when things don't happen right away. Replacing a passion that was front and center, clear, and meaningful with brunch with a few friends once a month doesn't quite do the trick. We get restless and frustrated. If we struggle with anxiety and depression on top of that frustration, it's easy to disconnect and just give up.

Life coach, Marie Forleo, wondered for several years what it would be like to be a dancer, though she had never before entered a dance studio. Knowing that most dancers start when they are five, Forleo thought it was a ridiculous idea to show up in her twenties. She told herself, "It sounds exciting, but dance as a career is crazy and irresponsible. There's no money in that. You studied business finance, so you should do something more stable and related to what you know." After more self-talk and debate, she took her first lesson and cried because it felt so right for her. Her action paid off, and Forleo became the world's first Nike Elite Dance Athlete and, she says, carved out a niche for herself in the world of dance and fitness. She's learned that passion can't be found in your head because it lives in your heart. "Clarity comes from engagement, not thought," she says.[3]

Remember that passion is sensual. We feel it in our bodies, which is not something those of us coming from the fundamentalist faith do well. Writer Neil Carter says, "It's not that religion always directly shames people for their desires and their pleasures. But the Christian faith in particular teaches you never to be totally at home in your own body."[4] The key to finding our passion is to throw our entire selves into the process of *doing*. Do everything you have the least bit of interest in doing. Go to the opera, shop at garage sales, go windsurfing, become a hairdresser or an entrepreneur. Become a secret shopper or a firefighter. Check activities off your list that you know for sure you don't like to do, and don't stop pursuing your interests until something clicks.

When I started dating again I included in my profile all the typical things people say they are interested in, such as hiking, camping, working out, going to movies, and so on. I knew I didn't like to camp, but I was willing to be adventurous if it meant making a human connection. Fortunately, I was never put in that situation. Truth be told, I complain a lot when I have to do things I don't like to do.

Once, Abel and I signed up with a Meetup group to go snowshoeing. We persuaded a friend to go with us, partially because he got a discount on snow rental equipment. Early on a beautiful but cold Saturday morning, we convoyed up the mountain with other members of the group. Once parked, group members gleefully poured out of their cars, and we all put on our snowsuits, jackets, gloves, and shoes, ready to trek along the mountainside.

The mood was light. Lively conversations ensued as old friends reunited and others of us made new friends. Abel and I were trailing behind most of the other hikers, simply enjoying each other's company. And then somewhere around halfway through the hike, I looked up at the snow-covered trees glistening in the sunlight and then down at the tops of rocks sticking out of the snow on the ground. I stopped moving and stuck my poles into the ground. "I *hate* hiking," I said to Abel out of the blue. "It's just one tree after another, followed by a rock that looks like the last rock." With that, I discovered my passion was likely *not* going to be outside.

Trust Your Feelings

I obsessively went over the details of "God's confirmation" after my marriage fell apart. I couldn't have been any more sincere in my prayers asking God for direction, spending time in the Word, and seeking godly advice. I had done my due diligence, and I felt I was doing the right thing. Fundamentalism, with all its emphasis on faith, is a religion built on absolute certainty in absolute truth. Consequently, it produces followers who believe they are absolutely right. How do they know they are right? They *feel* it.

It's no wonder, then, we distrust our feelings when we see one thing with our eyes but are admonished to follow the party line with our hearts. And it's certainly no mystery why we distrust our feelings when we begin to question our faith. They were supposed to guide us. After all, we *felt* conviction. We *felt* God speaking to us. We *felt* God's presence. When we prayed in sincerity, we *felt* an answer. The scriptures we heard from the pulpit, memorized, and cited confirmed exactly what we felt to be true. But it wasn't true. Our feelings betrayed us, and now we don't know what to think or believe. How can we possibly trust our feelings to lead us in the right direction?

In theory, rationalization without emotions sounds good. Excel spreadsheets don't have emotions, and as long as the formulas are entered correctly, the answers are perfect every time. When formulas are wrong, Excel immediately provides feedback telling the user the input is incorrect. But our brains are not databases, and unlike a spreadsheet, they don't only look at information entered in a cell. Our brains are multisensory and pull in quantitative and qualitative data. Even our emotions are used to make decisions; in fact, they are essential.

Neuroscientist Antonio Damasio told about a well-to-do businessman who suffered damage in an area in the middle of the front of the brain. He lost his marriage and business ventures, which he described to Damasio in dispassionate tones. The tumor that damaged his brain so strongly affected his emotions he could no longer make decisions. Damasio said of his patient, "He was always controlled. Nowhere was there a sense of his own suffering, even though he was the protagonist. I never saw a tinge of emotion in my many hours of conversation with him: no sadness, no impatience, no frustration."[5]

Philosopher David Hume argued, "Reason is, and ought only to be, the slave of the passions, and can never pretend to any other office than to serve and obey them."[6] And author Jonah Lehrer said, "Motivation is driven by feeling, not intellect."[7]

For years I distrusted my emotions after leaving the church. I didn't want to be lied to by anyone, including me. But that's not how emotions work. Emotions don't guide our motivations; they follow them. When our motivations change, so do our feelings. Our feelings, in fact, do exactly what they are designed to do and *substantiate* our passions, motivations, and goals.

The emotions we feel shape the depth of the thoughts we have, both positively and negatively. We process those thoughts in one of two ways: heuristically, using what we know or rely on to be true, as in the case of our deeply ingrained faith, and systematically, which involves more critical thinking. We can use these processes separately or in combination. Neither is wrong and both have value. The heuristic process relies heavily on how much we trust the source of information. We evaluate what we hear based on what we feel about the source and what we believe to be true according to our gut instincts and experiences.

For example, if the pastor of our holiness church tells us going to the movies is sinful, we believe he has our best interest at heart. Our gut instinct, based on our experiences and indoctrination, tells us we should trust his judgment. The systematic process, on the other hand, tends to lead us to more critical thinking about the content *and* the source. In other words, while we trust the pastor and believe he has our best interest at heart, we may also think that the

Bible says nothing about movies being inherently sinful. Yet we may choose to avoid the movies based on a number of scriptures provided by our pastor that cause us to believe attending a movie makes us less holy. Ultimately, what we *feel* about the information presented leads us to attend or avoid going to the movies. Concurrently, our emotions trigger a set of responses that help us quickly deal with problems or opportunities. Our feelings determine our decisions, and our decisions are determined by our goals. We need our feelings to make meaningful connections with the people we love, we need them to heal, and we need them to help us find direction and purpose. The bottom line is, not only is it okay to trust your feelings, it's necessary.

Life Isn't Over Yet

A late-night-talk-show host on an old television show once asked comedian Rodney Dangerfield where he was from.

"I'm from New York," Dangerfield said.

"Oh! Have you lived there your whole life?" the interviewer asked.

"I don't know," Dangerfield retorted, "I'm not dead yet."

Our stories don't have to be complete and our journeys don't have to have reached a destination for us to have meaning. Our stories are our history and the foundation of what is to come. The better we understand our history, the better we are at deciding our future. Don't discount the mistakes, embarrassing moments, or perceived failures from your history. They make up as much of who you are as your successes. And life is never linear like a movie. It's full of stops and starts and events that don't always fit neatly into your story but may have had a significant impact on who you are.

Neuroscientist Kenneth Hayworth divides the self into two major categories: the MEMself, made of our memories, and the POVself, made of our specific points of view. Our memories define us in the present and in the future, while our points of view are based on our experiences with the world around us.[8] Cognitive research shows us that memories are not filmed like single events with a camera, but instead, as psychologist Michael Shermer says, "Memory is a continually edited and fluid process that utterly depends on the neurons in your brain being functional."[9] Our brains change as we age and gain life experiences, usually shaping our memories and how we remember events. Consequently, those memories and the value placed on them sometimes guide our perspectives of past and current life events. We can no more separate who we are from those memories than we can separate our conscience existence from our bodies. Similarly, our points of view are uniquely our own. They are based on interactions and experiences, and our interpretations of those experiences, that have created the person we have become.

Journeys are all different. Some journeys last longer than others. Some are rich with details and others provide a memory of only one thing. We don't have to rush to the end or to find our ultimate purpose. To quote nearly every philosophical song ever written, life really is about the journey itself. Where we end up can't be rushed. It's our personal journey, and one in which we find meaning only when we are ready to receive it. The best way to honor that journey is to keep living our lives, keep experiencing our interests and passions, and let the work speak for itself.

Reinventing Yourself

Remember, no matter at what age or life stage you find yourself, it's never too late to do something different. Only you can decide when you've finished your journey. Beyond the mental fortitude required, the practical steps of reinvention will take you from where you are to where you want to be. My friend Tony decided to go back to school and get a degree in something besides biblical ministry. With kids in middle school and a stay-at-home wife, Tony had a lot of moving pieces to figure out. Online schools worked best for his schedule, but the cost was expensive. Tony had the foresight to start going to school before leaving his last position, which helped pay for his schooling and alleviated many of his worries.

It's important to set SMART (specific, measurable, attainable, results-oriented, and timely) goals. A goal to "one day" go back to school or call someone "later" is attainable, but it's not specific or measurable. On what date will you go back to school? What is the deadline for registration, and what items do you need to register on time? If you're going to call someone, what results are you looking for, and how will you know when you've achieved them?

In education, we differentiate between agendas, objectives, and goals in our classrooms. An agenda tells the audience, which in this case is an audience of one, what we plan to do; objectives are performance indicators, or the minigoals we need to meet to tell us we're on the right track; and the goals are where we want to end up. We can't jump from the agenda to the goals. For example, I can't write on a piece of paper that I'm going to be a professor and then stand up in front of a classroom the next day.

Most importantly, we must commit to making a plan and following the steps. All the talk about vision boards and dreams is irrelevant if we haven't put a plan in place and aren't actively doing something to reach our goals beyond attending self-help seminars and singing "Kumbaya" naked in a steam room. For those who never read or listened to *The Secret* when it was all the rage in the early 2000s, I'll save you the money and tell you what the secret is: the universe isn't paying any attention to you unless you are *doing* something.

Transforming into the person we were meant to be should never feel awkward or unnatural. If we're focused on our appearance and posturing to show people what we want them to see, we're not being authentic.

Here's an example. I was invited to appear on a local television show and I was terrified. I hadn't been in front of a camera in nearly twenty years and I was about to go speak on the most intimate parts of my life. I read everything I could find about appearing on television. I remembered rules from back in the day about acceptable clothing, such as solid, muted-colored shirts, and I watched videos on how to do a good interview. I even rehearsed what I wanted to say. Still, the day before my appearance, my stomach was in knots. I could only worry about turning it into a disaster and stopping the sale of my book before it ever got started.

My younger daughter, twelve at the time, said, "What are you so nervous about?"

"Humiliating myself!" I shot back.

"Look," she said calmly, "What's the worst thing that could happen? You say something stupid, it ends up on YouTube, and then it goes viral. What's the big deal?"

Instantly, my nerves were calmed. She was right. I had no obligation to do anything besides be the nervous, shaking, socially awkward person I am. I can simultaneously work on becoming more confident and professional, but I have to be honest about my insecurities. That person, more than the one who has all the answers, is the person people relate to best. If you think about the people you're drawn to, the characteristics that attract you are almost always honesty and vulnerability over perfection.

Commit to Life with Uncertainty

I'd just finished speaking at an organization of freethinkers and atheists, though the audience also included conservative Christians, and people who were questioning their faith. I spent quite a bit of time talking about the benefit of living in the uncertainty of faith and being okay with not having all the answers. But just as I finished my talk, one old man, an avowed atheist, shouted from the middle of the room, "You really should just come all the way over to being an atheist and give up on any idea of God. It's a lot easier that way." Indeed, it is.

All of us have an innate need to feel certain about life. Whether taking the same route to work every day or washing the sheets every Saturday, humans rely on routine and certainty to feel secure. Relationship expert, Grace Boyle, says, "We find comfort in regularity. When something out of the ordinary comes along, it forces us to dig deep and make a U-Turn instead of keep going straight, it's jarring."[10]

A false sense of security came from the certainty of our faith. We received simple answers for practically everything that happened to us, which left us with the belief that if we obeyed God, we would be spared the more horrific circumstances of life. And, of course, *he* would never allow anything more than we could bear. Unfortunately, those beliefs kept us in a bubble, confined our thoughts, and often prevented us from taking chances.

Uncertainty allows us to find answers instead of believing the ones we've been given. Uncertainty opens roads of possibilities that certainty had closed. Uncertainty changes the question from Why? to Why not? Uncertainty doesn't make assumptions. When it comes to humanity, uncertainty shows empathy and compassion first and asks questions later. A life of uncertainty is the greatest risk with no guarantees, except that we lived life on our terms.

Conclusion

Mary Jane McLeod Bethune had a passion for missionary work. Born in 1875 to former slave parents, Mary was the fifteenth out of seventeen children. Her mother worked for her former owner while her father picked cotton. Most of Mary's siblings had been born into slavery. But by the time she was born, her parents had saved enough money to buy five acres of land. With the help of Mary's brothers, her parents built a small cabin on the land, a rice and cotton field, where Mary was born.

Mary's parents taught her to survive in the postwar era. At five years old she went with her mother to drop off laundry for a white family when she spotted a book in a playroom where the family's child was playing. Mary picked up the book, but the other child quickly snatched it out of her hands and told her she couldn't have the book because she didn't know how to read. It was a moment that would eventually change Mary's life. Still, by age nine, Mary was picking up to two-hundred-fifty pounds of cotton a day.

Reconstruction after the war afforded Mary an opportunity for education, and she was able to attend classes in a one-room schoolhouse for black children. Each night she would go home and teach her family what she had learned. Following her days in the small schoolhouse, Mary attended a boarding school in North Carolina and graduated in 1894, at nineteen years old. Her eyes were set on becoming a missionary in Africa, so she moved to Chicago, Illinois to attend the newly founded Dwight Moody Institute for Home and Foreign Missions. But with no church to sponsor her, Mary said, "Africans in America needed Christ and schooling just as much. My life work lay not in Africa but in my own country."[11]

Mary spent the next year serving the growing homeless population of Chicago, as well as teaching in the prison system, but found no satisfaction in her work. In 1898, after having taught at several schools throughout the South, Mary met and married Albertus Bethune and had a son the following year. In Savannah, Georgia, where the couple lived, Mary did social work and took care of their child. At a chance meeting with a pastor visiting Savannah, Mary was asked to move to Florida and manage his new missions school. It was a big commitment for Mary and Albertus, but they agreed to go. After five years, Mary realized it still wasn't what she wanted to do.

Mary envisioned herself working with young black girls, which was the population she believed needed her most. It was work that wasn't widely done, but it also required resources Mary did not have. She determined that if a school was to be established, she would have to do it herself. Mary moved her family to Daytona, Florida, because of its economic stability. She rented an old building, which sat next to a dump, with a down payment of $1.50 and rent of $11.00 per month. Using the dump for resources, Mary built her own desks and created pencils out of burnt wood. She opened the door to young black girls, who paid her 50 cents a month in tuition. Within a year, thirty were attending the school. To raise funds, Mary went door-to-door and, with the help of black churches, sold sweet potato pies, ice cream, and fried fish. She put on concerts and reached out to both black and white donors who believed in her mission. Her board of trustees was uniquely racially mixed, and Mary served as a teacher, headmaster, mentor, and fundraiser for her school. By 1907, Mary was able to purchase land and build a brick building on it with the help of wealthy donors she had courted. In the same year, her husband, Albertus, moved back to South Carolina to leave Mary to her work. The two never filed for divorce but never lived together again.

By 1916, the school was a completely accredited high school, and by 1920 it had over three hundred-fifty students. Three years later, the school merged with Cookman Institute for Men and the coed school boasted over eight hundred students. Bethune-Cookman College ended up on a thirty-two-acre campus with fourteen buildings.

Mary lived her passion until her death at age eighty. What started out as a desire to win Africans for Jesus turned into a love affair with education. Yet beyond her tireless work in education, Mary was a champion of gender and race equality. She led voter registration drives for women following the passage of the nineteenth Amendment in 1920, she served as the chapter president of the National Association of Colored Women and president of the Southeastern Federation of Colored Women's Clubs, and she founded the National Council of Negro Women. She was the first black woman on an advisory board, which she formed, under Franklin Roosevelt and lobbied so aggressively for minority involvement on Roosevelt's National Youth Administration that he appointed her as the director of the Division of Negro Affairs.[12]

It was a book–a children's book, no less–that changed Mary's life. It was a book she never read because she was told she couldn't. It was a book whose story would go far beyond the pages of what was written inside, transcending its original purpose and lighting a fire without a match. She was a girl–a black girl, no less–born on the wrong side of the tracks at a time in history when she wasn't supposed to succeed. What drew both of them together was the need to tell a story. Whatever was written on the pages of the book Mary picked up we will never know. But their story together is a story of purpose, passion, human determination, and a drive to change the world one girl or boy at a time. Their story together transcends race, culture, socioeconomic status, and the word *can't*. That's your story, too.

Epilogue

I want to say a few words about politics, which wasn't the point of this book. But if we're going to rethink *everything*, then something must be said before we go. It's almost inevitable that a person's politics changes after he's taken a deep dive into understanding his own religion. Like leaving my faith, I went kicking and screaming out of far right politics. The first time I was old enough to vote was when Ronald Reagan was running for his second term as president. Since then, I voted almost exclusively along Republican Party lines all the way to Mitt Romney in the 2012 election. Yes, 2012! Much of the reason for my right-leaning politics was that I believed what I'd been told by the GOP, which was unwittingly reinforced through my faith. I never went searching for answers because I thought I already had them. Yet even as the foundation of fundamentalism began to crumble, my politics stayed intact. I've joked on more than one occasion with my therapist that I came to him as a Republican and left as a bleeding-heart liberal, vegan, conservationist. He's that good!

Abortion

I consider myself pro-life, but from the cradle to the grave, not just to the cradle. A death penalty stance, if you claim to be pro-life, makes sense only if you believe in an authoritative, punitive God who demands instant justice and shows no grace or mercy. This is often the angry, Old Testament God we call on when it comes to black and white issues, such as morality and patriotism. As stated in chapter 2, the pro-life, anti-choice political movement came to be as the direct result of consolidating political power under the Republican Party. After all, how could we as human beings–let alone God-fearing Americans–not be moved to save innocent babies from an unconscionable death at the hands of their own mothers and doctors? It's a question that naturally yanks the reigns of the reactionary emotions that resides in all of us with a seemingly simple answer. Clearly it's not that simple, or we'd all agree. I'd argue that *all* human beings are pro-life, no matter their political or religious affiliation.

The argument that life starts at conception was one that developed over time. In fact, W. A. Crisswell, the Southern Baptist Convention's former president, said of the abortion ruling in 1973, "I have always felt that it was only after a child was born and had a life separate from its mother that it became an individual person, and it has always, therefore, seemed to me that what is best for the mother and for the future should be allowed."[1] However, evangelicals jumped on the anti-abortion bandwagon "as a rallying-cry to deny President Jimmy Carter a second term."[2] The question is, when does a person become a viable human being?

Michael Shermer, in his book *The Moral Arc*, does a good job of reasoning through the issue. He breaks down the development process into the *probability* of human life as the cells develop within the womb. An egg and sperm separately are not considered human beings, but neither are a zygote, a fertilized egg, or a blastocyst, the mass of cells from which an embryo could potentially develop. These could turn into a partial human being and abort naturally or split into two human beings. By eight weeks, an embryo has recognizable human features–such as a face, hands and feet–but no neural connections, which means it has no feelings or thoughts. It is still a mass of cells with little difference from the uterus in which it sits.[3]

After eight weeks the embryo begins to show signs of "primitive response to movements," but at twenty-four weeks, about six months, it cannot live on its own. The critical organs needed for survival have not yet developed, and the lungs are not capable of gas exchange. Some variability exists at this point, but not until twenty-eight weeks does a fetus reach 77 percent of development and begin to show signs of cognitive capacities found in newborns. At thirty weeks, 83 percent of full-term development, it begins to show more signs of brain activity. Several weeks *after* birth the infant begins to show signs of thought.[4]

Shermer notes it's difficult to argue the case that abortion is murder in the first trimester, when nearly all abortions occur, as the mass of cells is not a sentient human being. The question becomes, Do we support the rights of a *potential* human being or the rights of a *living* human being?[5]

In countries where abortions are denied or severely limited, the human and economic consequences are devastating. In El Salvador, where abortion is illegal for any reason, suicide is the cause of death for 57 percent of pregnant females between ten and nineteen years old.[6] In Romania, where abortion was made a crime in the 1960s, over 170,000 children were dropped into state-run orphanages, leaving many of them mentally and physically impaired, and over 9,000 women died in back-alley abortions.[7]

Studies also show that women who are denied access to legal and safe abortions, and their offspring, are more likely to struggle socioeconomically. In one such study, "women denied abortion were three times as likely to end up below the federal poverty line two years later."[8] In a study of Czechoslovakian women denied abortions, their children were found to suffer from disadvantages including acute illnesses and lower grades, less social capability, less popularity among their peers and teachers and, if boys, even their own mothers.[9] In the United States, 75 percent of those who seek abortions are already living at or below the federal poverty level.[10]

The belief that life begins at conception was not a theological concept among evangelicals until Francis Schaeffer made it one in his 1979 film, *Whatever Happened to the Human Race?*, writes historian George Marsden.[11] The Bible does not say life begins at conception. To the contrary, the rule of thought for centuries had been that the soul could only inhabit a body with organs.[12] Thanks to the religiously infused battle against abortion, Republican politics have stayed afloat for decades, while abortion rights have remained virtually unchanged since 1973.

The twisted irony of the pro-life position is that most GOP policies favor the wealthiest among us while ignoring the most vulnerable. These policies reject much of the Christian doctrine of helping the poor, refugees, and those less fortunate. Christian fundamentalists mindlessly ignore the abject poverty many of these unwanted babies will likely grow up to experience. For example, according to Poverty Solutions 33.6 percent of black children, 28 percent of Hispanics, and 11.5 percent of white children under the age of eighteen, as of 2014, live in poverty in the United States.[13] Many of these kids, without support, will become part of the 9.4 percent of drug users in America.[14] Many are also likely to end up in prison, as the link between poverty, race, drug use, and prison is undeniable.[15] Yet pro-lifers pro-death-penalty stance conveniently ignores the factors that brought the unborn baby they were concerned about to its end point.

What happens when that baby turns out to have special needs or, God forbid, is gay? Conservatives voted down extending the Americans with Disabilities Act abroad in 2012 and introduced two hundred religious freedom bills in the first half of 2016, denying equal human rights to the LGBTQ+ community.[16] More recently, pro-life conservative Christians have lobbied to deny immigrants from war-torn countries entry into the United States. What no longer made sense to me, as I began to look more closely at the issue, was to continue supporting pro-life politicians who vote against funding for medical services for women; funding for sex education, which is proven to drastically reduce unwanted pregnancies and abortions; and living wages for people who are most at risk of unwanted pregnancies. Throwing our hands up and saying, in essence, "A woman's irresponsbility isn't my problem, but I'm going to force her to have the baby," is cruel, heartless, and short-sighted. It is anything but "pro-life."

Race, Social Justice, and White Privilege

The Ferguson, Missouri, riots following the death of Michael Brown were a turning point in my view of race and social justice. I remember scoffing at Brown's stepfather, who stood on the top of a car telling the community "Burn this bitch down" after police officer Darren Wilson was acquitted by a grand jury of any wrongdoing following an investigation. I shook my head in disgust at African Americans who looted their local businesses, broke windows, and burned down their own neighborhoods. And then Abel said, "What are they supposed to do?"

"Uh, not that," I said judgmentally. "How does burning down your own neighborhood help your cause?"

Abel, who had grown up poor in ghettos and attended low-performing schools, said, "Regardless of whether or not the cop rightfully or wrongfully killed Michael Brown, these people have been the targets of discrimination and racial profiling for decades. You can only keep a dog caged for so long before he starts to tear the cage apart."

I'd never given much thought to the plight of black communities as a white man. Both of my parents grew up poor yet worked hard and made enough money to retire comfortably. What was stopping African Americans from doing the same? With limited understanding of the history of race in our country, and only that from the perspective of predominantly white historians, I assumed black people and other minorities were primarily the cause of their own circumstances. I'd been fed the lie and believed that the wars on drugs and crime were about drugs and crime, not about race. I was challenged to see things differently.

White privilege is a concept thrown around by the left and ridiculed by the right. Many conservatives say it doesn't exist. When you are white, you don't see your life as privileged. When you've faced economic challenges, as my parents did, and fought to overcome them, you take pride in pulling yourself up by your bootstraps. You believe if you can do it, nothing is stopping anyone else besides one's own "stinking thinking." But even poor white people started at a higher rung on the ladder of success.

When the slaves were emancipated in 1863, they initially gained citizenship and men the right to vote with the fourteenth and fifteenth Amendments. Before long, however, angry former slaveholders and the frightened people of the South overturned any progress made, determined to stop social change. Manisha Sinha, professor of Afro-American studies and history at the University of Massachusetts, Amherst, says, "African American ideas about emancipation were deferred until the Civil Rights Movement led to the passage of new laws to implement black citizenship."[17] But there was more than one way to enslave black people.

Author Douglas Blackmon, in his book *Slavery by Any Other Name*, says:

> Vagrancy . . . [the inability to prove one's employment] was a new and flimsy concoction dredged up from legal obscurity at the end of the nineteenth century by the state legislatures of Alabama and other southern states. It was capriciously enforced by local sheriffs and constables, adjudicated by mayors and notaries public, recorded haphazardly or not at all in court records, and, most tellingly in a time of massive unemployment among all southern men, was reserved almost exclusively for black men.[18]

Once incarcerated, these men were put to work on farms and used as other free labor sources for local businesses. Blackmon discovered one encampment that "supplied tens of thousands of men over five decades to a succession of prison mines ultimately purchased by U.S. Steel in 1907." He said these men were "'leased' by state and county governments to U.S. Steel or the companies it had acquired."[19]

In 2016, it was discovered that Nixon aide John Ehrlichman made a shocking confession to *Harper's Magazine* twenty-two years earlier, saying,

> We knew we couldn't make it illegal to be either against the war or black, but by getting the public to associate the hippies with marijuana and blacks with heroin. And then criminalizing both heavily, we could disrupt those communities. We could arrest their leaders, raid their homes, break up their meetings, and vilify them night after night on the evening news. Did we know we were lying about the drugs? Of course we did.[20]

In 1982, Ronald Reagan upped the rhetoric on drugs, declaring a war on a problem that didn't exist. In fact, according to Ibram X. Kendi, author of *Stamped from the Beginning*, "It was an astonishing move. Drug crime was declining. Only 2 percent of Americans viewed drugs as the nation's most pressing problem. Drug treatment therapists were shocked by Reagan's unfounded claim that America could 'put drug abuse on the run through stronger law enforcement.'"[21]

The "war on drugs" has disproportionately impacted black and brown lives, though drug use is more often or equally prevalent among whites. The National Addiction and HIV Data Archive Program shows that 17.1 percent of the whites surveyed had used cocaine compared to 9.9 percent of blacks. When it comes to crack cocaine, the survey shows that 3.4 percent of whites had used crack cocaine compared to 5 percent of blacks. And 17.2 percent of whites had used hallucinogens compared to only 6.7 percent of blacks. Approximately 1.8 percent of both blacks and whites admit to using heroin equally.[22]

While African Americans represent only 12.5 percent of the drug use population, they make up 29 percent of those arrested for drug offenses and 33 percent of those in state prisons for drug use.[23] The Bureau of Justice Statistics shows that in 2011, of the 225,242 people serving time in state prisons for drug offenses, African Americans made up 41 percent, while whites made up just 30 percent.[24] Not so coincidentally, private prisons have been a $70 billion industry, using prisoners to make their fortunes. The industry is consistently supported by pro-life Republicans,[25] who often refuse attempts at any meaningful prison reform.

Civil rights attorney and author of *The New Jim Crow*, Michelle Alexander, says,

> Jim Crow laws were wiped off the books decades ago, but today an extraordinary percentage of the African American community is warehoused in prisons or trapped in a parallel social universe, denied basic civil and human rights—including the right to vote; the right to serve on juries; and the right to be free of legal discrimination in employment, housing, access to education and public benefits.[26]

For white evangelicals, privileges–being more likely to get employed, being more likely to receive a home loan, being less likely to go to prison for equal offenses, and holding a majority of governing leadership–are taken for granted. Yet remember, these are the evangelicals who went to court to keep their schools from being infiltrated by people of color, feeling it was their God-given duty to keep the races separated. The gerrymandering of the GOP continues to draw lines between people of color and white America, a declining majority as the races mix, as a way to ensure white America maintains its political power and fuels its out-of-proportion wealth. Racism is ingrained in our culture, and white people, particularly conservatives, refuse to acknowledge it. The conservative political party has a long history of racism. And as fundamentalist Christian groups tighten their grip on conservative politics, the likelihood of race relations and prison reform will only decline. As a pro-life person, I cannot in good conscience support conservative politics.

How Should We Then Live?

In light of so many secular influences, Francis Schaeffer asked in his 1976 book and subsequent films, How should we then live? But after almost fifty years of religious domination, we must revisit this question. Perhaps the question should be, How can we live in a world shrouded in fundamentalist religious ideologies and enveloped in public politics? Even if we are comfortable living in a society whose values and morals are determined by a single religion at the highest levels in the land, are we equally comfortable when that religion is not our own? The religious freedoms that liberate one segment of society often enslave another. Are we willing to change places with our religious counterparts when their religion inevitably overtakes ours?

The purpose of this book was never to dissuade those who believe in God but to challenge the foundation on which those beliefs exist. Those of us harmed directly or indirectly through fundamentalist, evangelical teaching have a clear path of rational exit. Nevertheless, this does not disprove God's existence. Our binary, anthropomorphic thinking creates a god who is male or female and looks, sounds, feels, and thinks like us. We have a more difficult time thinking of God as a cosmic force, a math equation, or an invisible spirit who unites all sentient and nonsentient life forms. (The latter is more common in Eastern cultures.) It's also more likely that any god figure who could create the intricate and magnificent details found in the universe would be impossible to encapsulate in a whole volume of books, let alone one.

Acknowledgments

With this as my third book, I think this section should be called "Apologies." I've ignored my children and family for so long that when I walk out of my office to say something, I'm met with blank stares until someone finally says, "And you are…" So I'm sorry. I apologize to my college-student daughter for putting her on speaker while I work until she finally says, "Yeah, I'm gonna go." I apologize to my high-school daughter for stacking books in the chair in the office so she wouldn't sit down and talk to me. I apologize to my husband for telling him every single thing I learned for the last three years in as much detail as I could remember and not listening to a word he said because it wasn't nearly as interesting. I apologize for ignoring him, coming late to dinner, letting the house fall apart, and being a recluse (more than normal). I apologize to the dog for missed walks, missed baths (mine, not his), and missed trips to the dog park. I apologize to the cat I've never liked for–actually, I think I did some of those things on purpose.

At the end of 2016, I decided 2017 would be better. I mean, it couldn't get worse, right? A mad man became the leader of what was once the free world, hate crimes were skyrocketing, and civil liberties were rolled back to the 1950s. I was seeing my shrink so often I paid for his kid's college tuition. She's seven. But we were barely in March of 2017 before things got worse. A lot worse. I had an aneurysm, my mom was diagnosed with cancer, and my father was diagnosed with Alzheimer's. Figuratively and literally, the next several months became a blur. Our family came together to do what needed to be done, often without much help from me. Our friends rallied around us with kind notes and phone calls to check on us and offer any help we needed. It's nearly impossible not to step back and feel gratitude for the people who love us every day. Despite the hurdles, this book was written because of the constant encouragement of the people in my life whom I depend on, love, and adore. I'm thankful for my husband, my children, my sister, and our extended family. I couldn't do what I do without them.

Special thanks to my nephew Justin for taking a stab at formatting notes, my friend Stephanie Chandler (whom Abel calls the "white Oprah") for all the positivity and encouragement; my new friend, developmental editor, and owner of WriteNow, Cristen Iris for her guidance and direction; and Sharon Goldinger for schooling me in the underworld of *The Chicago Manual of Style*. (Who makes up these rules?) Thank you to Mike Ralston for volunteering his story, John Smid for letting me share some of his insights, Bill Prickett for letting me vent, giving advice, and making me smile.

Lastly, I'd like to say a big nerdy thank you to all the scholars whose information I used for this book and whose books, articles, lectures, and research I use every day to satisfy my own curiosity. I have unhealthy crushes on many of you, stalk your social media, and fantasize about what I'll say if I ever meet you in person. Thank you for filling the world with knowledge and moving society toward a place where we recognize we are all on the same team, working toward the same goals of love, kindness, and unity, regardless of nationality, gender, race, or creed.

APPENDIX A

The Jewish Underpinnings of Christianity

Talmudic, or Jewish, writings are believed to have first appeared around the tenth century BCE,[1] though most of what has been discovered in the way of biblical texts are dated between 150 BCE and 70 CE,[2] right before or during the rise of Christianity. Thousands of these fragments came from the Dead Sea Scrolls, so named because they were found in eleven caves about a mile from the Dead Sea, in an area now known today as the West Bank.[3] Archeologists found between eight hundred and nine hundred manuscripts. While no one knows exactly who wrote them, the belief is that they came from a Jewish sect called the Essenes.[4]

Fragments of the Old Testament books were discovered there, with the exception of the book of Esther, which wasn't found, and Isaiah, which was found in its entirety. The copy of Isaiah was dated to 100 BCE. Also of interest is that these fragments were written in multiple languages, including Hebrew, paleo-Hebrew, a symbolic language seldom seen after the fifth century BCE, and Aramaic. Some texts were passages translated from Hebrew to Greek.[5] Greek culture and its influence was ubiquitous: the mythologies reached far and deep into the development of religious culture, including Christianity.

To date, no evidence has been found of an original Old Testament as we know it. Much of the Jewish tradition, as is the case for most historical religions, was oral and passed down through generations.[6] Jewish religious text, as found in the Christian biblical canon today, was pieced together from a variety of sources and canonized well after the Christian New Testament.[7] It's not difficult to imagine that some of the so-called prophecies and their fulfillment were written after the fact.

Lee Martin McDonald, author of *The Biblical Canon*, says, "Part of what complicates inquiry into the origins of the biblical canon is the lack of agreement among scholars on what precisely constitutes a biblical canon."[8] Indeed, the rabbinic Judaism Old Testament, or Tanakh, as it's called, contains twenty-four books. But the Protestant Christian version of the Old Testament contains thirty-nine books, the Catholic version contains forty-six books, and the Eastern Orthodox version contains fifty books. The Masoretic text, from which the Tanakh was composed, was copied and edited between the ninth and eleventh centuries CE, approximately four to seven centuries *after* the New Testament was canonized.[9] With the discovery of the Dead Sea Scrolls some eight hundred years later, differences between the Septuagint and Masoretic texts brought many questions about which one was more accurate.[10]

The Septuagint text was the first translation of the Hebrew scriptures, created around 300 BCE at a time when Greek culture became prominent and was rapidly proliferating throughout the region. Aristobulus, the first known Jewish philosopher of religion, attests that the Torah was translated under Ptolemy II Philadelphus, who reigned as king in Egypt between 283 and 246 BCE.[11] Given the large population of Jews in the area, it is highly likely this "king legitimized the translation in some form since he, the first truly 'absolutist' ruler in antiquity, would have been interested in the laws followed by a large ethno-religious minority in his realm," according to historians.[12] The translation was primarily focused on the Pentateuch, the first five books of the Old Testament, with "the later historical and prophetic tradition diminish[ed] strikingly in significance in relation to its importance in the Palestinian motherland."[13] Pagan authors also confirm that other books concerning the prophets were not mentioned, which is "quite in contrast to later Christian interpretation."[14] The Apostle Paul even "relies on a Hebrew-oriented revision of the Greek translation for his citations from Isaiah, Job and 1 Kings," and "the possibility cannot be excluded that the Apostle himself undertook such a revision."[15]

The creation and translation of the Septuagint, which is Latin for "seventy," in itself is rather suspicious. The Letter of Aristeas, written around the second century BCE, purported that Ptolemy II Philadelphus was urged by his chief librarian to have the Hebrew Law translated for his vast library.[16] The king sent gifts to the Temple in Jerusalem, and the high priests responded by sending seventy-two translators, six from each of the twelve tribes of Israel. The Letter of Aristeas states that the translation came to be through comparisons and majority decisions.[17] Hellenistic Jewish philosopher Philo of Alexandria, or Philo Judaeus (30 BCE–50 CE), however, said the Septuagint happened through divine inspiration: each of these translators was isolated in a separate room, yet they all rendered exactly the same translation in seventy-two days.[18] Philo was convinced that all people would accept the law as divine inspiration, and indeed, his view "holds inestimable significance for Christian estimation of the LXX as inspired Scripture."[19] The idea of divine inspiration would later influence Christians, who included the Jewish prophetic writings in their Bible. Philo, however, was speaking only of the first five books as the other books were added much later.[20]

The view that Moses wrote the first five books of the Bible was virtually unchallenged until the seventeenth century.[21] Surprisingly, few questioned how Moses could write about his own death and burial in Deuteronomy, a question I remember asking my mother when I was a kid. Scholars have identified at least four different groups of scribes writing over several hundred years, as evidenced by contradicting scriptures.[22] For example, in the flood story alone, Genesis 7:2 says God told Noah to bring seven pairs of every clean animal and two pairs of every unclean animal, but in Genesis 6:19, God tells Noah to bring two of every living animal.

The Exodus story of the flood cannot be corroborated by archaeologists. Neither can the story of the mass exodus of Israelites from Egypt's control and purported conquering of Canaan. Instead, the Israelites seem to have originated in Canaan, an offshoot of Mesopotamia. The Israelites were not from the outside but "a social and economic revolution" from *within* Canaan, archaeologist William Dever says.[23] Peter Machinist added that the Israelites were always in the land of Israel, but they were "basically the have-nots."[24] The rising of Israel is an *outcome* of the collapse of the Canaanite society, not the *reason* for the collapse.[25]

The sources of the Hebrew Bible can be determined from "geographical terminology and religious symbols, and the roles played by various tribes."[26] Clearly, some of the text was written in Jerusalem, estimated between 970 and 930 BCE, as it represents the "united monarchy or the kingdom of Judah."[27] Other texts were written north of Judah between 930 and 720 BCE and represent the kingdom of Israel in that era. The book of Deuteronomy was determined to have been written independently because of its "distinctive message and style," and several passages throughout the Pentateuch dealing with ritual matters have been assigned by scholars to a "priestly source. These texts display a "special interest in purity, cult, and laws of sacrifice."[28]

According to archaeologists Finklestein and Silberman, "Scholars gradually came to the conclusion that the first five books of the Bible as we know them were the result of a complex editorial process . . . were skillfully combined and linked by scribal compilers or 'redactors' whose literary traces . . . consisted of transitional sentences and editorial asides. The latest of those redactions took place in the post-exilic period [between 538 BCE and 1 CE]."[29]

As is the case with most writings of the ancient era, particularly in regard to religious writing, historical accuracy was not a consideration. Dever noted that writing objective history is a modern concept and that Biblical writers were simply telling stories.[30] They did not use footnotes or quote sources. Writings were not peer-reviewed, and no one corroborated facts. The purpose was to convey thoughts, ideas, and stories. These writings answered questions about the origins of man and how tribes came into existence, and they offered a purpose and understanding of the world. Since writing came into existence long after oral tradition, the details of these stories changed throughout generations, often influenced and reinterpreted in the current context of societal norms.

Judaism, like most religions, evolved over time. It didn't start with a single god and likely not with a burning bush. There were sects and divisions, struggles for power, and collusion to tell a more unified story as the centuries progressed. Like the foundations of the faiths themselves, it was a centuries-long process.

APPENDIX B

God – in the Beginning

It's important to call out that monotheism, which is what the Jewish religion ultimately became, is not older than polytheism. Additionally, monotheism and polytheism are not opposites of each other, but monotheism speaks more to the uniqueness of a god than anything else.[1] Monotheism means not just the sole worship of one god, as in the case of the Jewish god, but the sole worship *to the exclusion and negation* of all other gods.[2] Reza Aslan says monotheism rejects subjective truth, which explains why monotheistic systems are often "brutally enforced in order to overcome people's natural beliefs and assumptions."[3]

When exactly monotheism began is debated among archaeologists. Some argue that evidence of monotheism first appeared around the fourteenth century BCE with the reign of Egyptian pharaoh Akhenaten.[4] Akhenaten worshipped the sun disk god, Aten. Five years into his reign, Akhenaten decreed that Aten would be the only god Egyptians would worship, which was a massive departure from his predecessors. Zoroastrianism, formed around the teachings of the prophet Zarathustra around the tenth century BCE–which would later influence the development of the Abrahamic religions and also parallel stories of Jesus–cast aside the polytheism of the day and "unified the various notions of divinity found within these faiths into one all-encompassing deity called *Ahura Mazda*."[5]

The Israelites, before they formed a state, were also *not* monotheists. Rainer Albertz said the idea of "God of the father" initially denoted family gods: "The

God worshipped in the family is regarded as a God of the father or forefather."[6] The description of Yahweh as seen in Genesis, Albertz and other scholars contend, is a revision of the texts. "The ancestors are connected with a series of El deities," including El-Elyon in Jerusalem, El-Bethel in Bethel, and El, the God of Israel, in Shechem.[7] Those family gods had little more in common with the Great God of heaven than the name. Even the name of the Isra-*el*-ites was based on the El gods. Genesis 1:26 provides some evidence of this: "And God said, 'Let *us* make mankind in *our* image, in *our* likeness'" The word translated as "God" in this verse is Elohim, which is morphologically plural.[8]

Diana Edelman noted that the prominence in biblical texts of Yahweh and El, excluding other gods, with the exception of Baal, should be seen as "monotheizing" religious tradition.[9] Several inscriptions showing the names of other gods have been excavated in the area of ancient Judah.[10] Focusing on the name Yahweh, Edelman says, "merely indicates that the worship of Yahweh was particularly strong among the upper class of the state at the end of the monarchy; a person who wanted his son to advance in the governmental bureaucracy would name him after the head male deity of the state pantheon, Yahweh."[11] Jewish monotheism developed over centuries, culminating, by the second century BCE, in exclusive monotheism during the Hellenistic period.[12]

But the Hebrew texts do little to hide the fact that the Israelites had an infatuation with polytheism. The very first commandment written in Exodus 20:3 was "You shall have no other God before me." So what happened to all those gods, and how do the Hebrew texts reconcile their removal from the foundation of Jewish theology?

One answer is subsequent revisions to the texts through later translations. "The stratum of Priestly editing in Exodus 6 depicts things rather differently. Here the revelation of the name of Yahweh first takes place to Moses . . . which only subsequently is identified with Yahweh. Here the religion of the patriarchs appears as a kind of prelude to the 'full' Yahweh religion of Israel," Albertz writes.[13] Many scholars argue that developing a monotheistic point of view was strategic for the survival of the Israelites by unifying them.

Yahweh's Story

Unifying the Hebrew gods into one god can be clearly seen in the story of Moses in Exodus–whom God raised up to lead the Israelites out of slavery–when he says to Moses in Exodus 6:2, "I am the Lord," or Jehovah. Both names for God were translated from the Hebrew word YHWH. Since the Hebrew language does not have vowels, they were added to make words pronounceable. YHWH appears only in the Hebrew Bible and is not found in Canaanite texts or stories. This was an interesting omission to scholars, as it initially seemed the god YHWH suddenly appeared from nowhere. However, YHWH does indeed have a history, which can be found in the Syrian city of Ugarit, as well as in the stories of ancient Egypt.

On the north wall of the Karnak, an ancient mix of decayed temples, chapels, pylons, and other buildings in Egypt, can be found YHW mentioned by Ramses II's father, Seti I.[14] Seti I commemorates one of his great victories over the Shasu, who lived in the deserts of southern Canaan.[15] The southern kingdom of what was once Canaan came to be known as Judea.[16] The Shasu emerged around the same time as the Israelites, and one of the places they lived was YHW, which likely was the name of their patron god.[17] Evidence suggests YHWH already existed in the mountain region south of Palestine and was already being worshipped.[18] In the Exodus story, Moses encounters YHWH for the first time among the Shasu, or Midianites. Moses, according to Exodus 3:1, was married to a Midianite woman. Albertz notes that YHWH was a god who "came from the outside, an alien god who had not yet been incorporated into the structure of the Egyptian pantheon and was thus in a position to break up this religious system which gave political stability to society."[19] YHWH is associated with storm and thunder gods in the pre-Israelite era; however, "the special feature of the Israelite history of Yahweh is that the dynamic properties of this former storm god are twisted round into the political and historical sphere."[20]

In 1928, an archeological dig in the northwest Syrian city of Ugaritic uncovered clay tablets that contained mythological content regarding YHWH.[21] "YHWH had reached his supreme status as a god by taking over traits from the gods of El and Baal as they are depicted in Ugaritic mythology," says theologian Herbert Niehr.[22] Ugaritic religion is "not simply identical with the 'syro-Canaanite religion;' it constitutes one local perspective of the Late Bronze Age (1200–500 BCE) Syrian religion."[23]

While no archaeological evidence has been found of a mass exodus of slaves from Egypt, a small group of ex-slaves likely brought the message of deliverance from Shasu to Canaan. Professor Carol Meyers says these former slaves spread the word to the highlanders about a god who represented freedom.[24] A *messiah*, or savior who delivers, is a common theme found throughout history and often appears among oppressed groups, including Native Americans, slaves, and, in this case, the Jews. An 1875 book by Kersey Graves entitled *The World's 16 Crucified Saviors* provides historical examples of stories similar to the Christian one.[25] Nevertheless, these former Canaanites were primed for just such a message of salvation. This new group began uniting under the name of a single god. But, of course, the switch to monotheism isn't as clean as the Bible implies.

Yahweh's Wife

According to William Dever, Yahweh's wife, Asherah, was a popular Canaanite mother goddess in Israel. Evidence of Asherah first surfaced in an Israelite archeological dig in 1968 when Dever was carrying out salvage excavations in a tomb in southern Israel. He discovered an eighth-century tomb inscription that gave the name of the deceased as well as blessings given by Yahweh and Asherah. Subsequently, more inscriptions were discovered along with thousands of figurines. Dever says it was a common belief that Asherah was Yahweh's wife, and it was an accepted practice among the Israelites to worship both of them.[26]

Asherah was a pagan goddess who appeared throughout history in the region under a variety of names and titles. She appeared in Ugarit, the port city of northern Syria, before 1200 BCE as the "Lady Athirat of the Sea."[27] She is also known as Elat, the goddess, which is the feminine form of El.[28] Theologian Lowell Handy says, "It appears clear that Asherah was seen to be on par with El as far as divine levels were concerned."[29] In Ugarit, Handy says, the god El "was the highest king of a series of deities who were kings over various aspects of the universe."[30] Asherah was believed to be the "divine

Queen Mother, with both authority and power."[31] Theologian and professor of the Hebrew Bible and ancient religion Francesca Stavrakopoulou agrees: "After years of research specializing in the history and religion of Israel, I have come to a colorful and what could seem, to some, uncomfortable conclusion that God had a wife."[32]

Since Yahweh first appeared, he seems to have been connected with Asherah. An 825 BCE inscription on a clay pot found in what was once ancient Samaria, where Israel was centered, reads, "YHWH of Samaria and his wife Asherah."[33] Another archeological site in the West Bank, in what was once the Kingdom of Judah, contained an inscription dated between 800 and 750 BCE that reads, "YHWH and his Asherah," indicating that Asherah was seen as Yahweh's counterpart.[34] Lowell Handy says, "When taken together, the Bible and the inscriptions prove fairly conclusively that the Judahites worshipped a goddess who was associated with the god YHWH."[35] Removing her from scriptures, Francesca Stavrakopoulou says, was revisionist Hebrew theology. "The idea that any variation from worship concentrated at the single central sanctuary represented apostasy from YHWH stems from a small coterie within Judah, the Deuteronomists, and does not correspond to what was believed by most people, though it has had an unfortunate effect on most later readers of the Bible."[36]

Yahweh's Divorce

Theologians surmise that Asherah was removed from the prominent position she once held due to political advantage and rewrites. Diana Edelman says the goddess's status was "whitewashed by adding a definite article to her name," such as *the* Asherah, and turning her into a common noun.[37]

J. Edward Wright, president of the Arizona Center for Judaic Studies and the Albright Institute for Archaeological Research, says Asherah wasn't completely removed from the Bible. "Traces of her remain, and based on those traces, archaeological evidence and references to her in texts from nations bordering Israel and Judah, we can reconstruct her role in the religions of the Southern Levant."[38] Wright went on to say, "Many English translations prefer to translate 'Asherah' as 'sacred Tree,'" which he sees as a modern desire to keep the current Biblical narratives and "to hide Asherah behind a veil once again."[39] Aaron Brody, who is an associate professor of Bible and archaeology at the Pacific School of Religion, noted that the Bible often refers to Asherah as a tree or symbol that was "chopped down and burned outside the Temple in acts of certain rulers who were trying to 'purify' the cult, and focus on the worship of a single male god, Yahweh."[40]

Professor Ellen White says, "The relationship between Asherah and Israel is a complicated one."[41] White points out that the Bible remained devoted to the cult symbol of Asherah, as found in Isaiah 27:9, Jeremiah 17:1, and Micah 5:14. Objections come mostly from Deuteronomistic literature "rather than the prophets."[42] However, the writers of both Deuteronomistic and prophetic literature appear to be more concerned about the worship of Baal, than the worship of Asherah. White concurs that most Judeo-Christian adherents have a difficulty wrapping their heads around the idea that Yahweh had a wife and reminds us that in the ancient world, the idea that gods who married and bore children was a common one. "This popular connection between Yahweh and Asherah, and the eventual purging of Asherah from the Israelite cult, is likely a reflection of the emergence of monotheism from the Israelites' previous polytheistic world-view," she says.[43]

Yahweh's Character Mirrors the Times

Women, according to this God, have no value, other than being property. Eve was created to help Adam, the man God created (Gen. 2:7). Adam then names her like he named the animals (Gen. 2:27). In Genesis 3:16, God tells Eve that Adam will rule over her. In the tenth and final commandment, God tells the men of Israel they should not covet their neighbor's wives, as they should not covet any other items the neighbor owns, such as slaves, animals, or property (Exod. 21:24). If a man has sex with a married woman, whether or not she wanted it, they are both to be put to death (Lev. 18:20). If a woman steps in to help her husband in a fight and grabs the testicles of her husband's enemy, her hand is to be cut off (Deut. 25:11). And of course, while men could marry as many women as they wanted, along with having an unlimited number of concubines, women could marry only one man. Polygamy was a recurring theme among Yahweh's chosen male leaders.

Yahweh never denounces slavery. Instead, he provides rules for how to treat slaves, none of which are humane. For example, a slave owner is permitted to beat his slave with abandon, as long as the slave doesn't die (Exod. 21:21). The slave may not be able to move for a couple of days, but if he's not dead, the slave owner has done nothing wrong. He can do whatever he wants to his property. However, if he knocks out an eye or a tooth, he has to let his slave go free (Exod. 21:26–27). Jewish slaves are to be emancipated every six years (Exod. 21:1–4). However if the owner gave his slave a wife and the slave and his wife had children, the wife and children still belong to the owner. The slave can leave but without his family. Unfortunately for women, once again, if a man sells his daughter into slavery, she is not allowed to leave as Jewish male slaves are (Exod. 21:7). Yahweh preferred that the Israelites make slaves out of people from surrounding countries, whom they could also pass down to their children (Lev. 25:44–46). They could treat these slaves however they wanted. And if a man raped or had consensual sex with a female slave engaged to another man, she was to be whipped, while he was only required to sacrifice an animal in the temple to be forgiven (Lev. 19:20–22).

Not surprisingly, Yahweh's personality and indifference toward human life, particularly of other nations, mirrored the leaders, tribes, and civilizations of the era. Xenophobia–fear and distrust of others–has its roots in evolution. Tribes needed to protect themselves from outsiders to prevent disease and avoid war. They needed to ensure their food and water supplies were safe from intruders for their own survival. Ethnocentricity–the tendency to judge another's culture by one's own cultural standards and practices and the belief that one's own standards and practices are the right way to approach life–is often how we determine who is in or out of our social circle. We look for people who believe, act, and perceive the world the way we do, and we feel safer when we are with our own kind. If you put Yahweh in the sandals of his creators, his overreaction to, and fear of, the outside world makes much more sense.

With El and Yahweh wrapped into one, Judaism became more cohesive in its history and theology. As the centuries passed, this God became more merciful, loving, and kind, as did humans. He became more palpable as the

God of grace around whom Christians would eventually rally, thanks mostly to the Apostle Paul's new and improved version. His bad behavior could be explained away because of the seriousness of sin, which must be dealt with by a just God. But a loving god called Father is much more approachable than a just God called Yahweh.

APPENDIX C

How God Became a Christian

God's transformation from Yahweh to Jesus happened over the span of several hundred years. Changes can be seen in the rewrites of Hebrew texts, along with the addition of poetic literature at the same time the world's population developed more of a universal consciousness. German philosopher Karl Jaspers coined the phrase "axial age" to represent this period, which was a confluence of simultaneous and independent "spiritual awakenings" roughly between 800 and 200 BCE.[1]

The shift turned the direction of humanity like a wheel on an axis. Religions around the globe went through an enlightenment metamorphosis that had a profound impact on the growth and evolution of humanity. Or perhaps the growth and evolution of humanity had a profound impact on the enlightenment of religion. Other historians disagree with the concept of an axial age. Given the time frame, they simply see the change as a maturing process in our evolutionary history. Either way, historian Karen Armstrong says that during this time, Confucianism and Taoism in China; Hinduism, Buddhism, and Jainism in India; monotheism in Israel; and philosophical rationalism in Greece, "without any collusion . . . came up with a remarkably similar solution to the spiritual ills of humanity."[2]

Armstrong says prior to this period there was no introspection. People were caught up in rituals, which gave them "intimations of greatness."[3] Psychologist John Mayer notes, "Before the Axial transformation, human beings told one another myths and other stories about how they came to be. The stories were not regarded as true or false; rather, their truth did not require questioning."[4] But during the axial age, questions such as "Who am I?" and "Why are people different?" began to emerge and "qualities such as courage, solidarity, and kindness occupied a new cultural place and were explicitly valued by religious and other wisdom writings."[5]

Part of the reason that all religions became more spiritually focused is that disparate groups of people had more interactions as they came together through commerce, so they experienced humanity outside their own tribes and nations.[6] Violence wasn't working toward the greater good anymore, so the idea that a person must abandon the ego, which was the cause of wars, emerged. Confucius was the first to espouse the golden rule (five hundred years before Christ) when he said, "Look into your own heart. Discover what it is that gives you pain. And then refuse to inflict that pain on anybody else."[7] When asked by his disciples what the greatest teaching was, he said, "Do not do to others as you would not have them do to you."

Another major influence on nearly all religions at the turn of the millennium was Hellenism, or Greek culture. Hellenism covered 1.5 million square miles and encompassed 54 million people across multiple nations. The Hellenistic period extended between 300 BCE and 31 CE. Historian Jonathan Smith says that during this time, religions experienced growing links to nationalism and messianic movements centered on overthrowing "Greco-Roman political and cultural domination. From Palestine to Persia one may trace the rise of Wisdom literature (the teachings of a sage concerning the hidden purposes of the deity) and apocalyptic traditions (referring to a belief in the dramatic intervention of a god in human and natural events)."[8]

According to Smith, People's concerns had to do with things like "national destiny, the saving power of kingship, and the revival of mythic images." Many of these ideas were modified by the influence of Greek culture, particularly among those who lived in cosmopolitan centers. This idea of God was less focused on the welfare of the native land. What evolved instead were "complicated techniques for achieving visions, epiphanies (manifestations of a god), or heavenly journeys to a transcendent god." The religious theme turned toward individual salvation, as well as concern for everyone. "The prophet or saviour replaced the priest and king as the chief religious figure."[9]

Many of the converts to the archaic religions were second- and third-generation immigrants who spoke Greek. Thus, the native languages of these religions required Greek translation for the new followers to understand. "In each case the material was reinterpreted both in light of common Hellenistic ideals" and for the special traditions and needs of the transplanted religious community. The members of the native group understood the text based on their own traditions, while immigrants and new converts often used allegory, reinterpreting what the texts meant to them.[10]

Books of the Believers

After the death of Jesus, somewhere around 30 CE, Christianity went silent. Neither Jesus nor his followers made the news or history books. The Apostle Paul's writings finally began to appear in the 50s. That's when things started to look up for the small Jewish cult. Paul was well-versed in Judaism, as an admitted Pharisee (Phil. 3:5), but highly influenced by the spiritual climate of his day. Of special interest, as scholar Raphael Lataster calls out, Paul made no mention of anything found in the four gospels, including Jesus's earthly events or his teachings. Paul didn't reference the man Jesus, as the gospels do, but referenced only a spiritual or heavenly Jesus. Paul's only proof of Jesus's deity came from personal revelation or indirect revelations from the Old Testament.[11] He also took allegorical liberty, as was common in his day. In Galatians 1:11–12, Paul specifically states that he never got his information from anyone human, but rather, "I received it by revelation from Jesus Christ." With that, Paul became the premier evangelist for the budding Christian religion and also wrote most of what we know about that period. But the influence of the four gospels themselves, which would appear 20–25 years later, is undebatable.

What *is* up for debate among scholars is who wrote the gospels. As is the case with most religions, Christianity began as an oral tradition. It was a combination of folklore, myths, legends, and wise sayings decades before the gospels themselves were written. The book of Mark was written somewhere between 70 and 75 CE, Matthew was written between 75 and 85 CE, Luke was written somewhere between 80 and 95 CE, and John was written somewhere around 95 CE or later.[12] Most scholars agree with this timeline, as well as the concept that Matthew and Luke were likely composed using Mark as source material. Historians generally believe gospel writers incorporated into their work a collection of Jesus's sayings known as Q from the German word quelle, which means "source."

Paula Fredriksen points out that the gospels are not biographies. She describes them as a "religious advertisement" of sorts.[13] The writings weren't meant to be completely factual accounts but to proliferate a narrative to the audiences to whom the books were written. Allen Callahan notes that none of the writers claimed to be eyewitnesses. In fact, he says, the writers wrote with the presumption that their audiences already knew something about Jesus.[14]

Biblical scholar, and former Christian fundamentalist Bart Ehrman says the gospels were written anonymously and later assigned names by editors and scribes. He also points out that none of the writers ever claimed to be eyewitnesses and that the book of Matthew was written in the third person. A closer look at John 21:24 reveals that the writer of the book of John differentiates himself from "the disciple who testifies" by notating "*we* know that his testimony is true." Here he is simply claiming to have gotten his information from John the disciple. Additionally, Mark and Luke were never disciples of Jesus. Mark was the companion of Peter, and Luke was the companion of Paul.[15]

The consensus among most scholars is that we don't know who wrote the gospels and cannot determine the answer with any certainty. The messages contained in the books are stand-alone messages for their specific audiences. Doing a side-by-side analysis of the "synoptic gospels," (Matthew, Mark, and Luke) proves difficult because of the inconsistencies of the details; however, early Christians weren't likely to do comparisons anyway. Scholar Harold Attridge says that since most early Christians couldn't read, they were dependent on hearing the gospels from other people, and they would have applied the message allegorically: "Since the Christians wanted to retain the Hebrew Bible as their scripture . . . it was necessary for them to make certain interpretive gestures to try to rein in the meaning of the Hebrew Bible text."[16] They would have noticed the inconsistencies between the stories and would have had a difficult time putting a literal message together.

But Did Jesus Even Exist?

Outside of the gospels, very little evidence suggests that Jesus ever existed. Professor Lawrence Mykytiuk points out that the Christian discussion of Jesus and his existence is often encased in more theological text by believers than can be found in history. However, he cites examples of mentions of Jesus by Publius Cornelius Tacitus (55/56–ca. 118 CE), a Roman senator and historian, and by Jewish theologian Flavius Josephus (37–100 CE). Tacitus, in his last major work entitled *Annals* (116–117 CE), refers to Christus, or Christ, as the founder of the group whose members are "hated for their shameful acts" and called "Chrestians." Mykytiuk notes that Tacitus mistakes the title of Jesus for his name, yet, he says, "The best-informed among the Romans understood *Christus* to be nothing more than a man's personal name. First-century Romans generally had no idea that calling someone 'Christus' was an exalted reference, implying belief that he was the chosen one, God's anointed."[17]

In Tacitus's brief description of the group of "Chrestians," he calls out a few key points: Jesus was associated with the members, he lived in the time of Pontius Pilate, and he was executed by the Roman governor of Judea. Tacitus clearly did not like Christians, as he refers to their religion as a "deadly superstition," Judea as "the origin of this evil," and Rome, where they were then living, as the place "where all things horrible and shameful from everywhere come together and become popular."[18] While Tacitus doesn't tell us much about the existence of Jesus, he does at least tell us that Christianity was a growing religion that wasn't appreciated by everyone.

Flavius Josephus's works are often referred to by Christian apologists as outside evidence of Jesus's existence. Josephus published two books to show Roman aristocrats that Judaism was to be admired as a religion for its moral and philosophical depth. His first book, *The Jewish War*, does not mention Jesus in its original text, but some later versions include the name.[19]

However, Josephus's book *Jewish Antiquities* mentions Jesus twice. The first mention is incidental in the story of Jesus's brother James, who was stoned to death by the high priest Ananus. The purpose of the story was to tell how Ananus lost his position. The reference to Jesus was to clarify which James Josephus was talking about, as James (Jacob) and Jesus (Yehoshua) were common names. Mykytiuk points out that Josephus was likely referring to a past reference to Jesus in another volume of his book, as most Romans would not have known the story of Jesus the Messiah.[20]

The second reference Josephus makes to Jesus is a little more suspicious. Here, in what is called the Testimonium Flavianum, he writes:

> Around this time there lived Jesus, a wise man, if indeed one ought to call him a man. For he was one who did surprising deeds, and a teacher of such people as accept the truth gladly. He won over many Jews and many of the Greeks. He was the Messiah. When Pilate, upon hearing him accused by men of the highest standing among us, had condemned him to be crucified, those who in the first place came to love him did not give up their affection for him, for on the third day, he appeared to them restored to life. The prophets of God had prophesied this and countless other marvelous things about him. And the tribe of Christians, so called after him, have still to this day not died out.[21]

Mykytiuk states that almost no scholars accept this passage as entirely authentic. Josephus was a passionate advocate for Judaism who did not exhibit belief in Christianity in any of his other works. Most scholars believe that the explicitly Christian elements of this passage–for example, "if indeed one ought to call him a man," and "He was the Messiah,"–were added later by Christian apologists. Mykytiuk states that because Josephus was a first-century Palestinian who grew up in a priestly family, he was in a position to know whether or not Jesus actually existed. Josephus tells us that Jesus was indeed a man, he had a brother named James, and he was crucified.[22]

In regard to what Jesus did, the biblical stories of his life and miracles were written decades after the presumed facts. The miraculous life he led seems to have gone unnoticed by the Jews. Scholar Marianne Bonz says, "Stories of heavenly portents, miraculous healings, mystical visions, and even resurrections were told about a number of demi-gods or heroes" and were commonplace in the first century.[23] For example, Greek historian Dio Cassius and Roman historian Tacitus credited the popular emperor Vespasian for healing a blind man and restoring a crippled man's hand. Greek and Roman citizens differentiated magicians from miracle workers in that magicians performed for profit while miracle workers were considered "exceptional human beings, in the service of a god, for the good of other people."[24]

Christianity arose during the Herodian era.[25] Herod the Great took the throne in Judea, with Roman support, in 40 BCE and remained in place until his death in 4 CE.[26] The Roman senate declared him king of the Jews, though he wouldn't control all the Jewish territories for a few more years. Herod converted to Judaism in 2 CE. His political ambitions, ties to Rome, and marriage to a princess made him a successful leader, and he was able to expand his territory well beyond Judah to include Palestine, parts of the kingdom of Jordan, and southern Lebanon and Syria. "Herod endowed his realm with massive fortresses and splendid cities, of which the two greatest were new, and largely pagan, foundations."[27] One of his greatest accomplishments was rebuilding the Temple of Jerusalem. However, Herod grew mentally unstable as he aged. He became paranoid and violent, eventually murdering his wife, her sons, her brothers, her mother, and her grandfather. He also disinherited his eldest son and murdered him. While the slaying of male children in Bethlehem before his death was "consistent with the disarray to which he had fallen," it doesn't bare historical accuracy.[28]

Tom Mueller, a *National Geographic* writer and researcher, describes Herod as "an astute and generous ruler, a brilliant general, and one of the most imaginative and energetic builders of the ancient world; Herod guided his kingdom to new prosperity and power."[29] However, Herod is "almost certainly innocent of this crime, of which there is no report apart from Matthew's account."[30] No other historical document mentions this act, including history written by Josephus, who was alive at the time of the supposed incident and who recorded many of the other murders carried out by Herod during his reign.[31] However, historians agree that Herod could have murdered these children and that the historical omission could have been because, despite the numbers reported by later church documents (ranging from three thousand to sixty-four thousand children) the number of deaths was closer to a dozen children, as the population of Bethlehem at the time of Jesus's birth would have been around three hundred people.[32]

Regardless of Herod's attempt at thwarting Christianity, many of the Jewish leaders themselves seemed unconcerned, or more likely unaware, of an up-and-coming Messiah. Dr. Kaufmann Kohler, president of the Hebrew Union College in Cincinnati, Ohio, says that Talmudic literature doesn't have a space for Christian beliefs and could only refer to them as a "distinctive species of belief," alongside Gnosticism and heresies.[33] Jews viewed Christianity as one of many messianic movements that targeted Roman rule and inevitably ended with the death of the messianic leader. Messiahs were commonplace toward the latter end of the old millennium and beginning of the new.[34] The idea of a personal messiah didn't appear in literature until later.[35] Outside of Galilee, most Jews had never heard of Jesus. His existence in the Talmud, which is the book of Jewish laws and legends, is the subject of much debate and decided upon only through theological rather than scientific interpretation.

Most Jews followed Pharisaical Judaism at the time, according to Josephus.[36] They represented what had become modern Judaism. However, three other groups warred for control: the Sicarii, the Zealots, and the Essenes. All four groups had their own distinct agendas, much the way American Christian sects divide along conservative and liberal political lines. The Pharisees, for example, "believed in Torah and were even prepared to exchange Jewish national independence for the survival of the Jewish people and the Torah." The Sicarii were considered the "Jewish mafia." They exhibited many aspects of the Jewish culture and life and were considered a state within a state but acted more like gangsters, robbing and extorting people in their communities. The Zealots were "extreme nationalists that wanted to free the Jewish people from the oppression of Rome–and who were convinced, somehow, that they had the strength to do it and drive Rome out of Judea." The Essenes, on the other hand, collaborated with Rome, believing the Jewish future was *with* Rome, not against it.[37]

The spiritual mentor for this last group was Philo, a well-known philosopher who "influenced a sizable percentage of the Jewish people (particularly outside Judea), and who consequently felt that the future of the Jewish people lay in the melding of the Jewish ideas with Roman ones."[38] Philo's introduction of allegory, revealing a hidden moral or political meaning behind stories, would prove to be of substantial importance to the introduction of Christianity. Allegory had been used in the Torah and by Jewish scholars in the past, but Philo's use of allegory proposed following the spirit of the law, rather than the letter of the law.[39] Examples of this use include descriptions of a "circumcision of the heart," in Romans 2:28–29 and lust as "adultery in the heart," even without the action, in Matthew 5:28. Scriptures were open to spiritual interpretation instead of being taken as direct commandments from God. (This allegorical practice of Christianity goes on steroids when it meets evangelical, experiential Christianity centuries later.)

The Essenes were a group of Jews who promoted piety, which often had them practicing rituals outside the scope of Judaism. Many of these rituals and beliefs can be seen in some of the early traditions of Christianity and include a belief in celibacy, and the practice not to marry. This, then, required them to "evangelize," or find new members outside their own group. They also purified themselves daily by immersing themselves in a mikvah, or ritual bath. This ritual among the Essenes is believed to have become the doctrine of baptism, and John the Baptist likely came from this group.[40]

Daniel Boyarin notes there was "shared and crisscrossing lines of history and religious development" between Jews and Christians during the first century.[41] He says, "One could travel, metaphorically, between rabbinic Jew to Christian along a continuum where one would hardly know where one stopped and the other began."[42] Most scholars credit the Council of Jerusalem (described in Acts 15) held around 50 CE, with hashing out the details of what Christianity would look like. For all practical purposes, Christianity looked a lot like modern Judaism with a Messiah, or leader. Additionally, in 70 AD, the Roman tax on Jews was deemed not applicable to Christians, further distancing the religions amid Christianity's emerging doctrines.[43] Most, however, attribute the separation between Christianity and Judaism to Paul.

According to the four gospels, Jesus's focus and emphasis was on the Mosaic law. He told his followers that if they wanted life, they needed to follow the law (Matt. 19:17). Jesus's kingdom was the kingdom of heaven, which, in context, was Israel's prophetic earthly kingdom, and Jesus said he was the promised Jewish Messiah and king. To the contrary, Paul's gospel was one of grace. He preached that faith alone was needed for salvation, that Jesus was the risen Lord and head of the church, and that Christians did not need to follow the laws of Moses (Rom. 6:14). Most scholars give Paul credit for salvaging Christianity and extolling it to the next level. Historian Berel Wein says, "Without Paul, Christianity would not exist today. He is its founder; the one who built and popularized it."[44]

Jesus Becomes God

Whether or not Jesus existed, a version of Jesus as some kind of deity begins to emerge in the second half of the first century. Paul's spiritualized version of Jesus clearly does not mirror the Jesus written about in the gospels. At no time in the first three gospels did Jesus ever claim to be God. Only in the book of John–written toward the end of the first century, following the writing of the other three gospels and after the writings of Paul–do we see a theological supposition for Jesus as God. Bart Ehrman says, "I think it is completely implausible that Matthew, Mark, and Luke would not mention that Jesus called himself God if that what's he was declaring about himself. That would be a rather important point to make."[45] Ehrman notes that Messiah meant something completely different to the Jews of Jesus's day than it did to the Christians. Messiah means "anointed one" in Hebrew, which is how Jews referred to their king. At the time of Jesus, there was no Jewish king or leader. Thus, many claimed the title and led small rebellions against the Romans, all of which were quickly quashed. Whenever Jesus refers to himself as the Messiah in Matthew, Mark, or Luke, the context is always that of an earthly ruler, as the Jews would have understood it.[46]

Anthropologist Pascal Boyer says these types of beliefs are likely to be shared and passed down because they are ideas that are "slightly anomalous."[47] In other words, we can relate to a humanlike god who is similar to us but better than us. Jesus was presented not as a weird green alien but as someone who understands our culture, our struggles, and our faults. He gets us. The gospels, written over a span of twenty-five years nearly forty years after the death of Jesus, provide material for all three perspectives and were written for different audiences who also "got him."

Interestingly enough, Ehrman says, Jesus's resurrection never led to any conversions. Instead, people were confused. The only result of the resurrection, according to the Bible, is that people saw Jesus in visions. Ehrman says this falls in line with what we know today about people who have visions. About one in eight of us will have a visionary experience at some point during our lifetimes, and the top two most common visions are dead loved ones and religious figures.[48] As an example, Ehrman points to the many sightings of the Virgin Mary. Catholic Online provided a video of one such sighting in June 2017, with the headline, "Accurately Predicted: Our Lady Appears to Thousands in Knock, Ireland."[49] More importantly, Ehrman says, Jesus appeared in bodily form to the Jews, which is what they would have expected, and this is what began the belief in Jesus's bodily resurrection.[50]

Jesus may have been crucified by Pontius Pilate, as Roman senator and historian Tacitus referred in his book *Annals*. Beyond this, we have no historical records about Jesus's death and burial. Ehrman notes that no literary descriptions of exactly how crucifixions were performed exist. However, he says, Jesus's body probably was not removed from the cross for burial based on two historical facts:

1. The character of Pontius Pilate didn't lean toward benevolence, meaning nothing in his character indicates that a request by Joseph of Arimathea to bury Jesus's body would have been granted. To the contrary, by all historical accounts, Pontius Pilate was ruthless and cruel.

2. People who were crucified on crosses were left there to rot for the public to see. No records indicate anyone was ever taken off a cross after dying. Criminals were left as warnings to others not to disobey the Roman laws.[51]

As stated above, between the time of Jesus's death and Paul's writing, no written literature was written about Jesus. However, scholars noted quotes in Paul's writing from what is called preliterary traditions. Ehrman says these writings indicate early Christians believed that Jesus became the Son of God at the time of his resurrection. Ehrman says the beliefs about the interaction of the divine with humans are found in Greek, Roman, and Jewish writings predating Jesus.[52]

According to tradition, a human being can become divine in three ways. The first way is that God sees the person as a superior human being because of beauty or wisdom or some other extraordinary quality and bestows divinity on him or her. The second way is that God has sex with a mortal and creates a divine human being. The third way is that a divine being takes on the form of a human, or temporarily becomes human. Ehrman says early Christianity encapsulated all three methods. First, Jesus was made into a god. Later, Jesus was believed to be born of God and a virgin, and finally, the theology stated Jesus was God in human form.[53]

The New Testament

The contents of the Protestant books of the New Testament didn't solidify until the latter part of the fourth century, over 350 years after the death of Jesus. This time gap allowed for a wide variety of beliefs and traditions to develop, including the solidification of the theology of hell and the devil. Of the thirteen books attributed to Paul, nearly all scholars agree he wrote seven of them. This includes Romans, Galatians, 1 Thessalonians, 1 and 2 Corinthians, Philippians, and Philemon. Most scholars believe Paul wrote at least parts of Ephesians, Colossians, and 2 Thessalonians, but questions remain around 1 and 2 Timothy and Titus. While Hebrews has been widely attributed to Paul by pastors, most scholars believe Paul is most likely not the author.

Professor Lincoln Blumel explains that discerning whether some of the books were written by Paul is difficult because of his use of scribes.[54] Only in Romans 16:22 does the scribe make himself known: "I Tertius, who wrote down this letter, greet you in the Lord." In Galatians 6:11, Paul picks up the pen to add, "See what large letters I use as I write to you with my own hand!" It appears a scribe wrote the rest of Galatians. Because of the use of scribes, it's more difficult to discern syntax differences. In other words, did Paul dictate all the books and they were written differently because different scribes paraphrased Paul, or do differences exist because someone else wrote the books and attributed them to Paul? One of the main reasons the latter books have been brought into question is that the sentence structure is unlike Paul's style in the first seven books. The writer employs what is called hypotaxis, or the frequent use of subordinate clauses, which creates long, complex sentences.[55]

How we address and what we consider New Testament scriptures go far beyond the twenty-seven books that ultimately became the Protestant New Testament. The Gnostic gospels are a collection of early Christian texts that were discovered in 1945 and dated to the beginning of the first and second centuries.[56] Of most interest is the book of Thomas, whose introduction claims the book contains the "hidden words that the living Jesus spoke." Many scholars think this might be a reference to the missing and hypothetical Q source from which they believe Mark was written. Thomas is mostly a collection of sayings by Jesus, with a few short parables Jesus told. While it does allude to Jesus's death, it does not reference his divinity, crucifixion, resurrection, or messianic purpose. It was referenced in third-century, early Christian writings but deemed heretical by the fourth century.[57]

Bishop Marcion of Sinope is generally credited as the first person to canonize a new testament, somewhere between 130 and 140 CE. His list of books included ten of Paul's letters and Luke's gospel, as well as his own version of the gospel, which disassociated Jesus from the Old Testament altogether. Marcion liked Paul's version of Christianity better than Jesus's version.[58] The writers of the four gospels clearly linked Jesus to the Old Testament, which Marcion found to be inferior to his new testament.[59] While Marcion was eventually labeled a heretic, he succeeded in pointing out to the church fathers the need for a Christian canonization of scriptures.

Early church history shows clear references to what would eventually become the canonized New Testament, quoting from many of the Pauline epistles and gospels in other church writings. Scholar Nicola Denzey Lewis, however, says the road to canonization was more complicated than just including scriptures that were quoted from specific sources. Documents were circulated by the early Christians that included prayers, poetry, and texts in which Jesus provided special knowledge to his disciples. Some of the more popular books that didn't make it into what is now the New Testament include the Gospel of Mary Magdalene, the Gospel of Judas, the Protoevangelium of James, the letters of Ignatius and Clement, and the apocryphal acts of the apostles.[60]

Lewis also calls out that even in modern Christianity, differences in New Testament canons exist. For example, the Catholic canon contains the Apocrypha, which early Christian theologians considered important but not "divinely inspired." Apocrypha is a Latin word that means "secret" or "non-canonical." While Catholicism became the predominant form of Christianity early on and the basis for Western evangelicalism, small ancient churches, such as the Syrian Orthodox Christians and the Ethiopian Orthodox Church, have their own New Testament canons. The latter has "as many as 70 different writings [that] are considered authoritative." Lewis points out that the Syrian Orthodox Christian canon "originally lacked writings in the Western New Testament canon, including 2 and 3 John, Jude, and 2 Peter."[61]

In addition, books were added to and removed from the New Testament canon throughout the centuries, including the Epistle of Barnabas, the Shepherd of Hermas, and Paul's Epistle to the Laodiceans. Revelation, Lewis says, was left out by orthodox Christians, but it is now included by nearly all modern Christian sects.[62] The New Testament, like the new religion of Christianity, was developed and shaped over the first four centuries. Yet even after its solidification, the documents that supported the canonization of the New Testament defining Christianity continued to change.

APPENDIX D

The Rise of Christianity

One could certainly argue that God made Christianity the powerful force it is today as evidenced by the number of people who practice it. However, if validity is measured by popularity, the same argument could be made of Islam, which is en route to become the world's largest religion by 2070.[1] If using the age of a religion is an indication of divine truth, Zoroastrianism, roughly a thousand years older than Judaism and still practiced in parts of the world, would win on that front. Why a religion fails or succeeds is based on a number of criteria, many of which have to do with what's happening at the time the religion develops. But the rapid growth of Christianity beyond the first century is an interesting phenomenon with many moving parts. Historians don't always agree on exactly how it happened, but some interesting facts surround the event.

Church Membership

By the middle of the first century, more Jews were living outside of Judea than in it.[2] In fact, a first-century Greek geographer, Strabo, said it was impossible to go anywhere in the civilized world without encountering a Jew.[3] Of course, Christianity first showed up wherever there was a Jewish presence,[4] and Paul, the traveling evangelist, was busy spreading its message. Additionally, early

Christianity and Judaism were virtually indistinguishable at that time as many Jews adopted the social and cultural traditions of the cities in which they lived.[5]

Religious historian Rodney Stark refutes the number of conversions reported in the book of Acts based on what is known about the population in Jerusalem at the time. Acts 1:15 states that the church started with 120 believers following the resurrection. Shortly thereafter, Acts 4:4 claims there were 5,000 believers. By Acts 21:20, which puts the time frame around 60 CE, "many thousands of Jews" in Jerusalem were believers. If that were the case, Stark says, Jerusalem would have been the first Christian city, as the population of Jerusalem was only between 10,000 and 20,000 people at the time.[6]

Furthermore, it stands to reason that more would have been written about such a large, dominating Christian sect. The figures used in the book of Acts, however, were never meant literally, as historians remind us those numbers are instead "rhetorical exercises."[7] By the middle of the third century, church father, Origen Adamantius says Christians made up "just a few" of the population.[8] This is in stark contrast to the situation sixty years later, when Constantine the Great adopted Christianity and helped make it the predominant religion.

Helmut Koester notes that Rome had a very strict hierarchical system and life at the lower end of the socioeconomic ladder left you with little money and little hope. As Christian churches increased, so did social services, such as hospitals, soup kitchens, money for the poor, and even education.[9] Christianity also flourished among some upper middle class and Hellenized Jews.[10] Christians took care of the poor and sick at a time when Romans were brutally killing people.[11] Women and children were especially unsafe. Infanticide was popular among the pagans, who valued male children more than females, producing an imbalance of the sexes in their population. Christians, on the other hand, who opposed such practices, had a more balanced population of the sexes. And Christians who could read and write found themselves in places of leadership in society at large.[12]

Citizens and immigrants in Rome held a wide variety of religious beliefs, which became a problem only when those people opposed Roman rule. What made Christianity stand out, Professor L. Michael White believes, is that Christianity assimilated the Roman culture: Christians conformed to the social values and norms Romans already regarded as important.[13]

Expansion by Persecution?

Persecution of Christians was almost unheard of in the first century. If persecution occurred, it came from disagreement among the Jewish sects since Christianity was virtually indistinguishable from one of them to outsiders. Researcher Claudia Setzer says that what some Christians referred to as persecution, the Jews referred to as discipline for the Christians' unusual beliefs.[14] Bart Ehrman even questioned the Apostle Paul's claim that he persecuted Christians, as Romans were not in the habit of jailing people over disputes of theology.[15] Paul claims in Acts 8:3 to have gone from house to house jailing early Christians. It's not clear where he was putting them.

The Jewish-Roman war took place between 66 and 73 CE, and mentions of Christians during this time are infrequent and usually as a superstitious group, which leads some historians to believe first-century persecution is a myth.[16] However, during the brief reign of Decius (249–251), when Christians refused to make sacrifices to the state gods on behalf of the Roman emperor, many of them were killed.[17] Otherwise, persecution was often at the whim of local authorities. In fact, White says, "By the end of the third century, Christian bishops [had] taken over the role of the old civic patrons that had led the processions at Ephesus and Corinth and Rome."[18]

By the beginning of the fourth century, however, Emperor Diocletian, who famously detested Christians, issued the last and most violent decree against them. Between 303 and 311, Christians were brutally tortured and murdered. Clergy were arrested, churches were destroyed, and scriptures were burned.[19] But by this time Christians were so numerous it was impossible to eradicate them all.[20] Diocletian's actions backfired. He instead created a sense of empathy among Roman citizens, which caused Christianity to further expand.[21]

Jesus Gets a Break

Constantine the Great became the emperor of the Western Roman Empire in 306 CE. In 313 he issued the Edict of Milan, which gave Christians legal status for the first time.[22] It decriminalized Christian worship and became the turning point of the faith. Constantine is often credited with saving Christianity from obscurity, and that period of time is often referred to as the Constantine Shift by historians. Why he did it is up for debate. Some historians believe his mother was a Christian and influenced his decision, while others believe it was because of his personal faith. Regardless of the reason, Constantine's interest unified church leaders and led to the first of several councils where church doctrine and orthodoxy would be established. Of interest at the First Council of Nicaea was the relationship between God the Father and the Son: were they the same person or only in divine interest? Also, were Christians who defected from the faith during the persecution allowed to repent and come back in, or were they cast out forever?[23] Church government was established and liturgical practice was determined at this meeting.[24]

Signs of Division

But before the ink dried on the agreements made at the First Council of Nicaea, vast chasms had already developed. Not all early Christians joined in the First Council, and vehement disagreements occurred, such as the Arian controversy in which the presbyter Arius believed God the Father's power was greater than the Son's. Arius believed Jesus was *created* by God rather than a divine part of God.[25]

Early Christians did not believe in a triune God.[26] The idea of the Trinity was first promulgated by the Gnostics and rejected by the council since Gnostics were seen as heretics.[27] Dale Tuggy says, "A common strategy for defending monotheism in this period is to emphasize the unique divinity of the Father."[28] Therefore, the early church saw God the Father as having more power than Jesus and the Holy Spirit. In the second and third centuries, Catholic Christianity developed "a divine nature," for Jesus, but the "Spirit" was not worshipped. Nevertheless, the Trinitarian concept was adopted as part of Nicene Christianity in the fourth century.[29] To this day, Jesus's relationship to God the Father continues to be debated among various denominations and sects.

In 380, Christianity was declared the state religion of the Roman Empire by Emperor Theodosius I.[30] Between 389 and 392, Theodosius "removed non-Nicene Christians from ecclesiastical office and abolished the last visible remnants of Roman religion by declaring pagan feasts as workdays, closing

Roman temples, and disbanding the Vestal Virgins of Rome."[31] While his actions didn't completely get rid of rival Christian sects, it did establish Nicene Christianity as the predominant form of Christianity.[32] Therefore, the bishop of Rome was the preeminent leader of the church, or pope, a position handed down to him in a succession of popes going back to the Apostle Peter himself, according to the Catholic Church.[33] The Catholic Church claims to keep a meticulous list of popes since St. Peter and maintains its authenticity, which can be found in the *Catholic Encyclopedia*. According to Catholic tradition, Peter was the first pope commissioned by Jesus, as related in Matthew 16:18.

By the time Christianity had been declared the state religion, Rome was no longer the capital of the empire. The capital had been moved to an ancient Greek city called Byzantium, which Constantine renamed Constantinople. "This seat of political power then became a center of ecclesiastical importance," according to theologians Stephen Brown and Khaled Anatolios. Constantinople, Antioch, Alexandria, and Jerusalem in the eastern half of the empire ran regional churches and made claims of independence. When Rome fell in 410, Eastern Orthodoxy continued to flourish.[34]

By 431, a now much larger and more politically powerful church faced another schism over the title given to the Virgin Mary. Should she be called Theotokos (God-bearer) or Christotokos (Christ-bearer)? The view of church leader Nestorius and many Eastern churches was that a distinction was needed between Jesus's human and divine natures. On the other hand, the Monophysites believed Jesus was simultaneously human and divine. Nestorian Christianity became the Church of the East, which became successful in spreading its message by the seventh century to China and Japan. The Monophysites were later condemned for their beliefs, but established churches in Armenia, Syria, Egypt, and India. Today they are known as the Oriental Orthodox Church.[35]

The term Caesaropapism was later coined to describe the influence emperors had over the church, specifically who ran it and how. From 330 to the tenth century, the Byzantine emperor controlled who held office in the Eastern Christian Church while maintaining strong control over its ecclesiastical hierarchy.[36] By 1054, the Eastern and Western sections of the Roman Empire split. Orthodox Christianity established its headquarters in Constantinople and the Catholic Church established its papacy and power in the Church of Rome.[37]

More schisms and changes in doctrine and theology continued through the Protestant Reformation of the 1600s. Heretics were quickly excommunicated until the eleventh century. Then heretics were burned at the stake in mass numbers. Scholar Bob Moore states that people were considered heretics for two main reasons: (1) religious leaders were in conflict with church authority, such as a priest who disagreed with a bishop, and (2) laypeople disagreed with how the church handled its resources and property. As the centuries progressed, the church amassed a great fortune and wanted greater autonomy from government influence. This is when priests were required to become celibate so they couldn't use church land to establish "rival dynasties" against government interests.[38] By the 1600s, the Christian Church had become a well-established, well-oiled political and religious machine throughout Europe. It outlasted and outgrew emperors, kings, and statesman. Yet it would undergo several changes to structure, theology, and meaning over the next two centuries in a new land, with a familiar political purpose.

The Birth of American Evangelical Christianity

Doctrines and biblical canons had been hashed out over a millennia earlier, though reformations still added and deleted books centuries later. As stated earlier, the Masoretic text of the Old Testament, or Tanakh, was copied and edited between the ninth and eleventh centuries CE.[39] Furthermore, kings and nobles who commanded newer translations often had an agenda that fit their political motivations. For example, King James I authorized the King James Bible as a way to consolidate his political power after a popular Puritan Bible diminished what he considered his divine rights.[39]

While historians see hints of Protestantism as far back as the twelfth century, religious and political leaders who saw the sect as a threat to the establishment quashed much of it. Martin Luther, in the early sixteenth century, felt the Catholic Church had become too corrupt and successfully challenged the status quo with his *95 Theses*. Luther believed the church was too involved in politics, nationalism, and culture for its divine message to be effective.

During and following Luther's reformation in the sixteenth and seventeenth centuries, Protestant theology, like the ancient church, grew and splintered.

The various groups argued over exactly how far to separate from the Catholic Church and what doctrines to take with them. The Puritans grew out of the Church of England with the intent to "purify" some of the doctrinal remnants left from its exit of the Catholic Church. Puritanism is largely attributed to King Henry VIII who developed the Church of England for political reasons. The Catholic Church wouldn't let him divorce his wife, who produced a daughter, and he wanted to marry someone else he believed would give him a son and heir to his throne.[40]

The Puritans were highly influenced by the non-Catholic and radical ideas of theologian John Calvin, who proliferated the doctrine of predestination, or the belief that one could be a Christian only by divine providence. No matter what a person did during her lifetime, it was of no consequence since she was already saved. Additionally, Calvin rejected transubstantiation, papal authority, and the use of holy images and musical instruments in church.[41]

The Puritans were driven by "moral and religious earnestness," and their mission was to pattern a lifestyle for their nation to follow. In fact, the Puritans believed the nation of England was chosen by God.[42] Bishops were appointed by the king, and those who refused to comply were punished financially and excluded from public offices. One hundred years later, a battle for what the church should be, and consequently how politics should be run, created a religious and political war known as the Puritan Revolution.[43] The execution of King Charles I in 1649 at the order of the Puritan-dominated parliament was the result. Subsequent leaders either oppressed or elevated the Protestant movement for political gain.[44] Ultimately, Puritans decided to take their brand of religion somewhere else.

Christianity across the Pond

The number of Christian denominations and sects was small in the new country compared to today's number, which has reached over forty-one thousand worldwide, with various versions, beliefs, and doctrines.[45] Nevertheless, those groups attempted to enforce their interpretation of Christianity through local laws and ordinances. In New England, a primarily Puritan establishment, "the civil government dealt harshly with religious dissenters...whipping Baptists or cropping the ears of Quakers for their determined efforts to proselytize."[46]

State laws regarding religion in early America varied greatly. Only Christians could hold public office in Massachusetts; Catholics could serve if they denounced papal authority. New York banned Catholics from public office, whereas Maryland gave Catholics full rights, but Jews were excluded. Delaware required public office seekers to take an oath affirming the Trinity, while several other states had state-sanctioned churches. Incidentally, this type of persecution and dissension would eventually lead the United States' founders to separate church and state activities. As James Madison said, "Who does not see that the same authority which can establish Christianity, in exclusion of all other religions, may establish with the same ease any particular sect of Christians, in exclusion of all other sects?"[47]

Pietism, like Puritanism, arose from the seventeenth century, stressing not only high moral standards but introducing the concept of "experiential" theology.[49] In the 1730s and 1740s, under charismatic preachers George Whitefield and Jonathan Edwards, religious revivals swept through the colonies. These revivals, called the Great Awakenings, challenged the clerical elite and the colonial establishment,[49] appealing to the poor and uneducated. Evangelical Christianity and its theology began to emerge for the first time, emphasizing a personal experience with God. Harkening back to the early days of Pauline Christianity, allegory allowed for Spirit-inspired scriptural interpretation and emotive experiences uncommon in churches framed in liturgy and doctrine. Historian Patricia Bonomi notes that rationalism remained the predominant religious underpinning and "was often present in the religion of gentlemen leaders by the late colonial period."[50]

Most of the history of Christianity did not include biblical literalism. This left the door open for acting religious leaders throughout history to amend canons and interpretations to fit their religious and often political narratives. Augustine of Hippo, considered to be the Christian Church father, saw much of the book of Genesis as extended metaphor with few exceptions.[51] Origen, a third-century biblical scholar, found literal interpretation of some parts of the biblical canon silly.[52] And reformist Martin Luther removed the Apocrypha, while attempting to also remove Hebrews, James,

Jude, and Revelation because he believed they went against the Protestant doctrines of grace and justification by faith alone.[53] Although evangelicals did not take an official stance on biblical inerrancy and authority until the twentieth century, biblical literalism became a staple of evangelical theology. This theological perspective would eventually divide evangelical Christianity from other types of Christianity around the world. A century later, it would solidify a radical corporate political agenda.

Christianity Is Not Unique

While American Christianity is unique to America, many other religions have developed their own versions or "brands." Nearly all major religions have multiple sects. For example, Islam has three main branches: the Sunnis, Shiites, and Kharijites. They divide further based on jurisprudence, theology, and subdenominations. Later branches of Islam include the African American movement, the Ahmadiyya movement, the Gülen, the Muslim Brotherhood, and a host of other branches whose doctrines remarkably resemble Christianity. Likewise, Muslim preachers and teachers deliver messages of "truth" with as much conviction and zeal as a celebrated Christian evangelist.

Dr. Zakir Naik, an articulate and charismatic physician-turned-preacher of Salafi Islam, an orthodox Sunni Muslim sect, advocates a return to the early Islam of the Qur'an and Sunna. He preaches that Jesus Christ was indeed the Messiah to the Jews, was born of a virgin, healed the blind, and brought the dead to life. Well versed in both the Bible and the Qur'an, Naik passionately preaches that God is a God of peace. For him and his sect, Muhammad was the last of twenty-five prophets, all of whom directed humankind to the one true religion, Islam. Naik effortlessly and seamlessly, with all the polished allure of a television evangelist, quotes and conjoins Bible verses with the Qur'an, in English and Arabic. His explanations and exegesis of the Scriptures are both admirable and astonishing. He believes that all humans are born as Muslims, but parents and environments lead them astray.[54] When people become Muslims, they aren't converting but "reverting" back to their original state. In one powerful video, reminiscent of many of the evangelical meetings and church services I've attended, Naik leads a British woman to conversion with roaring applause from the stadium-sized audience. The only thing missing was a church organ. Christianity doesn't have a corner market on charisma, persuasion or even showmanship.

Christianity also bears similarities to other ancient religions. Buddhism predates Christianity by around five hundred years, yet the stories of Buddha and Jesus are relatively similar. Celestial beings announced their births, both were tempted by the devil, both claimed to know the thoughts of others, both healed the blind and stated the reason for the blindness was previous sins, both asked their disciples to renounce their worldly possessions, and both had a disciple who walked on water. Additionally, Buddha himself walked on water, challenged the religious order, was born through a miraculous birth, fed a large crowd of five hundred, and spread his teachings and wisdom through parables and sayings–stories that sound familiar to Christians.

Similarly, the Hindu god Krishna is seen as an incarnation of the god Vishnu. Krishna's story goes back eight hundred years before the birth of Jesus and, like Buddha's story, is similar to that of Jesus with elements similar to the story of Moses. Krishna's birth was heralded by angels and attended by angels and shepherds. An evil king attempted to prevent the birth of Krishna and went on a killing spree, murdering babies. But while the king's guards slept, Krishna's father was told to flee with his family, where he crossed a river and the waters were miraculously parted. Where Jesus had John the Baptist going before him, Krishna's brother Baladeva went before him to tell others about him. Krishna is seen as the supreme god who descends to earth to fight evil. Hindus also create nativity scenes of Krishna and his mother when they annually celebrate his birth. And where Christians often navigate the Holy Land of Israel, followers of Krishna can be found at Radha Kunda for ritual baths, where it is believed Krishna performed miracles. Krishna devotees believe they must forsake all else and follow him.

APPENDIX E

Hell, Fear, and Freedom

For a child of the Jesus movement in the 1970s, hell was a hot topic–pun intended. Demons and hell were the stuff of which sermons and confessions of faith were made. Award-winning box office and popular movies on the subject at the time included *The Exorcist* (1973), *The Exorcist II* (1977), and *The Amityville Horror* (1979). Trinity Broadcasting Network's Paul Crouch accused Led Zeppelin of writing subliminal satanic messages into their music, which could only be heard by playing the album backward.[1]

By the time I was involved in the church youth group in the 1980s, my youth pastor had written a book on this phenomenon and frequently warned us about the evils of secular music. Persuaded by his leadership and "expertise" on the subject, I went home and destroyed all my secular albums–both of them. One was by the Osmond Brothers and the other was by Elvis Presley. I only bought the Elvis Presley album because he had died a few years earlier and I thought it would be worth something later. Still, no sacrifice was too great for God. As was the case for many fundamentalist kids in my era, my ideology of hell was as inextricable from my faith as the theology of heaven. After all, if there is good, then there must also be evil.

The Snake in the Garden

Like the rest of theology, hell is a concept that evolved over time. The idea of an evil entity is not initially seen in literature. Monotheism, as detailed earlier, didn't suddenly appear either. The details about good and evil, God and Satan, and heaven and hell were hashed out over a millennium. Consequently, stories such as the temptation of Adam and Eve in the Garden of Eden by the serpent came to mean something different as Hebrew texts were rewritten and revised. With the rise of Christian theology, Satan, demons, and hell became more fully developed concepts.

Still, as you'll see, much more influence on these concepts was to come, and would eventually entrench them in Christendom. At the time the first five books of the Old Testament were written, Jews did not believe a devil existed, nor did they believe in an afterlife. Graves were understood to be the final resting place of human beings.[2] Referring to the concept of the serpent as a devil is not something the writers would have comprehended. Professor Shawna Dolansky says after the Hebrew Bible was completed with the book of Daniel around 162 BCE, "beliefs in angels, demons and a final apocalyptic battle arose in a divided and turbulent Jewish community. In light of this impending end, many turned to a renewed understanding of the beginning, and the Garden of Eden was re-read—and re-written—to reflect the changing ideas of a changed world."[3]

"Could It Be Satan?"

Satan has been blamed for a lot of things. Dana Carvey, in the character of his famous *Saturday Night Live* Church Lady, often inquired about someone's motivation for carnal behavior, attitude, or actions by asking, "Could it be Satan?" Some believe it most certainly is. Jeff Mateer, assistant attorney general of Texas and Donald Trump's nominee for Texas federal judge, inferred transgender children were being used by Satan to destroy American morality.[4] Cardinal Carlo Caffarra gave a speech giving credit to Satan for destroying God's creation through homosexuality and abortion.[5] When a man ran over a Ten Commandments monument in Oklahoma, he claimed the devil told him to do it and "piss on it" after he did.[6] Televangelist Pat Robertson claimed God punished Americans with Hurricane Katrina and Haitians with an earthquake for making a pact with the devil.[7] Pastor Mel Bond echoed what many other pastors have uttered from evangelical pulpits across America for decades: "All sickness and all disease is from the devil. If there is sickness and if there is disease there is literally a demon involved."[8] Satan's seemingly infinite power source goes back centuries. In fact, after the Christian reformation destroyed any hope of a single church, "both sides were quick to see the devil's hand manipulating their rivals."[9]

Satan became synonymous with any deity, creed, or political ideology that opposed the current Christian theology. Extreme examples, like those above, have become the norm in many fundamentalist circles. Conservative talk-show host Jesse Lee Peterson called Democrats "children of Satan,"[10] and a similar sentiment was shared by Donald Trump a few months earlier during the presidential race.[11] Baptist Pastor Gerald Harris, editor of the *Christian Index*, said liberal theology "has its roots in the deception of the Devil."[12] Of course, once the devil is introduced as the definitive reason for an opposing theological or political position, there is no longer a discussion to be had.

Who Is This Guy?

The devil is now primarily seen as a member of the extended Christian family,[13] though the concept goes back many centuries before Christianity. The term satan is a Hebrew noun meaning "adversary" or "accuser." It occurs nine times in the Hebrew Bible, usually in the context of a human military, political, or legal opponent. *Satan* is used four times to reference a supernatural or divine being. In these cases, "the satan" is either acting on behalf of God or is part of God's council.[14] In the story of Job, for example, the satan challenges God's assertion that Job is a blameless and upright man on his own, as opposed to being a good person because God rewards him. The story of Job, of course, presents a theological conundrum. It's troubling enough that God would let Satan kill Job's family if Satan were an opposing deity, but to allow such inhumane treatment just to settle a dispute between the two of them is unconscionable.

However, since the concept of a separate evil entity didn't exist at the time of the writing, God and "the satan" were working on the same team. This story paints an even worse picture of God as a sadistic being with a sociopathic lack of compassion and empathy for his own human creation. Greek philosopher Epicurus famously wrote of this God, "Is he willing to prevent evil, but not able? Then he is impotent. Is he able, but not willing? Then he is malevolent. Is he both able and willing? Whence then evil?"[15]

Researchers have found no direct line to or sudden appearance of the devil. "The devil should not be seen as a character invented by one civilization and handed on to others." Many cultures grappled with the ideas of good and evil and systems of "divine opposites."[16] However, for some faiths, especially evangelical Christianity, the father of all that is evil has his own well-developed theology and a place firmly cemented in their roots.

The devil concept first emerged in Jewish texts around the first and second centuries BCE. The book of Enoch, an ancient Hebrew text found as part of the Dead Sea Scrolls and not admitted to the biblical canon, references Gadreel, a fallen watcher of the "wall of God" who is credited with leading Eve astray, introducing weapons of death to men, and enticing the angels to have sex with humans, thus creating the Nephilim, a giant demigod species. Also around the first century, the Wisdom of Solomon contains the concept that the devil's envy allowed death to enter the world. Dolansky points out, "Though this may very well be the earliest reference to Eden's serpent as the devil, in neither text, nor in any document we have until *after* the New Testament, is *satan* clearly understood as the serpent in Eden."[17] Satan emerged as a stand-alone antigod as Christianity evolved alongside the cultural influences of Greek mythology. As a side note, Dolansky says there is no clear link between Satan and the "ancient serpent" mentioned in the book of Revelation: "The ancient Near Eastern combat myth motif, exemplified in the battle between Marduk and Tiamat in Enuma Elish and Baal and Yam/Mot in ancient Canaan, typically depicted the bad guy as a serpent."[18] The correlation between Eve's talking serpent and Revelation's serpent came much later.

There's No Place Like Hell

An interpretation of the doctrine of hell is up for grabs. Fundamentalists create word mazes to uphold the belief, while most nonfundamentalist biblical and historical scholars agree the doctrine has no basis at all. Hell is clearly a confluence of pagan and Greek mythology and scriptures. Still, it is an intricate part of many cultures and religions. It holds sway over the mind whether by morbid fascination or fearful pondering.

Author Alice K. Turner, produced an impressive book about the topic entitled *The History of Hell*, which priest and scholar Andrew Greeley called, "an insightful and balanced popular history of the growth and, one might almost say, the flowering of imagination about that place at the entrance of which all hope is abandoned."[19] Turner's book chronicles the evolution of hell from historical records beginning some four thousand years ago, noting it has gone in and out of style throughout millenia.[20]

Turner says, "These very early, surprisingly sophisticated stories of gods and heroes have been extraordinarily pervasive in later religious thought, myth, literature, and eschatology."[21] The stories were baked on clay tablets in an area called Sumer. The Sumerians were eventually conquered by the Semitic Akkadians, after which the area became known as Babylonia. The neighboring Akkadians, Babylonians, and Assyrians shared many of the same beliefs, although, as Turner notes, "their gods sometimes went by different names."[22]

Many of the stories, though told centuries earlier, mimic the Christian versions of a savior hanging on a stake or a tree, his spending three days and nights underground, the underworld lord asking for a ransom or substitute for the transgressions of the person he or she is holding, and the idea of death and rebirth. The devil, or underworld leader, continues to form, as well. Charun was the name of the lead demon for the Etruscans, whereas the Greeks, hundreds of years later, called theirs Charon. Charon was a ferryman for dead souls.[23]

Egypt first believed in an afterlife only for the "right-living nobility," somewhere between 2130 and 1770 BCE. This is when Osiris first emerged as the god of the dead but with characteristics similar to Jesus. Osiris was sacrificed and resurrected, and his son, Horus, ruled the living. Turner purports that the idea of a judgment after death might have first come from the Egyptians, not the Persians.[24]

Plato, 428–348 BCE, told stories as a way to describe what less-religious Greeks might have believed about the afterlife. His writings were, "reinterpreted by Neoplatonists of the Hellenistic period" and "carefully read by both Gnostic and orthodox early Christians," which "profoundly influenced such very un-Greek ideas as those of Original Sin and subsequent salvation," Turner says. Plato describes the "true earth" as the place where gods dwell, while Tartarus is a "vast chasm" that "pierces through the earth's center."[25]

Tartarus is found once in the Bible in 2 Peter 2:4: "For if God did not spare angels when they sinned, but sent them to hell (Tartarus), putting them in chains of darkness to be held for judgment." Scholars generally accept that Peter did not write this epistle, and it was written somewhere between 60 and 150 A.D. The word Tartarus originated within the Hellenistic period when Greek culture was prevalent throughout the Mediterranean, between 323 and 31 BCE. Tartarus, in Greek mythology, is "a dark abyss, place of imprisonment of the Titans, as far below Hades as the earth is below the heavens."[26] Titans were, of course, second-generation divine beings.

The description of hell had evolved to an eternal destination for some, as Plato wrote, "But those who appear to be incurable by reason of the greatness of their crimes–who have committed many and terrible deeds of sacrilege, murders foul and violent, or the like–such are hurled into the Tartarus which is their suitable destiny, and they never come out."[27] Turner notes that interestingly that the "incurables" about which Plato writes always seem to be public figures.

The word *hell* is found nowhere in the original text of the Bible, as we understand it today. *Hell,* in fact, wasn't a word until around 725 CE, when it first appeared in Old English during the Anglo-Saxon pagan period. Even then, it meant the "netherworld of the dead," or that mysterious place where dead people go.

According to most Biblical scholars, the idea of what happens after someone dies has always been vague at best when it comes to biblical interpretation. The Greek word Hades was used to translate the Hebrew word Sheol. While Sheol means "grave," Greek mythology says that Hades was the lord of the underworld and ruler of the dead. It's easy to see how Greek mythology commingled with biblical interpretation at the time, adding a new theological dimension.

Despite English transliterations of the Greek and Hebrew scriptures, no direct references to hell are found in the New or Old Testament. Words translated as "hell" were infused with cultural interpretations and meanings at the times the words were translated, often ignoring, or simply not understanding, the cultural context in which the ancient texts were written. For example, Gehenna is translated eleven times as "hell" in the New Testament in verses such as Matthew 5:30: "It is better for you to lose one part of your body than for your whole body to go into hell." But Gehenna was an actual place used as a perpetually burning garbage dump, where carcases of humans and animals were also thrown for sanitary purposes. It is also where children were sacrificed in Canaanite rituals.[28] Jesus's audience would have known exactly what he was talking about when he referred to Gehenna; however, they would have been lost on the notion of hell. Though the Apostle's Creed, written hundreds of years after the gospels, says Jesus descended into hell, no canonized scriptures support this. Some denominations have removed the phrase.

Fourth-century Bishop, Augustine of Hippo, who is credited with defining Christianity, wrote, "hell, which also is called a lake of fire and brimstone, will be material fire, and will torment the bodies of the damned."[29] Augustine had adopted one of Plato's ideas that humans possess an immortal soul. Thus, Augustine believed that even newborn children were automatically condemned to hell because humans were born into sin. Dante's *Inferno*, published in the 14th century lived a thousand years after Augustine and which was part of his poem *Divine Comedy*, added color and significance to the concept of hell. Before Dante put visual context around demons and hell, Latin poets and Greek stories contributed "a few additions to the underworld anthology."[30] But the vivid pictorial and dialectical imagery Dante created has defined evil in all its glory for over six hundred years. Theologians Richard Burky and Jeanette Anderson say that "to understand the source of the idea that people are tortured in an ever-burning hell, we have to go *outside* the Scriptures."[31]

The Jewish orthodoxy does not have a consensus on an afterlife. In fact, the Pentateuch, the first five books of the Bible, makes no reference to an afterlife at all. Many of the other Old Testament books were not written until well into the Mesopotamian era, between 3,100 and 539 BCE, which also happens to be the time when other cultures began writing, as noted in chapter 4. The book of Daniel, for example, which is believed to have been written around the sixth century BCE, says, "Multitudes who sleep in the dust of the earth will awake: some to everlasting life, others to shame and everlasting contempt" (Dan. 12:2). This aligns with a widely adopted religion called Zoroastrianism, which followed the Babylonian period and lasted until around the seventh century CE.[32]

Much of the history of the religion was handed down verbally as "The art of writing had been lost to the area by the time of the prophet, and was religiously forbidden for many centuries afterward."[33] It was a dualistic religion of good and evil. Eventually, it was believed, a battle would ensue between the forces, and a resurrection would occur. So, while the concept of an afterlife didn't occur at the founding of the Jewish faith, as the faith progressed, so did the cultural influence of supernatural thoughts and beliefs. Coincidentally, Zoroastrianism also taught that a savior, named Soshyans, would be born of a virgin, impregnated by the prophet Zoroaster, and sinners in hell would be forgiven.

Isaiah also appears to reference hell: "The realm of the dead below is all astir to meet you at your coming; it rouses the spirits of the departed to greet you — all those who were leaders in the world; it makes them rise from their thrones — all those who were kings over the nations" (ISA. 14:9). King James replaces "The realm of the dead" with the word hell. However, as Turner notes, put in context, this passage is directed to the king of Babylon and alludes to the story from 1 Enoch but only metaphorically: "Its message is exactly the same as the one Enkidu reported to Gilgamesh that great kings are brought low in Ereshkigal's domain."[34] In Mesopotamian mythology, Enkidu was a creature created out of clay and saliva by the goddess of creation for the purpose of ridding Gilgamesh, a demigod, of his arrogance. Ereshkigal was the goddess of the underworld.

By the time books of the Christian faith were written, decades after the birth and death of Christ, a culture of the underworld had become deeply entrenched in religious and mythological thought. Gnostics believed that hell was the physical realm of the earth, which was ruled by the devil. Satan as the "prince of this world" was a common theme in the early centuries. Satan also found his place in the New Testament. The devil tempted Jesus with food, protection, and riches if he would just bow down to him, as seen in Matthew 4:1–11. And 2 Corinthians 4:4 refers to the devil as "the god of this age" (NIV) or "the god of this world" (RSV, KJV). Judaism, just prior to this time, also began incorporating ideas about never-ending torture, something that had never before appeared in its literature or the earliest literature of the Christian Church.[35]

Strabo, a first century BCE Greek geographer and philosopher, noted that states and lawmakers sanctioned such beliefs as a "useful expedient" because people "are deterred from evil courses when, either through descriptions or through typical representations of objects unseen, they learn of divine punishments, terrors, and threats." Strabo also noted that Eastern philosophers wove myths "like Plato, about the immortality of the soul and the judgments in Hades and other things of this kind."[36]

While the era in which many of the New Testament canonical books were written is relatively the same, the concept of hell is not. Paul talks about "destruction" in Romans 5:6, where he said the "wages of sin is death." He makes lists of those not included in the "kingdom of God," found in 1 Corinthians 6:9–10, Galatians 5:19–21, and Ephesians 5:5, but never once references the more common themes of hell found in his era. Paul seemed more aligned with traditional Jewish thinking that those who died simply ceased to exist.

Perhaps even more interesting than what Paul wrote are the English interpretations later produced. For example, the English interpretation of 2 Thessalonians 1:9 says, "They will be punished with everlasting destruction and shut out from the presence of the Lord and from the glory of his might" (NIV). The Greek word for "everlasting," *aiōnion*, according to the Strong's definition, "does not focus on the future *per se*, but rather on the *quality* of the *age* it relates to."[37] In other words, Paul's words reference something more like a tragic death than the eternal fires of hell.

Nevertheless, the idea of hell and Satan became a staple in the various iterations of the Christian faith throughout the centuries, at times becoming more hell-centered than Christ-centered. Most denominations have some sort of doctrine or theology on hell, which sits alongside their doctrines of the virgin birth, Jesus's resurrection, and the second coming. And more often than not, the doctrine of hell is used to scare people into a salvation experience.

Hell houses, usually set up by churches around October each year as a way to compete for the Halloween audience, are used to demonstrate the fire and fury of the devil to those who don't accept their version of Christ. R. Marie

Griffith, director of the John C. Danforth Center on Religion and Politics, says, "Scaring people into salvation has often been a part of the Christian tradition."[38] The theme in hell houses is usually the same. Participants are taken through a series of worldly scenarios, such as dancing in a club, drinking alcohol, or going on a bad date, and something goes horribly wrong. Their "sin" leads them into consequences such as a nightclub shooting, a car accident, or an abortion, with an emphasis on the devil that led them there and the hell that awaits them for eternity if they don't turn their lives over to Jesus.

"Brainwashing techniques like this traumatized me as a child," explains former fundamentalist Josiah Hesse. "Atheism has been the only tool I've found to combat the fear of hell that still haunts my dreams."[39] Hesse's statements have been echoed by countless former fundamentalists I've met. Their own research leads them to believe that hell is an imaginary place with a centuries-long, evolving storyline, but formidable teachings by parents and pastors stay with them. Dr. Marlene Winell, a religious trauma researcher and psychologist, shared a statement from one client, who expressed similar sentiments: "As a child I had an awful fear of hell, and I used to fall asleep crying cause I thought I wasn't saved. Irrational fear leads to irrational decisions. Now with my career in the tank, having lost contact with friends and family over my leaving the church, I am trying to put my life back together."[40]

A Gospel of Fear

I'm terrible at plugging my own stuff. I'd rather be researching and writing than sitting on social media talking about it. So in January 2017, I paid for a Twitter campaign, which tweeted an advertisement about *Going Gay* multiple times a day for several weeks. While I didn't see the sales activity I was hoping for, the campaign did generate a certain amount of buzz among the Twitter community–but mostly from the "crazies." I received a tweet from a self-identified "Prophetess" who had a direct message for me from God. Here is the unedited message:

> God says to Mr. Rymel: Tim, I'll punish you for your GREAT SINS and your "Book" about GAYS! Did you read in BIBLE how I punished

> Lot's wife who just took her look at SODOM and Gomorrah? I turned her into column! I'll do the same with you: Short life+CANCER+painful End+ more after death! God

It was as if God just learned about my nearly three-year-old book. With a message that important, I would have expected to hear something from him much sooner!

Belief in hell can make people do and say crazy things, and if they are mentally unstable to begin with, a doctrine of hell quickly becomes hysteria in a box. How people treat others based on their belief in hell tends to move rather quickly from the sublime to the subversive.

For example, Betty and Dick Odgaard owned a wedding chapel in Grimes, Iowa. When they were sued for declining to host a gay wedding, they decided that rather than perform weddings at all, they would just close the doors to their business. That's when they launched the website Gods-Design.org. There they raise money to post billboards similar to the one they erected in their small hometown, which simply read as follows:

> Marriage = 1 + 1
> Please...I need your help with this!
> – God.

It's not clever, but it aptly states the rhetoric of their beliefs. A few other noteworthy statements about the Odgaards reaction can be found on their sparsely worded website. Outside of a single fragment of a Bible verse quoted from John 3:14, which says, " . . . so must the Son of Man be lifted up," they do not use theological arguments to support their point of view. They believe God is rendered impotent without the footwork of "God's children," and they seem to believe that putting up similar billboards across the country, or "1,000 points of light," as they call it, will change the social tide toward what they believe is "God's design." Clearly, the Odgaards are a simple-minded couple reacting to their world in a state of panic. The more challenged they feel, the louder they declare their version of truth. But it's also clear they feel obligated to defend their God. As they state on their website, "If His children won't stand in his defense, who will?" It's an odd question to ask, given the fundamentalist belief in an all-powerful God.

Many of us were taught that unless we stand in obedience for our beliefs, we will be cast into hell. Plenty of scriptures have been translated or interpreted to reflect this position:

- But whoever disowns me before others, I will disown before my Father in heaven (Matt. 10:33).

- [E]ternal life to those who by perseverance in good works seek glory and honor and immortality, but wrath and anger to those who live in selfish ambition and do not obey the truth but follow unrighteousness (Rom. 2:7-8).

- With flaming fire he will mete out punishment on those who do not know God and do not obey the gospel of our Lord Jesus (2 Thess. 1:8).

Many plausible interpretations exist regarding exactly what is meant by "disowns" and "unrighteousness," as well as "punishment" and "obeying God." That's one reason there are so many denominations. But to those of us raised in evangelical Christian theology, those scriptures clearly mean one thing: God will send us to hell if we don't remain faithful to him and pure in thought and deed. The enormous love that sent Jesus to the cross and the casting of sinners into an eternal lake of fire are two sides of the same coin. We gingerly tout the one while dreadfully fearing the other.

The Bible is fraught with horrendous examples of what happens when God's children make him angry, as discussed in chapter 4. Somehow, as evangelicals, we tend to overlook, ignore, or justify the actions of a God we have been taught is "the same yesterday, today and forever" (Heb. 13:8). This is likely the reason many evangelical Christians react so strongly to social changes such as gay marriage, abortion, and, as they once did, racial equality. They are driven by fears of inciting an angry God who has a clear and documented history of annihilating anyone and everyone who makes him angry for even the slightest of offenses. While we don't worry so much about being struck by lightning, we mentally cower at the thought of being sent to hell after we die. Some Christians are so terrified at the thought, they take a sociopathic stance against the behaviors of others for fear God will destroy the entire nation for the ungodly actions of a few.

Famed evangelist and speaker Tony Campolo says, Christianity was redefined in the mid-'70s as being "pro-life" and opposing gay marriage. "Suddenly theology fell to the background."[41] Somewhere in the middle of all the change, evangelical Christianity, as expressed by many of today's prominent leaders, crossed the line of faith and belief to hatred and abuse. After the 2016 election, evangelical leaders lined up in droves to support their conservative political potentate, Donald Trump, whose policies were clearly at odds with once embraced theological positions.

Kim Higginbotham, a minister's wife and special education teacher, wrote a blog entitled "Giving Your Child to the Devil," in which she stated, "Being a disciple of Jesus demands our relationship to him be greater than our relationship to our own family, even our own children."[42] She listed Matthew 10:37 as justification, which says, "Anyone who loves their father or mother more than me is not worthy of me; anyone who loves their son or daughter more than me is not worthy of me." She then went on a self-righteous, self-aggrandizing, martyr's rant, claiming her son turned his back on God, and she was left with no other option but to abandon him. Her son came out as gay and–it turns out–she posted her diatribe on his wedding day.

Psychologist M. E. Thomas cited sixteen behavioral characteristics of sociopaths, which include insincerity, lack of remorse or shame, poor judgment and failure to learn by experience, pathologic egocentricity and incapacity for love, unresponsiveness in general interpersonal relations, specific loss of insight, and general poverty in major affective reactions (e.g., appropriate emotional responses).[43] Driven by the fear of disrespecting God, making him angry, or simply being seen with those believed not to be living in God's holiness can cause some Christians to turn their backs on those who often need help the most, including their own children. Driven by the dread of hell, people like the Odgaards and Higgenbotham react to their social system with an "extreme moral vigilance" and "strong sense of interpersonal obligations" to the exclusion of everyone else who does not subscribe to the same line of thinking.[44] They perceive a very real threat, believing God's wrath will be invoked by the disobedience of others. They see themselves as the ambassadors of God who must either stop the wickedness of others or incur his wrath for not doing so. Not surprisingly, one study found that people who believe in a literal Satan were less tolerant of gay people and generally more prejudiced against minorities.[45]

In their black-and-white worlds of right and wrong, no compromise is allowed. When confronted, many of these Christians, encouraged by politically conservative news organizations, cry "persecution." Never mind that a majority of their fellow citizens and political leaders also identify as Christians and that there are no laws against them or their churches, no arrests of pastors, no imprisonment, no marginalization, and no death threats or killings for their beliefs.

The 1954 Johnson Amendment, which restricts nonprofit religious organizations from getting involved in politics, is rarely enacted. And it doesn't matter that they are often the aggressors, holding a significant amount of political power and enforcing their rules on nonbelievers with religious freedom laws. The real problem, according to Baptist University professor Alan Noble, is that they "fetishize suffering." He says, "Believers can come to see victimhood as part of their identity."[46] A 2016 report from the Public Religion Research Institute found that nearly 75 percent of Republicans and nearly 80 percent of white evangelicals believed discrimination against Christians was as much of a problem as discrimination against blacks and other minorities.[47]

Much of the evangelical Christian faith, when it comes to dealing with other people, is based in fear, though it's often called love. The decision to hold up signs where crowds gather that say "Heaven or hell, your choice" or "Turn or burn" is often precipitated by long, sincere prayers begging God to save souls and pleas for his mercy. Years ago I stood along a freeway with a group of pro-lifers and held signs that declared Jesus's love, along with the usual "A child is not a choice" messages. Some drivers honked in agreement as they drove by, while others yelled profanities. I felt I had done my righteous deed getting the message out, though it was one I would need to do again and again if I were to remain faithful to spreading the word of God's love and salvation.

Letting Go of Fear

I have participated in countless email exchanges with people struggling to reconcile their sexual orientation with their faith. For some of these people, regardless of all our back-and-forth discussions on the science of sexuality and theological interpretations, their greatest hurdle is the fear of being wrong. The question is posed as, "What if I'm wrong?" or "What if *you're* wrong?" The undercurrent of both is a deep-seated fear of one or both of us approaching an angry God and facing all of eternity on the wrong side of theology.

After several years of study, slowly letting go of my own fears, I came to realize the fundamentalist God and fundamentalist interpretation of scripture made no logical sense. I like to think that God is the master educator, and understands how humans perceive and learn. If that is the case, the syllabus and rubrics, provided in the form of the fundamentalist Bible and theology, are a kludge. They were pieced together using white-out, staples, tape, a red pen, and paper clips. Even if the students were graded on a curve it would be impossible for them to get the exam answers right, sending conscientious students into a tailspin.

The negative effects of fear impact us on a number of levels, including our physical health, memory, mental health, and even how our brain works. Studies show,

> Fear can interrupt processes in our brains that allow us to regulate emotions, read non-verbal cues and other information presented to us, reflect before acting, and act ethically. This impacts our thinking and decision-making in negative ways, leaving us susceptible to intense emotions and impulsive reactions. All of these effects can leave us unable to act appropriately.[48]

Fear is a terrible long-term motivator! Parents who control their children with fear will raise neurotic, emotionally stunted, socially inept, shame-filled kids with a lot of secrets and compulsive behaviors. Fear does not instill confidence, independence, and productivity. What it does well is create followers who ask very few questions and do what they are told. While it might produce loyalty, it doesn't provoke feelings of love and security. Fear is an excellent tool for dictators, oligarchs, and authoritarians. Fear isn't an option for a God who represents eternal love and unending grace.

Theology cannot put our fears to rest. The same number of arguments can be made on one side as they can the other. If the Bible runs out of scriptures to justify our position, thousands of others that were once canonized and went in and out of fashion take their place. Even *wrong* is a relative term because it is likely *right* in light of another theological position or equally established denomination.

Many years ago my family became friends with Janet, the real estate agent who sold my parents their house after we moved to Sacramento. My sister babysat her daughter and I once watched the family's St. Bernard when they went out of town. Our friend was a devout Lutheran who attended church regularly, involving herself in many of its extracurricular activities. She was close friends with her pastor and fellow congregants. So when her daughter came out as a lesbian, following a disastrous heterosexual marriage and a baby, Janet went to her pastor for advice. She was told, based on the church's theological point of view, her daughter was a sinner and going to hell. A friend asked Janet, "Well, what are you going to do?"

Without missing a beat Janet said, "I'm going to find a new church!"

Throughout the centuries, theological interpretation has often been tied to political or personal motivation. I've heard countless stories of people who changed their positions on divorce when they either went through one or married someone who was divorced. Priests who sign contracts of celibacy often change their theology and give up their priestly positions after they fall in love. Racism and segregation were once unabashed staples in the evangelical church, women weren't allowed to be pastors or priests, and gay Christians were unheard of. All these theological positions have changed or are changing as society naturally becomes more inclusive and educated. Similarly, embracing our own humanity helps alleviate many of the fears that motivated thoughts and behaviors in the past.

I realized a week after I sent my older daughter off to college in San Francisco that she was woefully unprepared. Just two hours away, she kept coming home on the weekends, between classes, and, I swear, between meals.

I knew something was wrong when I started seeing her more after she moved out than when she lived with me. She was in unfamiliar territory with unfamiliar people. Her fears and anxiety overwhelmed her. I happened to be in San Francisco for an appointment a few weeks into her first semester and decided to stop by the campus and meet her for lunch. I saw rows of students sitting alone on benches, leaning against buildings, or walking aimlessly around campus staring at their phones. When my daughter caught up with me after her class I asked, "What do you mean you don't have any friends? Why aren't you talking to these people?"

She scoffed at the idea and said, "No one wants you to talk to them. And that would be weird." I had just read a study on the loneliness students face at college, which I shared with her, and mentioned that she wasn't the only homesick student who had no friends. The remedy for loneliness is to talk to other people. But of course, that would require facing fears of rejection. Around a month into school she met someone who told her about a sorority, which she joined. She started working as a freelance sitter for dogs and children and soon had more friends than time. More than just facing her fears, my daughter did something that was emotionally healthy for her and the people around her. The moral of the story is that she *did something.*

While some fears may be logical, fear of hell is not one of them. Reason ultimately helps, but fear of hell is an emotional response to conditioning. I hesitate to say something as trite as "love conquers all fear," but I'll say it with the caveat that love requires us to do something proactive for ourselves or others. When we do, we not only gain more confidence but also gain control. We see ourselves as part of something bigger than ourselves and then we see how we fit into it. Fear is the result of danger or threat, and its byproducts include shame and dissociation. Love, on the other hand, is the result of security, which brings, by definition, belonging, intimacy, and attachment. When given a choice between the two, choosing love and putting it into practice forces fear to lose its grip.

Notes

Preface

1. Bob Seidensticker, Can Christian Scholars Be Objective? *Cross Examined* (blog), Patheos, July 19, 2013, http://www.patheos.com/blogs/crossexamined/2013/07/can-christian-scholars-be-objective-2/.
2. The National Academies of Sciences Engineering Medicine, "Is Evolution a Theory or a Fact?," accessed June 26, 2018, http://www.nas.edu/evolution/TheoryOrFact.html.

Chapter 1

1. Duke University, "Emergence of Advertising in America," accessed January 10, 2018, https://library.duke.edu/digitalcollections/eaa/timeline/.
2. Daniel Delis Hill, *Advertising to the American Woman: 1900–1999*, (Columbus, OH: Ohio State University Press, 2002), 18.
3. Kevin Allor, "*The Rise of Advertisement and American Consumer Culture*," Maryland State Archives, accessed January 10, 2018, http://teaching.msa.maryland.gov/000001/000000/000129/html/t129.html.

4. George Marsden, *The Twilight of the American Enlightenment: The 1950s and the Crisis of Liberal Belief,* [Blackstone Audio, Inc., 2014], audiobook
5. Stephanie Coontz, "*The Way We Never Were,*" The New Republic, March 29, 2016, https://newrepublic.com/article/132001/way-never.
6. Laurel Moglen, "*What is the 'traditional American Family'?*" The Mother Company, November 13, 2014, http://www.themotherco.com/2014/11/what-is-the-traditional-family/.
7. Ashley Lutz, "*These 6 Corporations Control 90% Of The Media In America,*" Business Insider, June 14, 2012, http://www.businessinsider.com/these-6-corporations-control-90-of-the-media-in-america-2012-6.
8. Ashley Lutz, "These 10 Corporations Control Almost Everything You Buy," Business Insider, April 25, 2012, http://www.businessinsider.com/these-10-corporations-control-almost-everything-you-buy-2012-4.
9. Michael Lipka, "Americans' faith in God may be eroding," Pew Research Center, November 4, 2015, http://www.pewresearch.org/fact-tank/2015/11/04/americans-faith-in-god-may-be-eroding/.
10. Pew Research Center, "*America's Changing Religious Landscape,*" May 12, 2015, http://www.pewforum.org/2015/05/12/americas-changing-religious-landscape/.
11. Pew Research Center.
12. Gilad Feldman, Huiwein Lian, Michal Kosinski, David Stillwell, "Frankly, we do give a damn: The relationship between profanity and honesty, *Social Psychological and Personality Science*, October 23, 2016, https://www.scribd.com/document/362843295/Profanity-pdf.
13. Robert P. Ericksen, Susannah Heschel, *Betrayal: German Churches and the Holocaust*, (Minneapolis: Fortress Press, 1999), 10.
14. Ericksen and Heschel, 10
15. Brittany Page, Douglas J. Navarick, "*The Three Shades of Atheism: How Atheists Differ in Their Views on God,*" eSkeptic, June 2017, http://bit.ly/2rZWzew.
16. Lena H. Sun, Juliet Eilperman, "*CDC gets list of forbidden words: Fetus, transgender, diversity,*" The Washington Post,

December 15, 2017, https://www.washingtonpost.com/national/health-science/cdc-gets-list-of-forbidden-words-fetus-transgender-diversity/2017/12/15/f503837a-e1cf-11e7-89e8-edec16379010_story.html?utm_term=.53f8be43d5af.

17. Alex Kasprak, "Trump Administration Bans CDC Officials from Using Certain Words?," Snopes, December 18, 2017, https://www.snopes.com/2017/12/15/trump-administration-bans-cdc-officials-using-certain-words/.
18. Marsden, "*American Enlightenment.*"

Chapter 2

1. Kathy Baldock, "*Walking the Bridgeless Canyon: Repairing the Breach between the church and the LGBT Community,*" (Reno, NV: CanyonWalker Press, 2014), 119.
2. Lauren Feeney, "Timeline: The Religious Right and the Republican Platform," *Moyers & Company* (blog), August 31, 2012, http://billmoyers.com/content/timeline-the-religious-right-and-the-republican-platform/.
3. Kevin Kruse, *One Nation Under God: How Corporate America Invented Christian America* (NewYork: Basic Books, 2016), 116.
4. Randall Balmer, "The Real Origins of the Religious Right," *Politico*, May 27, 2014, https://www.politico.com/magazine/story/2014/05/religious-right-real-origins-107133.
5. Fred Clark, "The 'Biblical View' That's Younger Than The Happy Meal," *Slacktivist* (blog) Patheos, February 18, 2012, http://www.patheos.com/blogs/slacktivist/2012/02/18/the-biblical-view-thats-younger-than-the-happy-meal/#LxxmQV4FtF4jCqjy.99.
6. Clark
7. Frank Schaeffer, "God in America Interview," PBS, October 23, 2009, http://www.pbs.org/godinamerica/interviews/frank-schaeffer.html#3.
8. Philipp Adorf, *How the South was Won and the Nation Lost: The Roots and Repercussions of the Republican Party's Southernization and Evangelicalization* (Bonn: University Press, 2016), 124.

9. Sonseeahray Tonsall, "Sacramento Baptist Pastor Applauds Orlando Shooting," Fox News, June 13, 2016, http://fox40.com/2016/06/13/sacramento-baptist-pastor-applauds-orlando-shooting/.

Chapter 3

1. Hal Hellman, "Two Views of the Universe, Galileo Vs. the Pope," *The Washington Post*, September 9, 1998, http://www.washingtonpost.com/wp-srv/national/horizon/sept98/galileo.htm.
2. Hellman
3. Hellman
4. Julia Sweeney, "*Letting Go of God*," (Los Angeles: Indefatigable, 2006), 2 CDs.
5. Pew Research Center, "The Changing Global Religious Landscape," April 5, 2017, http://www.pewforum.org/2017/04/05/the-changing-global-religious-landscape/.
6. Pew Research Center, "The Global Catholic Population," February 13, 2013, http://www.pewforum.org/2013/02/13/the-global-catholic-population/.
7. Jehovah's Witnesses, "How Many of Jehovah's Witnesses Are There Worldwide," accessed January 3, 2018, https://www.jw.org/en/jehovahs-witnesses/faq/how-many-jw-members/.
8. The Church of Jesus Christ of Latter Day Saints, "Facts and Statistics," accessed January 3, 2018, https://www.mormonnewsroom.org/facts-and-statistics.
9. Pew Research Center, "The Global Religious Landscape," December 18, 2012, http://www.pewforum.org/2012/12/18/global-religious-landscape-exec/.
10. Pew Research Center.
11. Pew Research Center, "The Future of World Religions: Population Growth Projections, 2010–2050," April 2, 2015, http://www.pewforum.org/2015/04/02/religious-projections-2010-2050/.
12. About Missions, "Statistics," accessed September 12, 2017, http://www.aboutmissions.org/statistics.html.

13. Pew Research Center, "The Future of the Global Muslim Population," January 27, 2011, http://www.pewforum.org/2011/01/27/future-of-the-global-muslim-population-related-factors/.
14. Clifford Geertz, "Religion as a Cultural System in the Interpretation of Cultures," (London:Fontana Press, 1993), 89–90,
15. Stefan Koelsch, "Brain correlates of Music-Evoked Emotions," *Nature Reviews Neuroscience*, 15, (March 2014): 170-180, http://stefan-koelsch.de/papers/koelsch_2014_brain_music_emotion.pdf
16. Koelsch, 178.
17. Michael Shermer, *The Believing Brain: From Ghosts and Gods to Politics and Conspiracies–How We Construct Beliefs and Reinforce Them as Truths*, (New York: St. Martin's Griffin, 2012), 117.
18. Shermer, 119.
19. D. F. Swaab, *We Are Our Brains: A Neurobiography of the Brain, from the Womb to Alzheimer's*, quoted in "This Is Your Brain on Religion: Uncovering the Science of Belief," *Salon*, January 4, 2014, http://www.salon.com/2014/01/04/this_is_your_brain_on_religion_uncovering_the_science_of_belief/.
20. Swaab.
21. Shermer, 153.
22. Swaab, *We Are Our Brains*
23. Dictionary.com, accessed June 7, 2017, http://www.dictionary.com/browse/fundamentalism.

Chapter 4

1. Joshua J. Mark, "Religion in the Ancient World," Ancient History Encyclopedia, March 23, 2018, http://www.ancient.eu/religion/.
2. William Schniedewind, "Origins of the Written Bible," *NOVA*, PBS November 18, 2008, http://www.pbs.org/wgbh/nova/ancient/origins-written-bible.html.
3. Isabel Kershner, "New Evidence on When Bible Was Written: Ancient Shopping Lists," *The New York Times*, April 11, 2016,

https://www.nytimes.com/2016/04/12/world/middleeast/new-evidence-onwhen-bible-was-written-ancient-shopping-lists.html.
4. Kershner.
5. Rainer Albertz, *A History of Israelite Religion in the Old Testament Period,* Volume I: *From the Beginnings to the End of the Monarchy*, trans. John Bowden (Louisville, KY: Westminster/John Knox Press, 1994), 42.
6. Nir Hasson, "Is the Bible a True Story?," *Haaretz*, November 1, 2017, https://www.haaretz.com/archaeology/1.818795.
7. Hasson.
8. William Dever, interview for "The Bible's Buried Secrets," directed by Gary Glassman, *NOVA*, PBS, aired November 18, 2008, http://www.pbs.org/wgbh/nova/ancient/bibles-buried-secrets.html.
9. "Narcissistic Personality Disorder," *Psychology Today*, April 17, 2017, https://www.psychologytoday.com/conditions/narcissistic-personality-disorder.
10. Michael Shermer, *The Moral Arc, How Science Makes Us Better People*, (New York: St. Martin's Griffin, 2015), 177.
11. Shermer, 179
12. Reza Aslan, *God: A Human History*, (New York: Random House, New York, 2017), 100.
13. David W. Bebbington, *Evangelicalism in Modern Britain: A History from the 1730s to the 1980s*, (London: Routledge), 2003, 1.
14. Randall Balmer, *Encyclopedia of Evangelicalism*, (Waco, TX: Baylor University Press, November 1, 2004), 23.
15. Kathy Baldock, *Walking the Bridgeless Canyon: Repairing the Breach Between the Church and the LGBT Community*, (Reno, NV: Canyonwalker Press, 2014), 115.
16. Baldock, 116.
17. Darren Dochuk, *From Bible Belt to Sunbelt: Plain-Folk Religion, Grassroots Politics, and the Rise of Evangelical Conservatism*, (New York: W. W. Norton, 2012), introduction, ebook.
18. Dochuk, ch. 11.

19. Jonathan Dudley, "The Real Story of the Religious Right–a Movement Born to Defend Racial Segregation," *Alternet*, February 11, 2013, https://www.alternet.org/tea-party-and-right/real-story-religious-right-movement-born-defend-racial-segregation.
20. George Thomas Kurian, Mark A. Lamport, eds. *Encyclopedia of Christianity in the United States*, (Lanham, MD: Rowman and Littlefield Publishing, 2016), 441.
21. Harold Lindsell, *The Battle for the Bible: The Book that Rocked the Evangelical World*, (Grand Rapids, MI: Zondervan, 1978).
22. Carl J. Rasmussen, *Monstrous Fictions: Reflections on John Calvin in a Time of Culture War*, (Lanham, MD: Lexington Books, September 14, 2016), 30.
23. John J. McDermott, *Reading the Pentateuch: A Historical Introduction*, (Mahwah, NJ: Paulist Press, 2002), 7.
24. Randall Balmer, "Jimmy Carter's Evangelical Downfall: Reagan, Religion and the 1980 Presidential Election," *Salon*, May 25, 2014, https://www.salon.com/2014/05/25/jimmy_carters_evangelical_downfall_reagan_religion_and_the_1980_presidential_election/.
25. Jonathan Merritt, "Trump-Loving Christians Owe Bill Clinton an Apology," *Atlantic*, August 10, 2016, https://www.theatlantic.com/politics/archive/2016/08/evangelicalchristians-trump-bill-clinton-apology/495224/.
26. Danielle, Kurtzleben, "Poll: White Evangelicals Have Warmed To Politicians Who Commit 'Immoral' Acts," NPR, October 23, 2016, https://www.npr.org/2016/10/23/498890836/poll-white-evangelicals-have-warmed-topoliticians-who-commit-immoral-acts.
27. Kevin Kruse, *One Nation Under God: How Corporate America Invented Christian America*, (New York: Basic Books, 2016).
28. Claudia Setzer, "The Historical Jesus," *Tikkan*, 10, no. 4, July 17, 1995, 73, reprint available at http://www.pbs.org/wgbh/pages/frontline/shows/religion/jesus/tikkun.html.
29. Timothy Rowe, "Religion, and Moral Influence," *TheHumanist.com*, October 23, 2014, https://thehumanist.com/commentary/reza-aslan-religion-and-moral-influence.

30. Pew Research Center, "America's Changing Religious Landscape," May 12, 2015, http://www.pewforum.org/2015/05/12/americas-changing-religious-landscape/.

Chapter 5

1. Kathy Baldock, *Walking the Bridgeless Canyon: Repairing the Breach between the church and LGBT Community*, (Reno, NV: CanyonWalker Press, 2014), 19, 109.
2. US House of Representatives, "Individuals Who Have Lain in State or in Honor," History, Art & Archives, February 28, 2018, http://history.house.gov/Institution/Lie-In-State/Lie-In-State/.
3. Ron Elving, "Billy Graham Walked A Line, And Regretted Crossing over It, When It Came To Politics," NPR, February 24, 2018, https://www.npr.org/2018/02/24/587809173/billy-graham-walked-a-line-and-regretted-crossing-over-it-when-it-came-to-politi.
4. Billy Graham Evangelistic Association, "Billy Graham: Pastor to the Presidents," February 21, 2018, https://billygraham.org/gallery/billy-graham-pastor-to-the-presidents/.
5. Elving, "Billy Graham."
6. Elving.
7. Rom Kampeas, "Billy Graham, Who Championed Israel in Public and Derided Jews in Private, Dies at 99," JTA, Feburary 21, 2018, https://www.jta.org/2018/02/21/news-opinion/politics/billy-graham-who-championed-israel-in-public-and-derided-jews-in-private-dies-at-99.
8. Kampeas.
9. Elving, "Billy Graham."
10. Elward Gilbreath, *Birmingham Revolution Martin Luther King Jr.'s Epic Challenge to the Church*, (Downers Grove, IL: InterVarsity Press, 2013), 78.
11. Emma Green, "Billy Graham, the Great Uniter, Leaves Behind a Divided Evangelicalism," *Atlantic*, February 21, 2018, https://www.theatlantic.com/politics/archive/2018/02/billy-graham-death/553850/.

12. Jay Reeves, "Billy Graham Had Pride And Regret on Civil Rights Issues," US News & World Report, February 25, 2018, https://www.usnews.com/news/best-states/alabama/articles/2018-02-25/billy-graham-played-complicated-role-in-us-race-relations.
13. Frank Schaeffer, "Billy Graham is Lying in State. Why? We are not Iran. We are not a Theocracy," *Frank Schaeffer* (blog), February 28, 2018, https://frankschaefferblog.com/2018/02/billy-graham-lying-state-not-iran-not-theocracy/.
14. Schaeffer.
15. Noah Davis, "Billy Graham's Son Jumps On The Birther Bandwagon," Business Insider, April 25, 2011, http://www.businessinsider.com/franklin-billy-graham-birther-donald-trump-sarah-palin-barack-obama-2011-4.
16. Asher Stockler, "Evangelist Franklin Graham Defends Trump Against Stormy Daniels Reports," NBC News, January 20, 2018, https://www.nbcnews.com/politics/donald-trump/evangelist-franklin-graham-defends-trump-against-stormy-daniels-reports-n839496.
17. Samaritan's Purse, Mission Statement, accessed February 28, 2018, https://www.samaritanspurse.org/our-ministry/about-us/.
18. Joel Baden, "Franklin Graham Said Immigration Is 'Not a Bible Issue.' Here's What the Bible Says," *Washington Post*, February 10, 2017, https://www.washingtonpost.com/news/acts-of-faith/wp/2017/02/10/franklin-graham-said-immigration-is-not-a-bible-issue-heres-what-the-bible-says/?utm_term=.d32826ec8add.
19. "The Southern Argument for Slavery," USHistory.org, accessed March 1, 2018, http://www.ushistory.org/us/27f.asp.
20. Camille Lewis, "'Is Segregation Scriptural?' by Bob Jones Sr.," *A Time to Laugh*, (blog), March 15, 2013, http://www.drslewis.org/camille/2013/03/15/is-segregation-scriptural-by-bob-jones-sr-1960/.
21. People for the American Way, "Jerry Falwell and Pat Robertson Blame 9/11 on Organizations like People For the American Way," YouTube, April 2, 2010, https://youtu.be/kMkBgA9_oQ4.
22. Gregory S. Paul, "Cross-National Correlations of Quantifiable Societal Health with Popular Religiosity and Secularism in the

Prosperous Democracies," *Journal of Religion & Society* 7 (2005), https://ffrf.org/uploads/timely/Religion%26Society.pdf.
23. Nurith Aizenman, "Gun Violence: How the U.S. Compares with Other Countries," NPR, October 6, 2017, https://www.npr.org/sections/goatsandsoda/2017/10/06/555861898/gun-violence-how-the-u-s-compares-to-other-countries.
24. Paul, "Cross-National Correlations."
25. Pew Research Center, "Global Christianity–Report on the Size and Distribution of the World's Christian Population," December 19, 2011, http://www.pewforum.org/2011/12/19/global-christianity-exec/; and World Atlas, "Which Countries Have The Most Christians around The World?," last modified March 8, 2018, https://www.worldatlas.com/articles/which-countries-have-the-most-christians-around-the-world.html.
26. Pew Research Center, "Religious Landscape Study," accessed March 1, 2018, http://www.pewforum.org/religious-landscape-study/.
27. Claudia Setzer, "The Historical Jesus," *Tikkun* 10, no. 4, July 17, 1995: 73, reprint available at http://www.pbs.org/wgbh/pages/frontline/shows/religion/jesus/tikkun.html.
28. TMZ, "Randy Travis DWI Naked Arrest Vid Released," December 4, 2017, http://www.tmz.com/2017/12/04/randy-travis-dwi-naked-arrest-video-released/.

Chapter 6

1. Daniel C. Dennett and Linda LaScola, "Preachers Who Are Not Believers," *Evolutionary Psychology* 8, no. 1 *EPJournal.Net*, (2010): 135, https://ase.tufts.edu/cogstud/dennett/papers/Preachers_who_are_not_believers.pdf.
2. Dennett and LaScola, 134–135
3. Dennett and LaScola, 136
4. Dennett and LaScola, 136
5. Wikipedia, s.v. "Bernard Madoff," last modified April 9, 2018, https://en.wikipedia.org/wiki/Bernard_Madoff.

6. Carol Tavris and Elliot Aronson, *Mistakes Were Made (But Not by Me): Why We Justify Foolish Beliefs, Bad Decisions, and Hurful Acts*, (New York: Mariner Books, 2015) 11–12
7. Nancy Faber, Clarence Busch, the Drunk Driver Who Inspired a Movement, Faces Prison After Another Accident, *People*, October 14, 1985, https://people.com/archive/clarence-busch-the-drunk-driver-who-inspired-a-movement-faces-prison-after-another-accident-vol-23-no-16/.

Chapter 7

1. Reklam.com.tr, "Dove France, Inner Critic Commercial," Youtube, April 10, 2015, https://www.youtube.com/watch?v=MOLike-Hkpg.
2. Kristin Neff, "The Motivational Power of Self-Compassion,", *Self-Compassion*, accessed August 4, 2016, http://self-compassion.org/the-motivational-power-of-self-compassion/.
3. Vyckie Garrison, "How Playing Good Christian Housewife Almost Killed Me," AlterNet, September 8, 2014, http://www.alternet.org/belief/how-playing-good-christian-housewife-almost-killed-me.
4. Brené Brown, *Rising Strong: How the Ability to Reset Transforms the Way We Live, Love, Parent, and Lead*, (New York: Random House, 2015), 64

Chapter 8

1. Mike Ralston, interview by author, January 9, 2017.
2. Marlene Winell, "Religious Trauma Syndrome: It's Time To Recognize It," *Marlene Winell, Ph.D.* (blog), June 28, 2011, http://marlenewinell.net/religious-trauma-syndrome-its-.
3. Reba Riley, "It's Called Post-Traumatic Church Syndrome, and Yes It's Real," *Faith Forward* (blog), Patheos, March 5, 2014, http://www.patheos.com/blogs/faithforward/2014/03/its-called-post-traumatic-church-syndrome-and-yes-its-real/.

4. Oliver Emberton, "If You're Not Pissing Someone Off, You Probably Aren't doing Anything Important," *Oliver Emberton* (blog),March 5, 2014, http://oliveremberton.com/2014/if-youre-not-pissin g-someone-off-you-probably-arent-doing-anything-important/.
5. Charles H. Elliott and Laura L. Smith, *Anger Management for Dummies*, 2nd ed., (Hoboken, NJ: John Wiley and Sons, 2015), 18.
6. Elliott and Smith, 20
7. Brené Brown, *The Gifts of Imperfection: Let Go of Who You Think You're Supposed to Be and Embrace Who You Are*, (Center City, MN: Hazelden Publishing, 2010), 70.
8. Bootie Cosgrove-Mather, "America the Medicated," CBS News, April 21, 2005,_http://www.cbsnews.com/news/america-the-medicated/.
9. Keri Blakinger, "What Countries Party Hardest? Here's a Look at Drug Use and Drinking in America vs. Europe," *New York Daily News*, September 17 2015,_http://www.nydailynews.com/news/national/drug-drinking-u-s-europe-article-1.2364210.
10. Zak Cheney Rice, "Here's How Much TV America Watches Compared to the Rest of the World," Mic.com, February 19, 2014, https://mic.com/articles/82809/here-s-how-much-tv-america-wat ches-compared-to-the-rest-of-the-world#.z2vRAOPfH.
11. Matthew Paul Turner, "5 Lingering Effects of Fundamentalism," *Matthew Paul Turner* (blog), August 28, 2014, http://matthew-paulturner.com/2014/08/28/5-lingering-effects-fundamentalism/.
12. Karyn Hall, "Self-Validation," *Psychology Today*, July 12, 2014,_https://www.psychologytoday.com/blog/pieces-mind/201407/self-validation.
13. Hall.
14. Hall.
15. Hall.

Chapter 9

1. James E. Kennedy, "Religious Guilt and Fear, Well-Being, and Fundamentalism," *Research Articles on Spirituality* (blog), 1999, http://jeksite.org/research/bv.pdf.

2. Kennedy
3. Susan Krauss Whitbourne, "The Definitive Guide to Guilt," *Psychology Today*, August 11, 2012, https://www.psychologytoday.com/blog/fulfillment-any-age/201208/the-definitive-guide-guilt.
4. David S. Wallace, Rene M. Paulson, Charles G. Lord, Charles F. Bond, Jr., "Which Behaviors Do Attitudes Predict? Meta-Analyzing the Effects of Social Pressure and Perceived Difficulty," *Review of General Psychology* 9, no. 3 (2005): 214–227, http://www.communicationcache.com/uploads/1/0/8/8/10887248/which_behaviors_do_attitudes_predict-_meta-analyzing_the_effects_of_social_pressure_and_perceived_difficulty.pdf.
5. Charles H. Hackney and Glenn S. Sanders, "Religiosity and Mental Health: A Meta-Analysis of Recent Studies," *Journal for the Scientific Study of Religion*, 42, no. 1 (2003): 43–55, http://www.aleciashepherd.com/writings/articles/other/Religiosity%20and%20Mental%20Health%20A%20Meta%20Analysis%20of%20Recent%20Studies.pdf.
6. Art Markman, "What Does Guilt Do?," *Psychology Today*, May 8, 2012, https://www.psychologytoday.com/blog/ulterior-motives/201205/what-does-guilt-do.
7. Karl Melvin, "6 Ways To Let Go Of The Toxic Guilt That's Keeping You in The Past," Elite Daily, March 4, 2016, http://elitedaily.com/life/let-go-toxic-guilt-past/1341839/.
8. Bob Neufeld and Marlene Neufeld, "Toxic Guilt," *Marlene & Bob* (blog), 2010, http://www.marleneandbob.com/Toxic_guilt.pdf.

Chapter 10

1. Tim Rymel, "An Open Letter To The GOP: 'We Are You'," *Huffington Post*, December 6, 2017, https://www.huffingtonpost.com/tim-rymel/an-open-letter-to-the-gop-we-are-you_b_10975536.html.
2. Michael Beschloss, "How an Experiment with Dolls Helped Lead to School Integration," *New York Times*, May 6, 2014, https://www.

nytimes.com/2014/05/07/upshot/how-an-experiment-with-dolls-helped-lead-to-school-integration.html.
3. Hazel Trice Edney, "New 'Doll Test' Produces Ugly Results," *Final Call*, September 14, 2006, http://www.finalcall.com/artman/publish/National_News_2/New_doll_test_produces_ugly_results_2919.shtml.

Chapter 11

1. Stacey Freedenthal, "How to Turn Self-Hatred into Self-Compassion," GoodTherapy.org, November 12, 2013, http://www.goodtherapy.org/blog/how-to-turn-self-hatred-into-self-compassion-1112135.
2. Anxiety and Depression Association of America, Facts and Statistics, accessed March 23, 2017, https://adaa.org/about-adaa/press-room/facts-statistics#.
3. Bruce Hennigan, "Depression: Reject the Guilt, Embrace the Cure," Focus on the Family, accessed March 23, 2017, http://www.focusonthefamily.com/marriage/facing-crisis/dealing-with-depression/depression-reject-the-guilt-embrace-the-cure.
4. Hennigan
5. CBN.com., "Overcoming Depression," Christian Broadcasting Network, accessed March 23, 2017, http://www1.cbn.com/overcoming-depression.
6. CBN.com
7. Austin Thompson, "Robin Williams, Death, Hell, and Denying Yourself," *What It Means to be a Christian* (blog), August 12, 2014, https://whatitmeanstobeachristian.wordpress.com/2014/08/12/robin-williams-death-hell-and-denying-yourself/.
8. Cheryl Meril, "Was Robin Williams an Atheist?," *Jesus Saved Cheryl Meril from Hell* (blog), August 11, 2014, http://cherylkicksass.blogspot.com/2014/08/was-robin-williams-atheist.html.
9. KPIX5, "Heartbreaking Essay from Robin Williams' Wife Says an Incurable Disease Ravaged His Mind," CBS San Francisco Bay Area, October 2, 2016, http://sanfrancisco.cbslocal.com/2016/10/02/

heartbreaking-essay-from-robin-williams-wife-says-an-incurable-disease-ravaged-his-mind/.

10. Samantha Schnurr, "Susan Schneider Reveals the Real Reason Behind Robin Williams' Suicide: 'We Were Living a Nightmare,'" ENews, November 3, 2015, http://www.eonline.com/news/712507/susan-schneider-reveals-the-real-reason-behind-robin-williams-suicide-we-were-living-a-nightmare.

Chapter 12

1. Marlene Winell, "Part 3: The Trauma of Leaving Religion," Journey Free, November, 2011, http://journeyfree.org/rts/the-trauma-of-leaving-religion-pt-3/.
2. James Moyer, "Psychological Issues of Former Fundamentalists," *Cultic Studies Journal* 11, no. 2 (1994):189-99, http://www.icsahome.com/articles/psychological-issues-former-fundamentalists-csj-11-2.
3. Marie Forleo, "The Secret to Finding Your Passion (Hint: It's Not What You Think)," Oprah.com, November 14, 2012, http://www.oprah.com/supersoulsunday/the-secret-to-finding-your-passion-hint-its-not-what-you-think_1#ixzz56wvs59y1.
4. Neil Carter, "What Leaving My Religion Did for Me," *Godless in Dixie*, (blog), Patheos, September 14, 2014, http://www.patheos.com/blogs/godlessindixie/2014/09/14/what-leaving-my-religion-did-for-me/.
5. Antonio Damasio, quoted in "How Emotion Shapes Decision Making," *The Intentional Workplace*, March 15, 2012, https://intentionalworkplace.com/2012/03/15/how-emotion-shapes-decision-making/.
6. David Hume, *A Treatise of Human Nature*, ed. L. A. Selby-Bigge (Oxford: Clarendon Press, 1896; repr. Zurich: International Relations and Security Network, 2007), https://people.rit.edu/wlrgsh/HumeTreatise.pdf.
7. Jonah Lehrer, quoted in Altman, "How Emotions Shame Decision Making."

8. Kenneth Hayworth, "Killed by Bad Philosophy," Brain Preservation Foundation, January 2010, http://www.brainpreservation.org/content-2/killed-bad-philosophy/.
9. Michael Shermer, "Who Are You?," *MichaelShermer.com* (blog), July 2017, https://michaelshermer.com/2017/07/who-are-you/.
10. Grace Goyle, "We Are Creatures of Habit," Life Without Pans (blog), accessed January 3, 2018, http://www.lifewithoutpants.com/theinconvenience-of-change-we-are-creatures-of-habit-grace-boyle/.
11. "Mary Mcleod Bethune: Early Life, Education, and School," *Self-Rescuing Princess Society*, (blog), July 14, 2014, https://selfrescuingprincesssociety.blogspot.com/2014/07/mary-mcleod-bethune-early-life.html.
12. "Mary McLeod Bethune Biography," Biography.com, last modified January 19,2018, https://www.biography.com/people/mary-mcleod-bethune-9211266; Debra Michals, "Mary McLeod Bethune", National Women's History Museum, 2015, www.womenshistory.org/education-resources/biographies/mary-mcleod-bethune; and New World Encyclopedia s.v. "Mary McLeod Bethune," last modified September 21, 2016, http://www.newworldencyclopedia.org/entry/Mary_McLeod_Bethune.

Epilogue

1. Randall Balmer, "The Real Origins of the Religious Right," *Politico*, May 27, 2014, https://www.politico.com/magazine/story/2014/05/religious-right-real-origins-107133.
2. Balmer.
3. Michael Shermer, *The Moral Arc: How Science Makes us Better People*, (New York: St. Martin's Griffin, 2015), 233–34.
4. Shermer, 233–34.
5. Shermer, 233–34.
6. Nathalie Baptiste, "This is What Happens When Abortion is Outlawed," *The American Prospect*, June 17, 2015, http://prospect.org/article/what-happens-when-abortion-outlawed.

7. Shermer, *The Moral Arc*, 232.
8. Joshua Lang, "What Happens to Women Who Are Denied Abortions?," *New York Times*, June 12, 2013, http://www.nytimes.com/2013/06/16/magazine/study-women-denied-abortions.html.
9. Lang.
10. Guttmacher Institute, "Abortion Patients are Disproportionately Poor and Low Income," 2016, https://www.guttmacher.org/infographic/2016/abortion-patients-are-disproportionately-poor-and-low-income.
11. George Marsden, *The Twilight of the American Enlightenment: The 1950s and the Crisis of Liberal Belief*, (Ashland, OR: Blackstone Audio, 2014), audiobook.
12. Jonathan Dudley, "The Real Story of the Religious Right–a Movement Born to Defend Racial Segregation," *Alternet*, February 11, 2013, http://www.alternet.org/tea-party-and-right/real-story-religious-right-movement-born-defend-racial-segregation.
13. Poverty Solutions, "Poverty in the US, accessed January 11, 2018, http://poverty.umich.edu/about/poverty-facts/us-poverty/.
14. National Institute on Drug Abuse, "Drug Facts," Nationwide Trends, 2015, https://www.drugabuse.gov/publications/drugfacts/nationwide-trends.
15. Bernadette Rabuy and Daniel Kopf, "Prisons of Poverty: Uncovering the Pre-Incarceration Incomes of the Imprisoned," Prison Policy Initiative, July 9, 2015, http://www.prisonpolicy.org/reports/income.html.
16. Brian Beutler, "Would Republicans Support the Americans with Disabilities Act Today?," *New Republic*, July 27, 2015, https://newrepublic.com/article/122380/would-republicans-support-americans-disabilities-act-today; and Eugene Scott, "ACLU Expecting More Religious Freedom Bills in 2017 Than Ever,", CNN, December 16, 2016, https://www.cnn.com/2016/12/16/politics/aclu-religious-freedom/index.html.
17. Manisha Sinha, "African Americans and Emancipation," Gilder Lehrman Institute of American History, accessed January 11, 2018,

https://www.gilderlehrman.org/history-now/african-americans-and-emancipation.

18. Douglas Blackmon, "Excerpt: *Slavery by Another Name*", NPR, March 25, 2008, https://www.npr.org/templates/story/story.php?storyId=89051115.
19. Blackmon.
20. Tom LoBianco, "Report: Aide says Nixon's War on Drugs Targeted Blacks, Hippies," CNN, March 24, 2016, http://www.cnn.com/2016/03/23/politics/john-ehrlichman-richard-nixon-drug-war-blacks-hippie/.
21. Ibram X. Kendi, "How Ronald Reagan's Drug War Fueled Americans' Addiction to Racist Ideas," Raw Story, June 23, 2016, https://www.rawstory.com/2016/06/how-ronald-reagans-drug-war-fueled-americans-addiction-to-racist-ideas/.
22. National Addiction and HIV Archive Program, accessed January 11, 2018, https://www.icpsr.umich.edu/quicktables/quickconfig.do?34481-0001_all.
23. National Association for the Advancement of Colored People, "Criminal Justice Fact Sheet," accessed January 11, 2018, http://www.naacp.org/criminal-justice-fact-sheet/.
24. E. Ann Carson and Daniela Golinelli, "Prisoners in 2012 - Advance Counts," US Department of Justice, July 2013, https://www.bjs.gov/content/pub/pdf/p12ac.pdf.
25. Lauren-Brooke Eisen, "Trump's First Year Has Been the Private Prison Industry's Best," Brennan Center for Justice, January 15, 2018, https://www.brennancenter.org/blog/trump%E2%80%99s-first-year-has-been-private-prison-industry-best.
26. Michelle Alexander, *The New Jim Crow: Mass Incarceration in the Age of Colorblindness*, (Prince Frederick, MD: Recorded Books, January 2012). audiobook.

Appendix A

1. Clara Moskowitz, "Bible Possibly Written Centuries Earlier, Text Suggests," *LiveScience*, January 15, 2010, https://www.livescience.com/8008-bible-possibly-written-centuries-earlier-text-suggests.html.
2. Jennie Cohen, "6 Things You May Not Know About The Dead Sea Scrolls," *History*, May 7, 2013, http://www.history.com/news/history-lists/6-things-you-may-not-know-about-the-dead-sea-scrolls.
3. Lydia Smith, "Newly-Excavated Skeletons Could Help to Reveal Who Wrote The Ancient Dead Sea Scrolls," *Independent*, November 18, 2017, http://www.independent.co.uk/news/science/dead-sea-scrolls-wrote-protected-excavated-skeletons-qumran-west-bank-archaeology-a8062341.html; and_Daniel K. Eisenbud, "Hebrew University Archeologists Find 12th Dead Sea Scrolls Cave," *Jerusalem Post*, February 8, 2017, http://www.jpost.com/Israel-News/Hebrew-University-archaeologists-find-12th-Dead-Sea-Scrolls-cave-480966.
4. Cohen, "Dead Sea Scrolls."
5. Cohen.
6. Kenneth Atkinson, *Judaism*, (Philadelphia: Chelsea House Publishers, 2004), 43._
7. Mark Hamilton, "From Hebrew Bible to Christian Bible: Jews, Christians and the Word of God," From Jesus to Christ, *Frontline*, PBS, April 1998, https://www.pbs.org/wgbh/pages/frontline/shows/religion/first/scriptures.html.
8. Lee Martin McDonald, *The Biblical Canon: It's Origin, Transmission and Authority*," 3rd ed. (Peabody, MA: Henderickson Publishers, 2007), 55.
9. Barry Hoberman, "Translating the Bible," *The Atlantic* 255, no. 2, (February 1985): 43–58, https://www.theatlantic.com/past/docs/issues/85feb/trans2.htm.
10. Richard N. Ostling, "'Dead Sea Scrolls' Yield 'Major' questions in Old Testament understanding," *Notre Dame News*, November

13, 2000, https://news.nd.edu/news/dead-sea-scrolls-yield-major-questions-in-old-testament-understanding/.
11. E. R. Bevan, "*The House of Ptolemy*," [London: Methuen Publishing, 1927], http://penelope.uchicago.edu/Thayer/E/Gazetteer/Places/Africa/Egypt/_Texts/BEVHOP/3*.html.
12. Martin Hengel, *The Septuagint as Christian Scripture: Its Prehistory and the Problem of Its Canon*, [Edinburgh: T&T Clark., 2002], 75.
13. Hengel, 76.
14. Hengel, 76.
15. Hengel, 83.
16. Hengel, 25.
17. Hengel, 25.
18. Hengel, 78.
19. Hengel, 78.
20. Hengel, 78.
21. Michael Coogan, interview for "The Bible's Buried Secrets", directed by Gary Glassman, *NOVA*, PBS, aired November 18, 2008, https://www.youtube.com/watch?v=qalTJzk4kO0.
22. Bruce Manning Metzger, *Manuscripts of the Greek Bible: An Introduction to Greek Paleography*, (Oxford: Oxford University Press, 2006), 76.
23. William Dever, "Archeology of the Hebrew Bible," *NOVA*, PBS, November 18, 2008, http://www.pbs.org/wgbh/nova/ancient/archeology-hebrew-bible.html.
24. Peter Machinist, interview for "The Bible's Buried Secrets", directed by Gary Glassman, *NOVA*, PBS, aired November 18, 2008, https://www.youtube.com/watch?v=qalTJzk4kO0.
25. Israel Finklestein and Neil Asher Silberman, *The Bible Unearthed: Archaeology's New Vision of Ancient Israel and the Origin of its Sacred Texts*, (New York: Touchstone, 2001), 118.
26. Finklestein and Silberman, *The Bible Unearthed*, 12.
27. Finklestein and Silberman, 12.
28. Finklestein and Silberman, 12.
29. Finklestein and Silberman, 12.

30. Dever, "The Bible's Buried Secrets."

Appendix B

1. *Encyclopedia Britannica*, s.v., "Monotheism,' by Theodorus P. Van Baaren, last modified January 24, 2018, https://www.britannica.com/topic/monotheism.
2. Reza Aslan, *God, A Human History* (New York: Random House, 2017), 98.
3. Aslan, 99.
4. Nicholas Reeves, *Akhenaten: Egypt's False Prophet* (London: Thames & Hudson, 2001), 36.
5. *New World Encyclopedia*, s.v. "Monotheism," last modified November 14, 2014, http://www.newworldencyclopedia.org/p/index.php?title=Monotheism&oldid=985355.
6. Rainer Albertz, *A History of Israelite Religion in the Old Testament Period,* Volume I: *From the Beginnings to the End of the Monarchy*, trans. John Bowden (Louisville, KY: Westminster/John Knox Press, 1994), 30.
7. Albertz. 30.
8. Albertz 30.
9. Diana Vikander Edelman, ed., *The Triumph of Elohim: From Yahwisms to Judaisms*, (Kampen, Netherlands: Kok Pharos Publishing House, 1995), 18.
10. Edelman, 19.
11. Edelman, 19.
12. Edelman, 19.
13. Albertz, *History of Israelite Religion*, 27.
14. Keith C. Seele, *The Coregency Of Ramses II With Seti I And The Date Of The Great Hypostyle Hall At Karnak*, (Chicago: University Chicago Press, 1940), https://oi.uchicago.edu/sites/oi.uchicago.edu/files/uploads/shared/docs/saoc19.pdf.

15. Carol Meyers, interview for "The Bible's Buried Secrets," directed by Gary Glassman, *NOVA*, PBS, aired November 18, 2008, http://www.pbs.org/wgbh/nova/ancient/bibles-buried-secrets.html.
16. Joshua J. Mark, "Religion in the Ancient World", Ancient History Encyclopedia, March 23, 2018, http://www.ancient.eu/religion/.
17. Meyers, "The Bible's Buried Secrets."
18. Albertz, *History of Israelite Religion*, 51.
19. Albertz, 52.
20. Albertz, 52.
21. Edelman, *Triumph of Elohim.*
22. Edelman, 45.
23. Edelman, 46.
24. Carol Meyers, interview for "The Bible's Buried Secrets," directed by Gary Glassman, *NOVA*, PBS, aired November 18, 2008, http://www.pbs.org/wgbh/nova/ancient/bibles-buried-secrets.html.
25. Kersey Graves, *The World's Sixteen Crucified Saviours Christianity Before Christ*, (Kempton, IL: Adventures Unlimited Press; Revised edition, 2001)
26. William Dever, interview for "The Bible's Buried Secrets," directed by Gary Glassman, *NOVA*, PBS, aired November 18, 2008, http://www.pbs.org/wgbh/nova/ancient/bibles-buried-secrets.html.
27. Mark S. Smith and Wayne T. Pitard, *The Ugaritic Baal Cycle*, volume 2, *Introduction with Text Translation and Commentary of KTU/CAT 1.3-1.4* (Leiden, Netherlands: Brill, 2009), 452.
28. Susan Ackerman, "Asherah/Asherim: Bible," Jewish Women's Archive, March 1, 2009, https://jwa.org/encyclopedia/article/asherahasherim-bible.
29. Edelman, *Triumph of Elohim*, 33.
30. Edelman, 33.
31. Edelman, 33.
32. Jen Viegas, "God's Wife Edited Out of the Bible–Almost", Seeker, November 27, 2012, https://www.seeker.com/gods-wife-edited-out-of-the-bible-almost-1766083399.html.
33. Edelman, *Triumph of Elohim*, 57.

34. Edelman, 54.
35. Edelman, 39.
36. Francesca Stavrakopoulou, John Barton, eds., *Religious Diversity in Ancient Israel and Judah*, (New York: T&T Clark, 2010), 4.
37. Edelman, *Triumph of Elohim*, 18.
38. Jen Viegas, "God's Wife Edited Out of the Bible–Almost", Seeker, November 27, 2012, https://www.seeker.com/gods-wife-edited-out-of-the-bible-almost-1766083399.html.
39. Viegas.
40. Viegas.
41. Ellen White, "Asherah and the Asherim: Goddess or Cult Symbol?, Bible History Daily, November 4, 2014, https://www.biblicalarchaeology.org/daily/ancient-cultures/ancient-israel/asherah-and-the-asherim-goddess-or-cult-symbol/.
42. White
43. White

Appendix C

1. Anthony Black, "The 'Axial Period': What Was It and What Does It Signify?," in "Special Issue on Comparative Political Theory," *The Review of Politics*, Vol. 70, no. 1 (Winter, 2008), 23–39, http://www.sfu.ca/~poitras/rp_axial_08.pdf.
2. Steven Paulson, "Going beyond God," *Salon*, May 30, 2006, https://bazaarmodel.net/phorum/read.php?1,6155.
3. Paulson.
4. John D. Mayer, "The Significance of the Axial Age, (the Great Transformation)," *The Personality Analyst* (blog), *Psychology Today*, May 25, 2009, https://www.psychologytoday.com/blog/the-personality-analyst/200905/the-significance-the-axial-age-the-great-transformation.
5. Mayer.

6. L. Michael White, quoted in "The Jewish Diaspora," From Jesus to Christ, *Frontline*, PBS, April 1998, https://www.pbs.org/wgbh/pages/frontline/shows/religion/portrait/diaspora.html.
7. Paulson, "Going Beyond God."
8. Paulson
9. *Encyclopedia Britannica*, s.v. "Hellenistic Religion", Jonathan Z. Smith, last modified April 27, 2017, https://www.britannica.com/topic/Hellenistic-religion.
10. Smith
11. Raphael Lataster, "Did historical Jesus Really Exist? The Evidence Just Doesn't Add Up," *The Washington Post*, December 18, 2014, https://www.washingtonpost.com/posteverything/wp/2014/12/18/did-historical-jesus-exist-the-traditional-evidenc e-doesnt-hold-up/?utm_term=.6996eaf22c92.
12. L. Michael White, quoted in "What Are the Gospels?," From Jesus to Christ, *Frontline*, PBS, April 1998, https://www.pbs.org/wgbh/pages/frontline/shows/religion/story/gospels.html.
13. Paula Fredriksen, quoted in "What Are the Gospels?," From Jesus to Christ, *Frontline*, PBS, April 1998, https://www.pbs.org/wgbh/pages/frontline/shows/religion/story/gospels.html.
14. Allen D. Callahan, quoted in "What Are the Gospels?," From Jesus to Christ, *Frontline*, PBS, April 1998, https://www.pbs.org/wgbh/pages/frontline/shows/religion/story/gospels.html
15. Bart Ehrman, quoted in "Jesus And The Hidden Contradictions Of The Gospels," *Fresh Air*, NPR, March 12, 2010, https://www.npr.org/templates/story/story.php?storyId=124572693.
16. Harold W. Attridge, quoted in "What Are the Gospels?," From Jesus to Christ, *Frontline*, PBS, April 1998, https://www.pbs.org/wgbh/pages/frontline/shows/religion/story/gospels.html.
17. Lawrence Mykytiuk, "Did Jesus Exist? Searching for Evidence beyond the Bible," Bible History Daily, September 5, 2017, https://www.biblicalarchaeology.org/daily/people-cultures-in-the-bible/jesus-historical-jesus/did-jesus-exist/.
18. Mykytiuk.

19. Mykytiuk.
20. Mykytiuk.
21. Mykytiuk.
22. Mykytiuk.
23. Marianne Bonz, "Religion in The Roman World," From Jesus to Christ, *Frontline*, PBS, April 1998, http://www.pbs.org/wgbh/pages/frontline/shows/religion/portrait/religions.html.
24. Bonz.
25. Berel Wein, "The Rise of Christianity," Free Crash Course in Jewish History, accessed June 10, 2016, http://www.jewishhistory.org/the-rise-of-christianity/.
26. *Encyclopedia Britannica*, s.v. "Herod: King of Judaea," by Stewart Henry Perowne, last modified February 22, 2018, https://www.britannica.com/biography/Herod-king-of-Judaea.
27. Perowne.
28. Perowne.
29. Tom Mueller, "King Herod Revealed, The Holy Land's Visionary Builder," *National Geographic* 214/6, December 2008, 34-59.
30. Mueller.
31. Gordon Franz, "The Slaughter of the Innocents: Historical Fact or Legendary Fiction?," BibleArchaeology.org, December 8, 2009, http://www.biblearchaeology.org/post/2009/12/08/The-Slaughter-of-the-Innocents-Historical-Fact-or-Legendary-Fiction.aspx.
32. Franz.
33. Kaufmann Kohler, "Christianity in its Relation to Judaism," Jewish Encyclopedia, accessed June 10, 2017, http://www.jewishencyclopedia.com/articles/4366-christianity-in-its-relation-to-judaism.
34. Kohler.
35. Julius Greenstone, *The Messiah Idea in Jewish History*, (Philadelphia: Jewish Publication Society, 1906), 21.
36. Wein, "Rise of Christianity."
37. Wein.
38. Wein.
39. Wein.

40. Wein.
41. Daniel Boyarin, *Dying for God: Martyrdom and the Making of Christianity and Judaism*, (Stanford, CA: Stanford Press), 8.
42. Boyarin, 9.
43. Bart Ehrman, *The Triumph of Christianity: How a Forbidden Religion Swept the World* (New York: Simon & Schuster, 2018), audiobook.
44. Wein, "Rise of Christianity."
45. Bart Ehrman, "How Jesus Became God–An Interview With Bart Ehrman," *Fresh Air*, NPR, April 10, 2014, https://www.youtube.com/watch?v=AxiNy8mwHqM.
46. Ehrman.
47. Pascal Boyer quoted by Reza Aslan, *God: A Human History*, (New York: Random House, 2017) 42.
48. Ehrman, "How Jesus Became God."
49. Marshall Connolly, "Accurately Predicted: Our Lady appears to thousands in Knock, Ireland," Catholic Onine, June 13, 2017, http://www.catholic.org/news/hf/faith/story.php?id=75183.
50. Ehrman, "How Jesus Became God."
51. Ehrman.
52. Ehrman.
53. Ehrman.
54. Lincoln H. Blumell, "Scribes and Ancient Letters: Implications for the Pauline Epistles," in *How the New Testament Came to Be: The Thirty-fifth Annual Sidney B. Sperry Symposium*, ed. Kent P. Jackson and Frank F. Judd Jr. (Salt Lake City: Deseret Book, 2006), 208–226, https://rsc.byu.edu/archived/selected-articles/scribes-and-ancient-letters-implications-pauline-epistles.
55. Blumell.
56. Elaine Pagels, *The Gnostic Gospels*, (New York: Random House, 1979), http://archonmatrix.com/wp-content/uploads/2017/01/Elaine-Pagels-The-Gnostic-Gospels-Vintage-1989-1.pdf.
57. Pagels.
58. R.A. Baker, *A Concise History of the Christian Church, From the Apostles to the Council of Nicea 325 A.D.*, 2005, https://books.google.

com/books?id=g4hRx8ofSYYC&printsec=frontcover&source=gbs_ge_summary_r&cad=0#v=onepage&q&f=false.

59. 59. Adolf von Harnack, *The Origin of the New Testament*, (London: Williams and Norgate, 1925), http://www.ccel.org/ccel/harnack/origin_nt.
60. Nicole Denzey Lewis, "What are Noncanonical Writings?," Bible Odyssey, accessed June 10, 2017, http://bibleodyssey.org/tools/bible-basics/what-are-noncanonical-writings.
61. Lewis.
62. Lewis

Appendix D

1. Olivia Rudgard, "Islam will be largest religion in the world by 2070, says report," *Telegraph*, March 1, 2017, http://www.telegraph.co.uk/news/2017/03/01/islam-will-largest-religion-world-2070-says-report/.
2. L. Michael White, quoted in "The Jewish Diaspora," *Frontline*, PBS, April 1998, https://www.pbs.org/wgbh/pages/frontline/shows/religion/portrait/diaspora.html.
3. Shaye I.D. Cohen, quoted in "The Jewish Diaspora," *Frontline*, PBS, April 1998, https://www.pbs.org/wgbh/pages/frontline/shows/religion/portrait/diaspora.html.
4. Cohen
5. White, "Jewish Diaspora.
6. Rodney Stark, *The Rise of Christianity: A Sociologist Reconsiders History*, (Princeton, NJ: Princeton University Press, 1996), 5–7.
7. Stark, 5.
8. Stark, 5.
9. Helmut Koester, quoted in "The Great Appeal," From Jesus to Christ, *Frontline*, PBS, April 1998, https://www.pbs.org/wgbh/pages/front-line/shows/religion/why/appeal.html.
10. Stark, *Rise of Christianity*, 31.
11. Stark, 87.
12. Koester, "Great Appeal."

13. L. Michael White, quoted in "The Great Appeal," From Jesus to Christ, *Frontline*, PBS, April 1998, https://www.pbs.org/wgbh/pages/frontline/shows/religion/why/appeal.html.
14. Claudia Setzer, "The Historical Jesus," *Tikkan*, 10, no. 4, July 17, 1995, 73, reprint available at http://www.pbs.org/wgbh/pages/frontline/shows/religion/jesus/tikkun.html.
15. Bart Ehrman, *The Triumph of Christianity: How a Forbidden Religion Swept the World*, (New York: Simon & Schuster, 2018), audiobook.
16. Lauren Markoe, "Candida Moss Debunks the 'Myth' of Christian Persecution," *Washington Post*, May 14, 2013, https://www.washingtonpost.com/national/on-faith/candida-moss-debunks-the-myth-of-christian-persecution/2013/05/14/1b903b24-bcc7-11e2-b537-ab47f0325f7c_story.html?utm_term=.2e396f56e577.
17. Ehrman, *Triumph of Christianity*.
18. White, "Great Appeal".
19. Michael Gaddis, *There is No Crime for Those Who Have Christ: Religious Violence in the Christian Roman Empire*, (Berkeley: University of California Press, 2005), 29, 35.
20. White, "Great Appeal."
21. Wayne A. Meeks, quoted in "The Martyrs," From Jesus to Christ, *Frontline*, PBS, April 1998, https://www.pbs.org/wgbh/pages/frontline/shows/religion/why/martyrs.html.
22. *Encyclopedia Britannica,* s.v. "Constantine 1: Roman Emperor," by Donald McGillivray Nicol and J. F. Matthews, last modified May 18, 2018, https://www.britannica.com/biography/Constantine-I-Roman-emperor.
23. Ehrman, *Triumph of Christianity*.
24. Leo Donald Davis, *The First Seven Ecumenical Councils (325–787): Their History and Theology*, (Collegeville, MN: Liturgical Press), 67.
25. Ehrman, *Triumph of Christianity*.
26. Dale Tuggy, "Trinity", *Stanford Encyclopedia of Philosophy*, last modified March 18, 2016, https://plato.stanford.edu/archives/win2016/entries/trinity/.

27. William Barry, "Arianism," *The Catholic Encyclopedia* (New York: Robert Appleton Company, 1907), Retrieved from New Advent December 18, 2017, http://www.newadvent.org/cathen/01707c.htm.
28. Tuggy, "Trinity."
29. Tuggy.
30. Ehrman, *Triumph of Christianity.*
31. Madeleine Pelner Cosmon and Linda Gale Jones, *Handbook to Life in the Medieval World* (New York: Infobase Publishing, 2009), 4.
32. *Encyclopedia Britannica*, s.v. "Theodosius I: Roman Emperor," by Adolf Lippold, last modified August 30, 2016, https://www.britannica.com/biography/Theodosius-I.
33. The List of Popes, 1911, New Advent, accessed June 18, 2018, http://www.newadvent.org/cathen/12272b.htm.
34. Stephen F. Brown, Khaled Anatolios, *Catholicism & Orthodox Christianity*, 3rd ed., (New York: Chelsea House, 2009), 46
35. Brown and Anatolios, 47, 50.
36. Kenneth Scott Latourette, *A History of Christianity, vol. 1, Beginnings to 1500*, [San Francisco: Harper & Row, 1975], http://www.coptics.info/Books/Kenneth_Scott_Latourette_A_History_of_Christianity.pdf.
37. Brown and Anatolios, *Catholicism & Orthodox Christianity*, 50.
38. Emma Mason, "In case you missed it . . . Your 60-second guide to heresy," History Extra, September 5, 2014, http://www.historyextra.com/feature/your-60-second-guide-heresy.
39. Barry Hoberman, "Translating the Bible," *Atlantic*, Volume 255, No. 2 (February 1985): 43–58, https://www.theatlantic.com/past/docs/issues/85feb/trans2.htm.
40. Erin Blakemore, "The Origins of the King James Bible," Smithsonian.com, October 16, 2015, https://www.smithsonianmag.com/smart-news/origins-of-the-king-james-bible-180956949/.
41. John A. Grigg, *British Colonial America: People in Perspectives*, Perspectives in American Social History (Santa Barbara, California: ABC-CLIO, 2009), 42–43.
42. Grigg, 42–43

43. *Encyclopedia Britannica*, s.v., "Puritanism," by Oliver Cromwell, Jonathan Edwards, John Knox, last modified January 3, 2018, https://www.britannica.com/topic/Puritanism.
44. Grigg, *British Colonia America*, 2009.
45. Pew Forum, Appendix B: Methodology for Estimating Christian Movements," accessed January 1, 2018, http://www.pewforum.org/files/2011/12/ChristianityAppendixB.pdf
46. "Religion in Colonial America: Trends, Regulations, and Beliefs," Facing History and Ourselves, accessed June 18, 2018, https://www.facinghistory.org/nobigotry/religion-colonial-america-trend s-regulations-and-beliefs.
47. Kenneth C. Davis, "America's True History of Religious Tolerance," Smithsonian.com, October 2010, https://www. smithsonianmag.com/history/americas-true-history-ofreligious-tolerance-61312684.
48. Balmer, *Encyclopedia of Evangelicalism*, 38.
49. "Religion in Colonial America."
50. Patricia U. Bonomi, *Under the Cope of Heaven: Religion, Society, and Politics in Colonial America*, (Oxford: Oxford University Press, 2003), 104.
51. Augustine, *De Genesi Ad Litteram Libri Duodecim*, Landover Baptist Church, August 13, 2011, https://www.landoverbaptist.net/show-thread.php?t=68410.
52. Diarmaid MacCulloch, *Christianity: The First Three Thousand Years*, (New York: Viking Penguin, 2009), 151.
53. Algis Valiunas, "Martin Luther's Reformation," *The Claremont Review of Books* 17, no. 4 (Fall 2017), https://www.claremont.org/crb/article/martin-luthers-reformation/.
54. Zakir Naik, "Christian Sister Accept Islam After She Got Her 2 Answer," recorded August 27, 2009, at Dubai International Holy Quran Awards, Dubai, UAE, video, 4:00, https://www.youtube.com/watch?v=T5ZlSSOhbzQ.

Appendix E

1. Andrew C., "Top 10 Famous Cases of Backmasking," Listverse, August 28, 2011, http://listverse.com/2011/08/28/top-10-famous-cases-of-backmasking/.
2. Bart Ehrman, "The Afterlife in the Hebrew Bible: Sheol," *Bart Ehrman Blog*, March 29, 2017, https://ehrmanblog.org/the-afterlife-in-the-hebrew-bible-sheol/.
3. Shawna Dolansky, "How the Serpent Became Satan," Bible History Daily, Biblearcheology.org, October 13, 2017, https://www.biblicalarchaeology.org/daily/biblical-topics/bible-interpretation/how-the-serpent-became-satan/.
4. Chris Massie and Andrew Kaczynski, "Trump Judicial Nominee Said Transgender Children Are Part Of 'Satan's Plan,' Defended 'Conversion Therapy,'" CNN, September 20, 2017, http://www.cnn.com/2017/09/20/politics/kfile-jeff-mateer-lgbt-remarks/index.html.
5. Carlo Caffarra, "How Satan Destroys God's Creation Through Abortion and Homosexuality," LifeSite, May 19, 2017, https://www.lifesitenews.com/opinion/how-satan-destroys-gods-creation-through-abortion-and-homosexuality.
6. Anita Fuentas, "Man: 'Satan Told Me 'Destroy and Piss' on 10 Commandments," Youtube, October 26, 2014, https://www.youtube.com/watch?v=dpV_PhQm9uQ.
7. "Pat Robertson Says Haiti Paying for 'Pact to the Devil,'" CNN, January 13, 2010, http://www.cnn.com/2010/US/01/13/haiti.pat.robertson/index.html.
8. Mel Bond, "Sickness and Oppression from the Devil," February 21, 2012, Youtube, https://www.youtube.com/watch?v=gY-tBHzqJ4I.
9. Peter Stanford, *The Devil: A Biography*, (New York: Henry Holt & Company, 1996), 10.
10. Ed Mazza, "Democrats Are 'Children of Satan,' Right-Wing Radio Host Says," *Huffington Post*, June 19, 2017, https://www.huffingtonpost.com/entry/democrats-children-of-satan_us_5947325ce4b0f15cd5bc501c.

11. Maggie Severns, "Trump: Democratic Party Is 'the Devil,'" *Politico*, October 9, 2016,_https://www.politico.com/story/2016/10/2016-presidential-debate-donald-trump-democratic-party-devil-229456.
12. Gerald Harris, "Theological Liberalism's Primrose Path to Destruction," *Christian Index*, May 16, 2017, https://christianindex.org/theological-liberalisms-primrose-path-destruction/.
13. Stanford, *The Devil*, 17.
14. Dolansky, "The Serpent Became Satan."
15. Epicurus quoted in *Philosophical Papers*, by N.A. Nicolson, (London: Effingham Wilson, 1846), 40.
16. Stanford, *The Devil*, 19.
17. Dolansky, "The Serpent Became Satan."
18. Dolansky.
19. Sam Roberts, "Alice K. Turner Dies at 75; Playboy Editor Kept Fiction Alive," *New York Times*, January 24, 2015, http://www.nytimes.com/2015/01/24/business/media/alice-k-turner-fiction-editor-of-playboy-for-20-years-dies-at-75.html?_r=0.
20. Alice K. Turner, *The History of Hell*, (Orlando, FL: Harcourt Brace, 1993), 5
21. Turner, 5.
22. Turner, 5.
23. Turner, 5.
24. Turner, *History of Hell*, 12
25. Turner, *History of Hell*, 31
26. Georg Autenrieth, "Τάρταρος," Homeric Dictionary, 2001, http://www.perseus.tufts.edu/hopper/text?doc=Perseus%3Atext%3A1999.04.0073%3Aentry%3D*ta%2Frtaros.
27. Turner, *History of Hell*, 32
28. *New World Encyclopedia*, s.v. "Gehenna," Last modified May 24, 2017, http://www.newworldencyclopedia.org/entry/Gehenna.
29. Richard Burky and Jeanette B. Anderson, "Hell: Origins of an Idea," *Vision*, Winter 2011,_http://www.vision.org/visionmedia/origin-of-hell/41044.aspx.

30. Turner, *History of Hell*, 36
31. Burky and Anderson, "Hell."
32. *Encyclopedia Britannica*, s.v. "Zoroastrianism," by Jacques Duchesne-Guillemin, last updated March 9, 2018, https://www.britannica.com/topic/Zoroastrianism#ref9190.
33. Turner, *History of Hell*, 16
34. Turner, *The History of Hell*, 41
35. Burky and Anderson, "Hell."
36. Burky and Anderson
37. Strong's Concordance, "aiónios," Bible Hub, accessed June 21, 2018, http://biblehub.com/greek/166.htm.
38. Josiah Hesse, "Evangelical Hell Houses Are Waking Nightmares," Vice News, October 30, 2017, https://www.vice.com/en_us/article/3kvkmy/evangelical-hell-houses-are-waking-nightmares.
39. Hesse.
40. Marlene Winell, "Part 3: The Trauma of Leaving Religion," Journey Free, November 2011 http://journeyfree.org/rts/the-trauma-of-leavin g-religion-pt-3/.
41. Tony Campolo, "03052010-Hawaiian-Island-Ministries-830AM-Full.mp3," Soundcloud, June 12, 2013, audio, 29:40, http://bit.ly/2DWh0js.
42. Kim Higginbotham, "Giving Your Child to the Devil," TeachingHelp.Org, May 6, 2017, http://www.teachinghelp.org/giving-your-child-t o-the-devil/.
43. M. E. Thomas, "How to Spot a Sociopath," *Psychology Today*, May 7, 2013, https://www.psychologytoday.com/articles/201305/how-spot-sociopath.
44. Gary F. Jenson, "Religious Cosmologies and Homicide Rates among Nations," *Journal of Religion & Society* 8, (2006), http://moses.creighton.edu/jrs/2006/2006-7.pdf.
45. Scott A. McGreal, "Belief in Hell: Does it Benefit or Harm Society?," *Psychology Today*, December 24, 2013, https://www.psychologytoday.com/blog/unique-everybody-else/201312/belief-in-hell-does-it-benefi t-or-harm-society.

46. Alan Noble, "The Evangelical Persecution Complex," *Atlantic*, August 4, 2014,_https://www.theatlantic.com/national/archive/2014/08/the-evangelical-persecution-complex/375506/.
47. Emma Green, "Most American Christians Believe They're Victims of Discrimination," *Atlantic*, June 30, 2016, https://www.theatlantic.com/politics/archive/2016/06/the-christians-who-believ e-theyre-being-persecuted-in-america/488468/.
48. Susan Towey, "Impact of Fear and Anxiety," Taking Charge of Your Health & Wellbeing, 2016, https://www.takingcharge.csh.umn.edu/enhance-your-wellbeing/security/facing-fear/impact-fear.

About the Author

Tim Rymel was born into the Pentecostal Church of God. He served as an evangelical Christian minister for nearly twenty-five years, during which time he was credentialed with the Assemblies of God; was ordained through a non-denominational church in Memphis, Tennessee; worked as the development director for Youth for Christ; and served as the outreach director for Love in Action, once the world's oldest and most renowned "ex-gay" ministry. He is a conversion therapy survivor.

Tim holds a master's degree in education, for which he researched cognition and transformational learning. He is a member of the American Psychological Association in the Educational Psychology division, as well as the Society for the Psychological Study of Lesbian, Gay, Bisexual and Transexual Issues.

Tim's work has appeared frequently in the *Huffington Post* and the *Good Men Project* where he writes on the confluence of religion, politics, and sexuality. He has also appeared on multiple radio and television shows, including *Fox News Radio* and *Vice News Media*. Stories about him and his work can be found on *Buzzfeed*, *ThinkProgress*, the *Advocate*, and *Time*.

He is also the author of *Going Gay: My Journey from Evangelical Christian Minister to Self-Acceptance, Love, Life, and Meaning* (2014) and the business book *Everything I Learned about Management I Learned from Having a Kindergartner* (2012).

Tim lives in Northern California with his husband, Abel, and his daughter, G, a high-school student. His older daughter, Caity, is away at college studying psychology. He also has two rescue pets, Habib, the dog, and Sam, the cat.

Author/Speaker Details: TimRymel.com
Twitter: @TheRealTimRymel
Facebook: facebook.com/TimRymel.AuthorPage/
Instagram: TimRymel
Email: Tim@TimRymel.com

Index

A

Index

Index

Index

B

Index

C

Index

Index

D

E

F

G

H

Index

I

J

K

L

M

N

O

P

Q

R

S

T

U

Y

Z

www.ingramcontent.com/pod-product-compliance
Lightning Source LLC
Chambersburg PA
CBHW021218090426
42740CB00006B/277

9780985758042